Young Children Becoming Curriculum

This book contests a tradition and convention in educational thinking that dichoto-mizes children and curriculum, by developing the notion of re(con)ceiving children in curriculum. By presenting an innovative research project, in which she worked with children to share their understandings of the internationally renowned Te Whāriki curriculum, Marg Sellers explores what curriculum means to children and how it works, as demonstrated in games they played. In generating different ways for thinking, the author draws upon her work with the philosophical imagi-naries of Gilles Deleuze and Felix Guattari, whose ideas shape both the content and the non-linear structure of this book. Topics covered include:

- rhizome, rhizo-methodology and rhizoanalysis
- plateaus
- de~territorializing lines of flight
- dynamic spaces
- the notion of empowerment.

This assemblage of Deleuzo-Guattarian imaginaries generates ways for thinking differently about children's complex interrelationships with curriculum, and opens possibilities for re(con)ceiving – both reconceiving and receiving – children's understandings within adult conceptions of how curriculum works for young chil-dren. This book will be of interest to early childhood students, scholars and prac-titioners alike, also appealing to those interested in philosophical, theoretical and practical understandings of curriculum in general.

Marg Sellers is Lecturer in undergraduate and postgraduate Early Childhood teacher education programs in the School of Education at RMIT University, Melbourne, Australia.

Series Title: Contesting Early Childhood
Series Editors: Gunilla Dahlberg and Peter Moss

This groundbreaking series questions the current dominant discourses surrounding early childhood, and offers instead alternative narratives of an area that is now made up of a multitude of perspectives and debates.

The series examines the possibilities and risks arising from the accelerated development of early childhood services and policies, and illustrates how it has become increasingly steeped in regulation and control. Insightfully, this collection of books shows how early childhood services can in fact contribute to ethical and democratic practices. The authors explore new ideas taken from alternative working practices in both the western and developing world, and from other academic disciplines such as developmental psychology. Current theories and best practice are placed in relation to the major processes of political, social, economic, cultural and technological change occurring in the world today.

Titles in the *Contesting Early Childhood* series include:

Sellers (2013) *Young Children becoming Curriculum*

Taylor (2013) *Reconfiguring the Natures of Childhood*

Moss (2013) *Early Childhood and Compulsory Education*

Vecchi (2010) *Art and Creativity in Reggio Emilia*

Taguchi (2009) *Going Beyond the Theory/Practice Divide*

Olsson (2009) *Movement and Experimentation in Young Children's Learning*

Edmiston (2007) *Forming Ethical Identities in Early Childhood Play*

Rinaldi (2005) *In Dialogue with Reggio Emilia*

MacNaughton (2005) *Doing Foucault in Early Childhood Studies*

Penn (2005) *Unequal Childhoods*

Dahlberg and Moss (2005) *Ethics and Politics in Early Childhood*

Young Children
Becoming Curriculum

Deleuze, Te Whāriki and
curricular understandings

Marg Sellers

Routledge
Taylor & Francis Group

LONDON AND NEW YORK

First published 2013
by Routledge
2 Park Square, Milton Park, Abingdon, Oxon OX14 4RN

Simultaneously published in the USA and Canada
by Routledge
711 Third Avenue, New York, NY 10017

Routledge is an imprint of the Taylor & Francis Group, an informa business

British Library Cataloguing in Publication Data
A catalogue record for this book is available from the British Library

Library of Congress Cataloging in Publication Data
Sellers, Marg.
  Young children becoming curriculum : Deleuze, Te Whāriki and
  curricular understandings / authored by Marg Sellers.
  Pages cm
  Includes bibliographical references and index.
  1. Early childhood education—Curricula. 2. Curriculum planning.
  3. Deleuze, Gilles, 1925–1995. I. Title.
  LB1139.4.S46 2013
  375'.001—dc23
  2012047932

ISBN: 978-0-415-53610-3 (hbk)
ISBN: 978-0-415-53611-0 (pbk)
ISBN: 978-0-203-11181-9 (ebk)

Typeset in Times New Roman
by Swales & Willis Ltd, Exeter, Devon

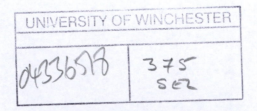

For Caelan, Leo, Taylah, Arran, Zach and Eden,
who move me to think differently about the
worlds of children, childhood and curriculum.

Contents

Acknowledgements

This book emerged through my doctoral research supervised by Eileen Honan (University of Queensland) and Noel Gough (La Trobe University). It is a response to the urge from Bronwyn Davies and Elizabeth St. Pierre – thesis assessors – to reproduce the text for a wider readership. Without this scholarly support, particularly that of Peter Moss and Gunilla Dahlberg, it would not have happened. For this collegiality, I am grateful, including that of the many workplace colleagues of the past decade from Whitireia Community Polytechnic, Porirua, Aotearoa New Zealand and RMIT University, Melbourne, Australia. I am also grateful to the teachers in an Aotearoa New Zealand kindergarten who welcomed me into their setting and to the children for their participation in generating the data, which continues to open possibilities for thinking differently about children, childhood and curriculum. Constant companions through this writing (ad)venture have been my children and grandchildren, never further away than *txt*, phone, email, Facetime or Skype. I thank them all for keeping me in touch with the(ir) world(s) when I was somewhere else – lost in books, papers and my own thinking. My Dad has always believed in me and I am grateful for his ever-loving support; my Mum inspired me to bring my educational dreams to life. However, my greatest ally in making this book happen has been Warren Sellers, my incomparable partner in love, life and educational endeavours. To him, I offer my heartfelt appreciation for the ongoing conversation around philosophy and living experiences of curriculum and learning, and for his technical expertise that enabled this rhizo production to emerge.

I wish to thank the following artists and scholars for permission to use their artwork.

Chris Harrison, Carnegie Mellon University, for his social networking image, *Internet Map: City-to-city Connections* (http://www.chrisharrison.net/projects/Internetmap/medium/euroblack.jpg).

Marc Ngui, Toronto, Canada, for his drawing from *1000 Plateaus Drawings: Intro Paragraph 15* (www.bumblenut.com).

Dr Warren Sellers, for his images of a botanical rhizome, Mobius strip de~territorialization and relations of play becoming spandrel.

Professor Carlo H. Séquin, University of California, Berkeley, for the photograph of his mathematical sculpture, *Symmetrical Half-way Point for Torus Eversion* (http://www.

cs.berkeley.edu/~sequin/ART/AMS_MathImagery/Torus-Eversion_Halfway-Point.jpg).

Paul Tricker, for his photograph of diffractive patterns of wind and sea waves(http://trickersinegypt.blogspot.com.au/2010_09_01_archive.html).

Z. Vrkast, fibre artist, for the photograph of her felted work, *Grey Suffolk and Banana Fibre* (http://www.flickr.com/photos/zedster01/7031516503/in/pool-1654385@N23).

Use of the following material is also acknowledged.

The Te Whāriki diagram is reproduced by permission of the New Zealand Ministry of Education, published in *Te Whāriki* by Learning Media Limited. Crown Copyright, 1996.

Reworked versions of material printed in the following publications is integrated throughout the plateaus with permission of the respective publishers; also with permission of co-author, Dr Eileen Honan.

Honan, E. & Sellers, M. (2006) So how does it work? – rhizomatic methodologiesed. Engaging Pedagogies: Australian Association for Research in Education 2006 International Conference, Adelaide, SA: AARE.

Honan, E. & Sellers, M. (2008) (E)merging methodologies: putting rhizomes to work. *In* I. Semetsky (ed.) *Nomadic Education: Variations on a Theme by Deleuze and Guattari.* Rotterdam: Sense Publishers, 111–28.

Sellers, M. (2005) Growing a rhizome: embodying early experiences in learning. *New Zealand Research in Early Childhood Education*, 8, 29–42.

Sellers, M. (2009) A rhizo-poiesis: children's play(ing) of games. *Complicity: An International Journal of Complexity and Education*, 6, 91–103 (http://ejournals.library.ualberta.ca/index.php/complicity/article/view/8819/7139).

Sellers, M. (2010) Re(con)ceiving young children's curricular performativity. *International Journal of Qualitative Studies in Education*, 23, 557–78 (http://www.tandfonline.com).

Sellers, M. & Honan, E. (2007) Putting rhizomes to work: (e)merging methodologies. *NZ Research in Early Childhood Education*, 10, 145–54.

Quotations from *A Thousand Plateaus: Capitalism and Schizophrenia* (Deleuze & Guattari, 1987, translated by B. Massumi) are used with permission.Copyright 1987 by the University of Minnesota Press. Originally published as *Mille Plateaux*, volume 2 of *Capitalisme et Schizophrénie* © 1980 by Les Editions de Minuit, Paris.

Series editors' introduction

Gunilla Dahlberg and Peter Moss

The present book is the eleventh in the series *Contesting Early Childhood*. The series has two main goals. On the one hand, it 'questions dominant discourses surrounding early childhood', those ways of thinking, talking and practising that make truth claims, implying or asserting they are inevitable, essential, self-evident and universal, seeking to enforce a dictatorship of no alternative and to stifle new thought and action. But, at the same time as being critical, the series aims to offer 'alternative narratives of an area that is now made up of a multitude of perspectives and debates'. The good news is that diversity has not been stifled despite the best efforts of dominant discourses, and this series provides one of the forums where that diversity of perspectives and debates can find expression, as well as vivid examples of how such diversity can be put into action and made to work. To borrow the title of one of the books in the series, we hope to contribute to 'movement and experimentation in early childhood education' (Olsson, 2009).

As editors we have found Marg Sellers' work, as it is presented in the present book, such an example of movement and experimentation in early childhood education. Working alongside children in a kindergarten in New Zealand, she has not only conceived of children differently but she has also conceived of curriculum differently. Instead of seeing curriculum from a perspective of implementation, which is the most common way of understanding curriculum, she has, through tracing the complexity of pedagogical relationships, shown how children perform curriculum: rather than curriculum as something done to children, children emerge as protagonists of curriculum, as doers of curriculum. In this sense curriculum becomes something children are experiencing in lived time.

The curriculum in this case is *Te Whāriki* (the Māori word for a woven mat), the New Zealand curriculum for early childhood education, covering all services for children from birth to school. Published in 1996, '[i]t was the product of a cross-cultural partnership with Māori, and the multiple perspectives of early childhood groups across the country' (Carr, 2013: 97). This highly original curriculum, created from an encounter between different cultures and languages, with its non-prescriptive tone, its recognition of context and its broad concept of education, has surely given Marg Sellers valuable conditions for moving outside essentializing and generalizing dominant discourses. For *Te Whāriki* creates a 'smooth space' both for children and teachers, as well as researchers. Such 'smooth spaces' are, in Marg Sellers' words, 'open spaces throughout which "things-flows" are distributed', in contrast to 'striated spaces', created for example by prescriptive curricula, which create 'closed spaces…plotted by points and positions and [which] are concerned with enclosing things linear and solid'. In her complex and challenging work, Marg Sellers has really made good use of the possibilities created by 'smooth space'.

We are here using 'challenging' as we know how hard it is to move beyond modernist trappings of the already taken for given, of representations and mental projections, and of reducing the complexity of a system, trappings that pervade dominant discourses in today's early childhood education. With inspiration from Gilles Deleuze's and Felix Guattari's most famous opus, *A Thousand Plateaus*, Marg Sellers has not only tried to move away from the Cartesian subject-centred view of the world, and the representational thinking that has characterized western metaphysics since Plato, but by using Deleuze and Guattari's rhizo-methodology she has also constructed new creative ways of conceptualizing the relations between children, childhood and curriculum. Through affirming children's play and through tracing instead of representing, she has opened up for rhizomatic processes of becoming and the flux of change. This she has done by continuously following her problematique in an attentive way and through a real concern for events, happenings and occurrences. By installing herself along with the children in events, she has been able to direct her attention towards the indecisive processes and life-giving potentialities that exist in specific moments – those unexpected processes and potentialities that are in a process of becoming anew and anew.

With inspiration from Michel Foucault, one could say that Marg Sellers in her work has *eventualized existence.* Foucault (1991) argued that we are, in our tradition of knowledge, so occupied with the general, the abstract and the hidden that we have non-eventualized existence. By so doing we have lost that which is immanent in the present moment of experience. We have lost Life and its rhythm. This is what Marg Sellers brings back by tracing children's play and curriculum as an event, as a process of becoming – as life.

The book as an assemblage

Marg Sellers' book is a challenge to dominant discourses on early childhood education, with their preoccupations with linearity and certainty of outcome. The challenge comes both in her interpretation of children's relationship to curriculum, but also in the way she has conceptualized and implemented the book. Both subject and format, what she writes about and how she writes, are inscribed with her theoretical perspectives. Like Gilles Deleuze and Felix Guattari (1999) in *A Thousand Plateaus*, she has presented her work as an assemblage of 'plateaus' that can be read in any order.

Deleuze and Guattari took the concept of 'plateau' from Gregory Bateson's work on Balinese culture. Bateson used the word 'plateau' to designate something very special: a continuous, self-vibrating region of intensities whose development reactivated or injected into other activities. In this way, a fabric of intensive states was created between which a number of connecting routes could exist. This avoids any idea of moving towards a culminating point or external end – the antithesis of the dominant discourses in today's early childhood education, with their fixation on predetermined and sequential outcomes. Instead we are always in-between, with many possibilities open to us.

Tracing such connecting routes and trajectories, and the unique events and intensive states that occur everyday in a kindergarten and in children's play, to produce her text, Marg Sellers has, in a very creative and poetic way, used several devices in her writing to enable her to move outside conventional, linear approaches. By using tildes (~), brackets, slashes, as well as 'and...and...and' instead of the essentializing'is, is, is', she has in her reading~writing~thinking managed to construct a multidimensional mode of composition that manages to trace the trajectories in the relational field of potentiality. And, as such, the data – to use Marg Sellers'own words – demonstrates children's 'sophisticated understandings about learning~living'. Hence, in her process of reading~writing~thinking she has in each plateau, like Deleuze and Guattari while writing *A Thousand Plateaus*, combined conceptual blocks in order to construct a dynamic holding-together of disparate elements.

Deleuze'sphilosophical concepts have here been crucial 'tools', but as Deleuze (Massumi, 2002: 244) has said, in order for philosophical concepts to become a tool, they have to cross a threshold by feeding into nonphilosophy. Brian Massumi calls this 'the pragmatic problem of the philosopher'. He argues that, to make an actual difference, philosophy has to be picked up by nonphilosophical hands that are engaged in collective experimentation (ibid.); such hands, Marg Sellers shows us, as she has got.

By picking up philosophical concepts and putting them to work, she has made a valuable contribution to rethinking democracy and political change. By listening and welcoming the wonder of minor experiences (Bennett, 2001), she has, as Humberto Maturana (1991) advocated, brought forth the world through the process of living, showing us what a body can do in an assemblage with other forces. By so doing, the reader, too, will find that children can help us learn new things, as they are not yet so inscribed in orthodox thought; rather they seem to be transversal and rhizomatic thinkers – far more so than adults.

In the translator's Foreword to Deleuze and Guattari's *A Thousand Plateaus*, Brian Massumi (1999: xiv) says that their book did not pretend to have the final word. The hope for them was that elements of it would stay with a certain number of its readers and weave into the melody of their everyday life. As series editors, we have a similar hope for this book. It has left us with a dynamism of intensity, just as it has left us also with new thoughts, new perceptions and new sensations. It has *tuned* into our bodies.

References

Bennett, J. (2001) *The Enchantment of Modern Life*. Princeton, NJ: Princeton University Press.

Carr, M. (2013) Making a borderland of contested spaces into a meeting place: the relationship from a New Zealand perspective. *In* P. Moss (ed.) *Early Childhood and Compulsory Education: Reconceptualising the Relationship*. London: Routledge.

Deleuze, G. & Guattari, F. (1999) *A Thousand Plateaus. Capitalism and Schizophrenia*. London: Athlone Press.

Foucault, M. (1991) Questions of methods. *In* H.L. Dreyfus and P. Rabinow (eds) *The Foucault Effect: Studies in Governmentality*. London: Harvester Wheatsheaf.

Massumi, B. (2002) *Parables for the Virtual: Movement, Affect, Sensation*. Durham, NC: Duke University Press.

Maturana, H. (1991) Science and daily life: the ontology of scientific explanations. *In* F. Steier (ed.) *Research and Reflexivity*. London: Sage.

Olsson, L. (2009) *Movement and Experimentation in Young Children's Learning: Deleuze and Guattari in Early Childhood Education*. London: Routledge.

...preambling...

The last conversation I had with my mother was after she sent me her most recent writings about her family history. We talked, not for the first time, about the impact on her life of her father not allowing her to continue on from primary to secondary school. At 12 years old she was a high-achieving student at a small, rural school in Aotearoa New Zealand but, within the authoritarian, patriarchal ways of her family, her role as eldest daughter caring for her seven brothers and sisters after their mother's death mattered more than her ongoing education. Her story was that she cried for days before accepting her father's unrelenting decision and, to her credit, she bore him no long-term resentment; in fact at 80 years of age she shielded his memory from my critique saying he did what he thought best. But in my feminist poststructuralist thinking, albeit seven decades on from the end of her schooling, contemplating her story and what she might have done in different times was not so easily put to rest. Taking my educational journey as far as I could was a way of honouring hers being stopped short. Somewhat synchronistically, at the moment she passed away in 2003 I was at a conference presentation about using narrative and metaphor for developing critical understandings of curriculum. In the presentation, 'Maggie's story',[1] the autobiographical text of a student teacher became the collective voice through which inescapable ethical issues of social control and power embedded in curriculum could be collaboratively read, pondered, debated and discussed. Considering this later, I appreciated the resonances of Maggie's narrative on control and power with the story of my mother's powerlessness in regard to her educational choices and of Marcy's story that follows below, which tells how she (pro)claimed her power-fullness with/in a living~learning moment.

A few months earlier I had met two-year-old Marcy while visiting a student teacher on placement in an early childhood setting. Marcy, according to the teachers was disruptive, although in regard to what they did not say, the term 'disruptive' commonly deemed an indisputable category and thus self-explanatory. However, my observation in that moment was that the programme and teachers were disruptive to Marcy and her learning, not the other way round. What I perceived was Marcy expressing her desires for her learning~living – that is, for her living experiences of her learning and her learning about living – and these were thwarted by the requirements of a routine. It was morning teatime but she was not yet ready to sit at the table and listen to a story while waiting for food to be served. She had not finished her puzzle and in all its complexity this puzzling moment intensified as she attempted to negotiate a way through both finishing the puzzle...*and*...listening to a story. She signalled she could do both but the teachers insisted that she sit with the other children at the table. Marcy was not being disruptive; rather the conditions of her desired living~learning experiences, her experiences of curriculum and her expressed curricular performativity were disrupted. (Marcy's story is detailed in the *Preceding echoes* plateau.)

From these interconnecting stories – my mother's, Maggie and Marcy's – ideas for researching young children's understandings of curriculum emerged. Weaving through these were scholarly connections, particularly Foucault's notions of power, control, discipline and surveillance alerting me to *thinking otherwise... and*...Deleuze and Guattari's imaginaries opening possibilities for (my) *thinking in other ways* in my doctoral research of bringing Deleuzo-Guattarian philosophical understandings alongside adult conceptions of curriculum and young children's curricular performativity.

(e)merging interests

In 2002, I happened upon Deleuze and Guatarri's (1987) 'Introduction: Rhizome' in *A Thousand Plateaus:Capitalism and Schizophrenia*. Here they introduce the botanical term 'rhizome' as a way to imagine a *multidimensional* system of thought different from, but not opposed to, *unidirectional*, binary logic, which operates in linear and sequentially ordered ways so that positions build on points already plotted. Deleuze and Guattari refer to this sequential linearity as arborescent thought; the metaphorical tree of knowledge fits with this root–tree thinking. In contrast, the rhizome works multidimensionally and dynamically to accrue knowing through ceaselessly establishing connections. As a way of thinking, rhizome operates through multitudes of nodes linked by paths or trajectories extending in all dimensions at once; positions assemble (assemblages form) only to be passed through as any point is linked with any other, endlessly extending the rhizome by generating more linkages. The idea of working with rhizome for thinking differently – non-hierarchically – about children, childhood and curriculum excited me. Further to this, Elizabeth St. Pierre and Donna Alvermann's use of the Deleuzo-Guattarian imaginaries, nomad thought and rhizoanalysis, in *Working the Ruins: Feminist Poststructural Theory and Methods in Education* (St. Pierre & Pillow, 2000) demonstrated ways of making rhizo thinking work; this encouraged my thinking about curriculum inquiry. What also mattered to any response I might make to Marcy's story being her expression of curricular performativity, was Gaile Cannella's (1997) poststructuralist challenge to conventional discourses of children and childhood in *Deconstructing Early Childhood Education: Social Justice and Revolution*. In this she calls for a renewed respect for reconceiving young children as younger human beings and for rethinking childhood outside the unequal power relations of the adult|child binary. Rhizo thinking with its non-hierarchical operations opened possibilities for these as well.

Yet, in a heartfelt way, it was Foucault's connections with Deleuze that urged me on. Foucault identifies his motivation as *curiosity*, as a passion not only for accruing knowledge but also for finding out how far he could take his thinking. What matters is 'knowing if one can think differently than one thinks, and perceive differently than one sees...[and] to know how and to what extent *it might be possible to think differently*, instead of legitimating what is already known' (Foucault, 1990: 8–9, italics added). As well as thinking differently, writing differently seems part of this endeavour. For Deleuze (1995: 8), how things work matters: '"Does it work, and how does it work?" How does it work for you?' Thinking differently through Deleuzo-Guattarian imaginaries, such as rhizome, meant putting them to work in the writing, using them as part of the process of talking about them; it seemed that how rhizome is put to work affects how philosophical notions of rhizome might be understood. So, in exploring how various imaginaries might work, I have used several writerly devices that move outside conventional, linear approaches to producing a text. In this (re)constitution of the rhizo work of my doctoral thesis (Sellers, 2009b) I use these devices as renderings of Deleuzo-Guattarian machines to generate rhizo activity of both thinking and writing.

writing~reading a rhizome

Avoiding the production of a strictly linear document in both content and in the presentation of sequentially numbered chapters, I use 'plateaus' (Deleuze & Guattari, 1987) that are connectable in various ways. Within these plateaus, which can be read in any order, the literature, data and analysis do not sit separately, rather they commingle, merging to tell stories of children's learning~living through play(ing) in different ways. For example, text is sometimes presented in various styles and formats, including: portrait and landscape juxtapositions of two or three columns, involving literature, data, analysis and commentary; storyboards of children's play and conversation generate more of the rhizoanalysis, in which children's words and actual activity are presented as mattering more than adult(erated) analyses; mostly the language used is academic but sometimes I venture into the poetic; all of this resonating with/in the complexity of children's play. In this, children's games, their play(ing) and scholarly discourses (e)merge as an always already forever-intensifying rhizome and what I offer here are but *encounters* with thinking~reading~writing and working differently. Ideas within any plateau slip slide alongside ideas in other plateaus. This means that the multiplicity of the research assemblage intensifies and moves outside structured academic limits as various ideas amass in different ways. However, the work of rhizome is only ever *towards* thinking differently, 'towards' as in avoiding this being (mis)interpreted as a concretizing endeavour; 'towards' also signals that any idea arrived at is instantly de~territorialized, dissolving and re-forming in cloud-like ways through relations of ideas through/with/in other spaces and lines of flight.

Already slipping in are other textual devices not yet explained – in the activity of talking about rhizome, rhizo activity is always already at work – such as, my use of tildes (~), brackets, slashes, and *and...and...and...*I use the tilde to join words~concepts that are in reciprocal relations, each co-implicated in the other. For example, a way of explaining de~territorialization is the thought that when we enter various spaces of thinking we territorialize that space, both our own thinking spaces and thinking spaces of others, but as soon as we enter any space our ongoing thoughts change it, this creating a simultaneously deterritorializing movement. In slippery movements through *territorialization* and *deterritorialization* each condition exists only in relation to the other. De~territorialization signals these constantly changing, commingling relations. In this, thought~thinking are similarly co-implicated as ideas are continually (e)merging – merging and emerging at once...*and...*(signalling there is more)...in thinking~writing each becomes the other as writing emerges from thinking and thinking happens within writing. The use of brackets points to an intentionally doubled reading so that re(con)ceiving means both reconceiving and receiving; mo(ve)ments means movements and moments. Similarly, slashes signal a multidimensional reading, the linkage of through/with/in, for example, opening simultaneously different readings from using the prepositions *through*, *with*, *within* and *in*, singularly and together. Illuminating a multidimensional reading, the Deleuzo-Guattarian 'and... and...and...' (Deleuze & Guattari, 1987: 25) works to make possible ongoing possibilities for thought~thinking. Deleuze and Guattari say the conjunction 'and' is the 'fabric of the rhizome' (p. 25); the stuff, the mess, the matter(s) of rhizo activity that is always already open so that specifics, certainty and conclusions are never finalized, only arrived at in the same mo(ve)ment that they are passed through in de~territorializing mo(ve)ments...*and...*there is always already more to be negotiated.

Words *sous rature* or under erasure (~~struck through~~) signal that the word is not entirely appropriate within a poststructuralist reading but for the moment there is no better word to describe a particular concept. Also, in working with Deleuze erasure de~territorializes the concept, opening a line of flight towards thinking something differently. For example, as a rhizome is continually growing, changing and moving in all dimensions at once it has no fixed beginning or end. But it can be difficult to talk about this without using the words 'beginning' or 'ending', thus placing ~~beginning~~ and ~~ending~~*sous rature* signals the contradictory activity. Similarly, I generally refer to my ~~thesis~~*sous rature*, as it is an assemblage of plateaus, readable in any order, not a sequence of conventional chapters, which is the expectation of a traditional academic thesis/dissertation. These poststructuralist workings of text open (to) possibilities for thinking differently, that is, opens *actual* (and virtual) possibilities and opens *to* the idea that there possibly are other possibilities for thinking otherwise in other ways, this expressing dynamic and changing, always already conditions of constant movement through space and time.

happening upon this curricular space

My work in early childhood began in the late 1960s as a kindergarten teacher in Aotearoa New Zealand and, over the next 25 years, I was involved as a teacher and parent in various state, community and private settings in urban, suburban and rural areas; also in distance learning. After a break from early childhood education through the 1990s, I returned to university to further my studies in the broader field of education but in 2003 I was drawn back to early childhood, into teacher education. It was while visiting a student teacher on practicum that I met two-year-old Marcy, whose story became the inspiration for my (ad)venture into doctoral research. Three years on, after much reading~writing~thinking about how I might make a research rhizome work, I took two video cameras into a kindergarten and with the children as participating researchers recorded 36 hours of play-full activity of them performing their curricular understandings, or their expressions of curricular performativity.

generating the research rhizome

State kindergartens in Aotearoa New Zealand have a history of free play and child-centred learning. This has evolved into an underpinning philosophy about learning spaces, in which children and teachers work together towards shared understandings, with children's desires for their learning to the fore. In the kindergarten selected for generating the data of this research, although routines were apparent they did not dominate the programme. The children's play was subject to minimal outside(r) disruption; for most of the session the children played unhurried and uninterrupted. While there was an array of activity common to many early childhood settings, the resources and materials provided were not only the focus of variously planned learning opportunities; they were regarded as tools for complex learning experiences generated by the children through the games they played. For example, the art area provided space for children to explore aesthetic potentialities of various paints, drawing and collage materials, but any exploration was likely to be part of a game in progress, which might also involve literacy/numeracy learning...and...conflict resolution...and...science-related discoveries...and...interactions with adults in the setting; all this opening (to) ongoing learning opportunities. As well, tidy-up time became less a routine and more an opportunity for children to continue their play(ing)~learning in various imaginative, social, physical, literacy and numeracy spaces. For example, a group of girls regularly tidied the sandpit, playing with trucks and ride-on diggers in the process; other children played with the puzzles, tipping them out to redo them before reorganizing them on the shelves. For others, tidy-up time seemed to be a last opportunity for the day to race the trollies the long way around the path to the shed, roll tyres down the steps from the top of the fort (and up again), don various hats and scarves while sorting dolls and beds in the family corner, and shape, slice and squish the clay before putting it and various tools into containers, and so on.

In these generative play spaces of the setting, programme and games the children played, the way the teachers operated was also significant; as with many teachers operating in these kinds of settings their approach afforded open play(ing)~learning spaces; while they interacted with the children, it was on the children's terms. But, most significantly, these teachers were *with* the children in their learning spaces, ever vigilant against assuming control and adept at not interacting needlessly. In this setting I anticipated optimum possibilities for working in rhizo ways; the largely uninterrupted play(ing) time afforded favourable opportunities for flowing with the children to generate data through video recordings of rhizo mo(ve)ments. Following their lead seemed a potentially productive way of coming to understand their desires for curriculum by considering the play(ing) of games as conditions and expressions of curricular performativity. Although I was not engaging in predetermined situations within a prescribed agenda, I avoid describing this rhizo process as random. It was both planned and unplanned – (un)planned – the ~~plan~~ being to have an open plan, not in a haphazard way but to follow lines of flight which inevitably opened (to) spaces of ongoing, (e)merging happenings. It was about engaging with the research process in ways that open possibilities for something to happen anew, not necessarily 'new' happenings but happenings that might be perceived as incipiently different – working with/in/through rhizome.

~~thesis~~ to book

As it is with rhizome, things intensify through a multiplicity of ongoing interconnections; everything is always already dynamic and changing. So although this book tells something of the rhizo research of my doctoral ~~thesis~~ – something as in not all and as always incomplete – the story of the research is constantly becoming something different. In this telling of the research story for a wider audience – early childhood scholars, students and teachers, also academics and practitioners with an interest in the workings of Deleuzo-Guattarian philosophy – the text is intended to in/vite/cite active engagement with an exploration of curriculum inquiry as it might relate epistemologically and ontologically to the underpinning philosophy and to how the plateaus are assembled. Some of the content of the ~~thesis~~ is not included here, such as the detailed explanation of putting rhizome work – here I just do it, making the rhizoanalysis a happening so that both conditions and expressions of rhizome might become perceptible. Also, ethical issues, details of the data collection and the implications for researching with young children are in the ~~thesis~~ but not here; and the discussion of historical understandings of children, childhood and curriculum is considerably reduced, my preference being to work (with) current ideas in different ways.

However, the rhizo activity of the ~~thesis~~ has continued through my ever (e)merging theoretical understandings, namely: notions of diffraction inspired by Barad (2007) and woven throughout – see the *Preceding echoes* plateau for more about this; further discussion of power-fullness in response to Bronwyn Davies', ~~thesis~~ assessor, comment that in reflecting on Tim's power-full activity I had inadvertently slipped into an 'institutional "ethics" discourse that relentlessly reduces children in stature and allocates all/knowing power to the researcher' – see the *Becoming-child(ren) becoming-power-full* plateau; and matters of materiality drawn to my attention through reading~thinking works of Liselott Mariett Olsson (2009) and Hillevi Lenz Taguchi (2010) – see the *Materiality matters* plateau. All together, these additions and omissions open to an incipiently different *Aftrwrding* through (re)connecting with *Te Whāriki* (Ministry of Education, 1996). Inasmuch as there is no ~~beginning~~ or ~~ending~~ in rhizome, some concluding thoughts – not specific conclusions – are offered in the *Aftrwrdng*. This title's textese form – where vowels are often elided – is intended to signal an always already incompleteness within which there are in-between spaces constantly being (re)negotiated, in ways appropriate to the reader, context, contact zones and relations in-between. Aspects of *Te Whāriki* useful to this approach are revisited and brought to the conversation that closes here but is likely still just opening for the reading~writing~thinking.

Through/with/in these mo(ve)ments I anticipate others negotiating this rhizome and generating more of the rhizo conversation about receiving young children's understandings...into adult conceptions of curriculum...made perceptible with/in/ through curricular performativity...through learning to think differently – about children, childhood and curriculum...generating productive living~learning experiences for young children in early childhood settings...all of this spilling into other worlds...of early childhood and beyond...In rhizo mo(ve)ments of poststructuralist performativity things inevitably slip slide through never ending (un)certainty, eluding being pinned down or concretized in a single space as a way of working with/in/through complex systems of living~learning. Young children's expressions of curricular performativity draw attention to this complexity and these expressed understandings excite~incite~invite exploration through/with/in their world(s). This is the learning journey of my text and as a provoking mo(ve)ment I invite readers to negotiate these spaces through my perceptions of what, how and why these might be...*and*...I incite you to negotiate space-times of your/my thought~thinking that opens the complexity of young children's curricular performativity...*and*...the power-fullness of this learning, towards re(con)ceiving children in curriculum...*and*...

Note

1   Deb Lean with a team from the University of Canterbury presented 'Maggie's story: narrative and metaphor as tools for developing critical understandings of the hidden curriculum in schools and teacher education' at the NZARE/AARE Conference, Educational Research, Risks & Dilemmas, Hyatt Regency Hotel and University of Auckland, 29 November–3 December 2003.

Mapping milieu(s)

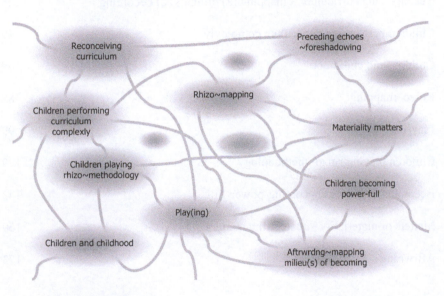

Map 0.1 Mapping milieu(s)

Plateau starting pages

Maps, figures and storyboards

Maps

Figures

Storyboards (colour plate section)

Preceding echoes ~ foreshadowing

starting up rhizome with foreshadowing ideas

The plateaus assembled as this book are a dynamically changing mass – a rhizome – of opening *Preceding echoes* that segue through the closing *Aftrwrdng*. The rhizome emerges through the boundless (ad)venture of my doctoral research (Sellers, 2009b), in an altered iteration continuing here. Transgressing conventional chaptering, the plateaus work non-linearly as an assemblage, a milieu of plateaus constituted in different ways by literature and data, variously telling the story of the research and re(con)ceiving children in curriculum. This is not a linear sequence of chapters containing specific segments of the research process. It is a research rhizome; it researches rhizome, recursively applying operations of research and rhizome working together. Thus the plateaus are written so they can be read in any order, according to readers' interests and in response to lines of flight that may emerge in the reading. The following mapping offers four ways through but with the suggestion that this plateau (*Preceding echoes*) be read first (Map 1.1) as it explicates the Deleuzo-Guattarian imaginaries (Deleuze & Guattari, 1987) deployed throughout. However, I invite readers to choose their own pathway, one that resonates with personal interests as they are now and as they emerge in the reading.

Aware that curriculum means different things to different people involving traditional discourses around the what, how and why, my interest is with, 'How does it work?' (Deleuze, 1995) but not in a conventional unpacking of curriculum. I am interested in understandings of curriculum as processual, as a lived experience, as *currere*, as always already becoming, working with the understanding that curriculum processes around us and we process through it. In this way of thinking, curriculum is less a thing and more about happening. Thus my inquiry circulates through how curriculum works, how we put it to work, how we work it as curriculum-ing, as curricular performativity, interwoven with Grumet's (1988) belief that we are curriculum. Curriculum – how it is played out in conditions and expressions of performativity – and the players as curricular performers, commingle. Questions that ease the productivity of this text are: How might Deleuzo-Guattarian imaginaries work with understandings of curriculum and with children's curricular performativity? How do children perform curriculum? How might children's curricular performativity contribute to reconceiving curriculum?

Understanding Children & Childhood	Curriculum
o Preceding echoes	o Preceding echoes
o Children & childhood	o Reconceiving curriculum
o Play(ing)	o Children performing curriculum complexly
o Children performing curriculum complexly	o Rhizo~mapping
o Becoming-child(ren) becoming-power-full	o Play(ing)
o Children playing rhizo~methodology	o Children playing rhizo~methodology
o Reconceiving curriculum	o Children & childhood
o Rhizo~mapping	o Becoming-child(ren) becoming-power-full
o Materiality matters	o Materiality matters
o Aftrwrdng	o Aftrwrdng

Research Methodology	The book-assemblage as presented
o Preceding echoes	o Preceding echoes
o Children playing rhizo~methodology	o Reconceiving curriculum
o Rhizo~mapping	o Children performing curriculum complexly
o Becoming-child(ren) becoming-power-full	o Children & childhood
o Children performing curriculum complexly	o Rhizo~mapping
o Play(ing)	o Play(ing)
o Children & childhood	o Children playing rhizo~methodology
o Reconceiving curriculum	o Becoming-child(ren) becoming-power-full
o Materiality matters	o Materiality matters
o Aftrwrdng	o Aftrwrdng

Map 1.1 Negotiating plateaus through leading interests

How are responses to these co-implicated in understandings of *Te Whāriki* (Ministry of Education, 1996), the Aotearoa New Zealand national early childhood curriculum statement?[1]

Considering young children's understandings of the world as significant as those of adults, my approach is to *receive* children, their childhoods and their understandings into adult *conceptions* of theorizing curriculum and into readings of *Te Whāriki*. This venture of *re(con)ceiving* children in curriculum becomes an adventure, a play-full exploration that works with young children's curricular performativity as expressed through/with/in games they play and their playing of those games, that is, in their play(ing). Similarly, I play with the literature, play-fully bringing it alongside children's play in the data and engaging play as oscillation to move back and forth through the literature. Play in these understandings belies linear progression, in itself generating con/di/verging plateaus rather than conventionally sequenced chapters. Play(ing) with the methodology in this rhizo way opens (to) possibilities[2] in a transgressive project of disturbing and perturbing the rationale of modernist thought. Already always (re)thinking the doctoral research, different notions of materiality emerge and I work to flatten another binary unnoticed in the doctoral ~~thesis~~, namely, the material|discursive hierarchy. This disrupts the primacy of logocentrism through actually naming material relations, some of which were already happening in various textual arrangements... *and*... in the closing moments of thinking and writing the *Aftrwrdng* another binary (e)merges,[3] namely, the hierarchical positioning of formal over informal (in|formal) learning that draws in to itself non|compulsory education and school|early childhood education binaries. These are not addressed, however, in the space-time of this book~assemblage,[4] they merely signal more of the milieu of rhizome...

The data generation of the doctoral research was a play-full rhizo adventure of flowing with the children in one kindergarten in Aotearoa New Zealand generating a random selection of games on video. Similarly, the rhizo analysis that both emerges through and merges with the various plateaus – (e)merges – becomes a play-full and serious (ad)venture of processing through the data and the writing of the research journey. For example, working with poietic inscriptions of ideas and style; also acknowledging the significance of the materiality of the text through different formatting arrangements; all challenging conventional linear readings. Curriculum as (a) milieu(s) of becoming emerges from/with/in shadows of my thinking and working with re(con)ceiving children in curriculum becomes a play-full (ad)venture with/of a multiplicity of children always already becoming something different.

Writing these introductory ideas of *Preceding echoes* is also a less structured venture than the logic of modernist academic realms dictates. Processing through the thought~thinking of this book~assemblage resists concretizing all the way. Both ~~beginning~~ and ~~end~~ are then *sous rature*, as rhizome has no beginnings or endings, only middle spaces in-between. Things slip and slide, continually tipping traditional thought and thinking off balance, creating an a-order and (dis)harmony that is chaotically complex. Within rhizo spaces of this textual assemblage the introduction becomes the conclusion – becomes as in both developing into and enhancing – and from within these (e)merging introductory~concluding ideas the middle story of the research project unfolds. Foreword becomes introducing ideas become concluding thoughts become after wording thinking becomes *Aftrwrdng*. Txt-ese, bracketing and slashes become useful for signalling different (in)completely ever changing ideas that this book becomes. The textual performance of research becoming book~assemblage becomes perceptible as textual performativity of research, a Deleuzo-Guattarian inspired milieu with *Preceding echoes* foreshadowing the *Aftrwrdng*...through a dynamic milieu of movements in-between. So, assembling introductory ideas here emerges as an ever changing mass that can only ever be some of this dynamic (ad)venture.

before ~~beginning~~ ~ a letter for Marcy

This letter was written as I readied the assemblage of plateaus for submission of my doctoral ~~thesis~~. It acknowledges the inspiration Marcy was and still is for my research activities.

Dear Marcy

It has taken many years to write this letter, to bring together the thoughts and thinking of ideas and inspiration, perceptions and conceptions, visions and suspicions, suggestions and intentions, images and imaginings, words and pictures, reading and writing, consciously and unconsciously in a way that befits my memory of you. The day I met you, you became every child in every early childhood setting everywhere; in my mind's eye, you became the children of many world(s), due unconditional respect from adult worlds. Working with/in my whitened, westernized understandings, you become a severalty of children that I wish to embody within incipiently different approaches to curriculum as commingling learning~living.

You continue to inspire me to think how I might think differently about children, childhood and curriculum and how I might think differently about thinking (differently). Many years have passed and it's hard to imagine that you were not yet three when our paths crossed, our lines of flight crisscrossing through the milieu(s) of our learning. As I write this, to assure myself you were that young~old, I (re)turn to my research journal. In August 2003, I wrote about your alerting me to the powerlessness of infants, toddlers and young children in some early childhood settings to eat, sleep or play when and how they want; also about the beginnings of a reconceiving of curriculum towards receiving young children's understandings of themselves and the world(s) around them. It was these thoughts about how you were (mis)understood by your teachers that opened to re(con)ceiving children in curriculum as my doctoral (ad)venture.

14 August 2003: Today Foucault likely turned in his grave. Foucault deconstructed surveillance, among other aspects of power, by analysing the relationship between discipline and punishment in prisons. Prisoners are watched over relentlessly; surveillance is everywhere, limitless, oppressive. While such disciplinary surveillance is an overt form of power, Foucault maintains that the notion of self-discipline, as promoted within the individualism of psychology, is a covert form of surveillance invented by bourgeois society to ensure and maintain cohesion. We have developed an individualized form of power exercised through the surveillance of individuals by themselves in such a way that they develop self-discipline – effectively we are then governed from within.

Valerie Walkerdine (1992) relates such discipline and surveillance to schooling, in that the child becomes the object of psychological theory and pedagogic practice, 'surveilled' by teachers, themselves responding to the same threat from above. Even when play is considered to be a child's work, the child is under the watchful and total gaze of the teacher, who is held responsible for the development of each individual. 'The teacher is there to help, to enable, to facilitate. Only those children with a poor grasp of reality, those poor pathological children, see her power' (p. 20).

Not knowing the pin number to open the door, I waited to be admitted into the custom built, privately owned early learning centre where you were – there was no one in sight, but at the push of a button the manager appeared. It felt like a corporate office and a prison, spacious with large grand managerial desk, designer reception and staff areas leading into a wide corridor that tracked through the building, giving views through large, well appointed internal windows of all areas where the children were cared for and played. Surveillance abounded, of both staff and children; even the cook was exposed to the view of passers-by. These were open plan spaces with (in)distinct boundaries that allowed (un)restricted flow from one area to another of children and teachers. I sensed something of the 'reality' of Foucault's notions of discipline and control, particularly of surveillance, and sensed Walkerdine's assessment of what this means for teaching practice and children's learning.

Walking into a room of under threes seated at two large round tables, I saw the children seemingly 'listening' to a story but apparently disengaged from the reading, the reader, and the surroundings. A lone child was doing a puzzle at another table and, as was soon to become apparent, she exemplified Walkerdine's facetious elaboration of a poor pathological child. This child may have been listening to the story being read as she worked on the puzzle, but that was not the issue. In her resistance to join the group, she was labelled 'a problem' and 'disruptive'. But, in her 'poor' grasp of reality, was she the (only) one who recognized the power and control she and her peers were subject to? Was she the one who appreciated the surroundings as oppressive to her as a person and to her learning, learning that mattered to her 'under three-year old' understanding of what she desired to know?

Although I think of this as your story, Marcy, it is not a story you actually told me, rather it is my storying of your way of connecting with the world in the short time I was part of that. As alluded to above, when I was ushered into your secured (in)secure world, it was like entering Foucault's vision of panopticon. In the under threes' room, I saw a group of children seated around a large round table waiting for a story to be read before morning tea. The teacher overseeing the group was finding it difficult to sustain the children's interest in the book. Admittedly my arrival was a distraction, but none of the children was seated for easy engagement with either teacher or book, and I suspect that the smells wafting from the kitchen were focusing their attention on food and eating, not on books and reading. Your attention, Marcy, was definitely elsewhere. Unnoticed by the teachers, you were engrossed in doing a puzzle, but once spotted you were ordered to join the group. Unsurprisingly, you refused despite further commands. By now, I was sitting on a small chair nearby and, before I could anticipate your next move, you hurtled across the room and planted yourself on my knee. Without thinking, I put my arms around you and you settled into listening to the story. For a moment, it seemed that the problem had been resolved. You were complying – you had abandoned the puzzle and had implicitly agreed to come and listen to the story.

But in the same moment, I realized that your terms of compliance were unacceptable, that you were required to sit at the table. I also realized in that moment that I was complicit in your resistance, in your preferred way of listening to the story and in what was later referred to as your disruptive behaviour. As I gently lifted you to the floor, my heart sank. Your teachers had denied your expression of engaging with curriculum – your curricular performativity – and I was now party to that. The puzzle was not to be completed; the chair at the table took precedence over the knee. It was not so much 'dis-empowerment' that you experienced, but that the flow of your power-fullness was quashed; Foucault's notions of power as force, as affect, through institutions of control and surveillance were illuminated. The implications for you and your learning were projected irrevocably and indelibly onto the screen of my understanding. Although I had only just happened upon the situation, knew nothing of you and little of the context, as an outsider~observer it appeared that you were resisting co-operating with a more powerful adult regime and, despite signalling a level of compliance by jumping onto my knee, your attempt to compromise was deemed unacceptable. The teachers might have justified their teaching practice by pointing to individualized learning outcomes, aligned to *Te Whāriki* principles and strands. Yet, I suspect your reading of *Te Whāriki* might be different, perhaps one of affirming your expression of what curriculum meant for you, enabling your flows of power-fullness and privileging your desires as a young human being to be heard, respected, understood and valued.

With this last thought, I close this long overdue letter of acknowledgment and appreciation, knowing that you may never read it, but, recorded in the annals of educational research, it may contribute to (an) opening (of) early childhood curricular worlds respectful of young children everywhere. I am ever hopeful that it will kindle some interest in opening (to) ways of thinking, incipiently different from the dominating ways that have got us thus far in early childhood education and curriculum. I am hopeful that my doctoral (ad)venture will become a way of opening (to) de~territorializing early childhood curricular spaces, through/with/in understandings of young children, such as yours Marcy, can flourish. It is for you, Marcy, and young children of other worlds, that I risk these spaces.

With respect, admiration and gratitude,

Marg

P.S. Marcy, the book~assemblage that follows is but a postscript to this letter and although the language of the text is not yours, I trust my expressions of your understandings resonate with your intentions for your learning~living.

~~beginning~~ ~ a note for the reader

Nothing ever 'begins', it only has tentative links to what has gone before and what is yet to come – threads (e)merging from/with/in heterogeneous space-times of past~present~future in mo(ve)ments[5] of middles. Uncertainly, the middle of the assemblage that constitutes this book is a processing through questions-without-answers, any pending 'answer' embodying another question, signalling (im)partiality, decentring expert authority, speeding up the intensity. And, an 'ending' is but a momentary pause, ebbing only until the flow again picks up speed, back/through/in/to the middle of more thoughts~thinking. So, how/where to ~~begin~~ with the desire to generate mo(ve)ments towards conceiving early childhood curriculum in ways that welcome young children as young people with views, opinions, understandings, experiences, capacities and skills as significant as adults' towards generating curricular performativity authentic to the worlds of children's living~learning? This big question becomes a milieu of ideas generated in rhizo ways, always already contemplating what else there might be. The muddle~middle of this quest with no specific starting point is perhaps not unusual. Deleuze and Guattari (1987) explain that ideas often occur, not in linear progression, but from within a middle space. Although this can be challenging, they urge: 'try it, you'll see that everything changes' (p. 23). So, I try negotiating the middle that is the milieu, from anywhere…I ~~begin~~ and it becomes something of a never-ending story…as the *aftrwrdng* tells…

foreshadowing the book~assemblage

The generative thinking of this textual assemblage involves bringing Deleuzian philosophy alongside conventional images of young children and their childhood(s) and their curricular performativity. A mass of rhizo connections is generated by exploring how Deleuzo-Guattarian philosophical imaginaries can be put to work, opening (to) possibilities for moving outside conventional, chaptered formatting and reading. Throughout this rhizo thinking~reading~writing~doing of research processes, several imaginaries areused to perturb linearity and generate an assemblage, which becomes a collection of conversations presented as plateaus that have no beginning or end, origin or destination, only linking ideas. As rhizome, the assemblage is heterogeneous, always in the middle, unconcerned with points, made only of lines of movement and speed (Deleuze & Guattari, 1987). Explaining how the plateaus work, presentation and content-wise, resonates with Deleuze's (1995) interest in the functional and practical of how things work. This (opening) plateau of *Preceding echoes* discusses how to go about reading the other plateaus, my use of Deleuzian imaginaries and the folds of my subjectivity around/with/in the thinking~reading~writing of the research.

For reading the plateaus, Map 1.1 *Negotiating the plateaus through leading interests* gives an overview of possible readings according to various interests, namely: conceptions of children and childhood; philosophy of curriculum; research methodology. A fourth possible reading is as the plateaus are presented here but other readings may follow other pathways. The plateaus as presented follow my line(s) of flight through the research. While there was an opening line of flight, processing with/through the writing was not linearly straightforward. Rather, it involved much to-ing and fro-ing in many directions, often all at once, particularly as I (re)turned to (re)work various pieces, expressions and characterizations. Also, the *Material(ity) matter(s)* plateau was generated relatively recently; engaging with a body of literature about human-nonhuman relations made more of the rhizome.

The mapping of the milieu(s) – the plateau map, *Mapping Milieu(s)* (Map 0.1) – is a way of linking the plateaus, of making a map to explicate the assemblage. Although the links are arbitrary, where they appear in the book~assemblage is intended to illuminate particular characteristics of the connectivity. For example, in the data the children's curricular performativity apparent in games they play illuminates their understandings of curriculum and also links with their mapping of their play(ing) of these games. Hence, *Reconceiving curriculum* comes before *Children performing curriculum complexly*, *Rhizo~mapping* coming after but not before *Children and Childhood*. Explaining rhizomethodology nearer the ~~beginning~~ may be useful to the reading, but it is by working through various snippets of data that I become aware of the children's performativity of rhizo understandings. Hence *Children playing rhizo~methodology* appears towards the ~~end~~. Situating this plateau in this later moment also leaves the children in their curricular performativity in the foreground of a latter reading. It signals the children's always already, tacit understandings of what the research project explores, leaving them the 'last say' and opening possibilities for understanding what young children know and what we can learn from them. The *Aftrwrdng* is my adult(erated) summary of what the children make perceptible with/in the data. In some ways I would have rather left the reader with the images, imagining and imagery performed by the children in their tacit, but working, understandings of Deleuzo-Guattarian imaginaries, but in that closing mo(ve)ment I somewhat reluctantly submit to convention and offer some concluding thoughts.

Following lines of flight that rise up in moments of reading is appropriate to any reading by any reader. When Deleuze (1995) is asked, 'So how are your *Thousand Plateaus* arranged?' he replies, 'It's like a set of split rings. You can fit any one of them into any other. Each ring, or each plateau, ought to have its own climate, its own tone or timbre' (p. 25). The (ad)venture here has been to make all these plateaus work – singularly and severally – acknowledging that a refrain of ideas risks repetition. However, in circles of con/di/vergence each (dis)connecting happens with/in different space-times of thinking and brings with it other dis/inter/rupted conceptions. The refrain always already opens (to) other understandings.

introducing imaginaries

Presenting Deleuzo-Guattarian philosophical concepts as imaginaries moves outside the notion of metaphor, that is, a figure of speech in which a word or phrase is transferred to an object or action so that something is regarded as representative, suggestive or symbolic of something else. Deleuze and Guattari (1994) explicate a concept as a multiplicity comprising inseparable components. It is asymmetrically constituted so that it is (only ever) a fragmentary~whole: 'Only in this condition can it escape the mental chaos constantly threatening it, stalking it, trying to reabsorb it' (p. 16). This fragmentary concept is fluid, always already relating to other concepts, (im)partially overlapping in 'a threshold of indiscernibility' (p. 19), each fragment and whole resonating singularly and severally as 'centers of vibrations' (p. 23). It is a non-totalizing movement that resists metaphorical representation.

The Deleuzo-Guattarian project of thinking differently – to 'think reality outside of representation' (Due, 2007: 9) – conceives philosophy as emerging from a perception of what it is to think, that is, what we do with/in thinking and what thinking does. 'Imaginary', as a multiplicitous 'concept', then becomes a way of working (with) complex thinking, different from the common understanding of 'imaginary' as existing in the imaginative mind's ability to be creative, inventive and resourceful. This understanding of (a Deleuzian) imaginary also differs from the Lacanian psychoanalytical imaginary, in which the word is perceived as being identical to what it represents (Clark, 2004). Working with/in folds of rhizo thinking, Warren Sellers (2008) uses imaginary as a 'characterising affect rather than a mental image referencing some thing, situation or circumstance' (p. 8) so as 'to avoid leaving any totalised major construct in mind' (p. 269). He perceives rhizome as imaginary, rather than metaphor or traditional trope, saying it is impossible to 'seize' rhizome as an entity – 'any attempt to represent it as such fails as soon as it is tried'. So that 'rhizome as imaginary in thinking' and 'imaginary as rhizome' is inseparable; together they work to 'reveal notions of understandings that are not otherwise conceivable' (p. 206).

To illuminate that which may be unthinkable in a representational mode, Braidotti and St. Pierre also avoid metaphorical thinking in relation to Deleuzo-Guattarian philosophical concepts, talking instead of figurations. Although there is slippage here into an emblematic or allegorical symbolism, Braidotti (2000) uses the term 'figuration' to characterize a 'conceptually charged use of the imagination' (p. 170) for thinking differently. St. Pierre (1997) similarly works with Deleuzian 'figurations' as a way of thinking outside a familiar use of language, opening (to) different questions that might affect understandings of educational theory and practice. Connecting explicitly with Braidotti and Deleuze, St. Pierre says:

> A figuration is not a graceful metaphor that provides coherency and unity to contradiction and disjunction; rather, it is a 'politically informed map' (Braidotti, 1994a: 181), a cartographic weapon, that charts a 'line of flight' (Deleuze & Parnet, 1987: 125) into turbulence masked by the simulacrum called coherence. A figuration is no protection from disorder, since its aim is to produce a most rigorous confusion as it jettisons clarity in favour of the unintelligible… Thinking with a figuration is 'living at a higher degree, at a faster pace, in a multidirectional manner' (Braidotti, 1994a: 167). Thinking with a figuration

may also lead to a seeming impasse where the desire to understand what is 'really going on' must be sacrificed, and the researcher must learn not to balk at the task of working bewilderment for all it's worth.

(St. Pierre, 1997: 280–1)

Not understood as pure imagination opposed to reason or as fantasy, imaginaries (figurations) function in spaces of transitions and transactions, as unstable and contingent, opening (to) possibilities for creating a different kind of work, for thinking and writing differently, outside modernist fixities. St. Pierre (1997) also says: 'Figurations, then, enable us to move toward realities in different ways…as we try to think our way out of the deadlock of epistemology' (p. 281). The Deleuzo-Guattarian imaginaries that I open with here – *rhizome, plateaus* and *assemblage~multiplicity* – in their complex relations of intra-activity mark the expression and content of this book~assemblage; and, when useful to the conversation, these imaginaries, in rhizo operations, are further explicated. Slip-sliding alongside, the imaginary of *nomad* informs and performs the process of the research and its writing, commingling with *de~territorializing lines of flight* and *smooth spaces*. Others, such as *milieu, becoming, singularities, monad, affect* and *desire* are introduced into the conversation in the moment they are put to work. To avoid overly fracturing the discussion, some are merely footnoted in passing. In using these imaginaries, no one is centralized. Rather, working together, they are co-implicated with/in complex arrangements that vary in different mo(ve)ments, with explanations of one drawing on/in others, some perhaps not yet explained.

Various researchers consider certain imaginaries of leading significance to their reading~writing~research methodology. For example, for Stagoll (2005), difference and becoming are central; for Boundas (2005), intensity is a key notion; Roffe (2005) says that multiplicity is basic and most important; Braidotti (1994a) claims rhizome as the leading figuration, although later the central figuration shifts to 'a general becoming-minority, or becoming-nomad, or becoming-molecular' (Braidotti, 2001: 392). As Colebrook (2005) says: 'Each definition of each term is a different path from a text, a different production of sense that itself opens further paths for definition' (p. 3). Thus, the order in which I present understandings of imaginaries that I use, relates to my (e)merging understandings of how they work and how I put them to work, conversationally, in this book~assemblage. Working with/in a rhizo middle that is horizontal and a-centred, there is no concern for one being more significant than any other, so I open with the one that first caught my attention – rhizome.

rhizome

Deleuze and Guattari's rhizo approach to thinking~reading~writing perturbs conventional order/ing, sequencing, categorizing and linearity, including that represented in/by the (metaphorical) tree of knowledge. The arborescent thinking of the tree of knowledge utilizes concepts of branches and roots through which we 'receive' knowledge from the past, develops it within the present and passes its fruits on to future generations. Such arborescence supports binary logic, representing linearly ordered systems of thinking, which are fixed and rooted, that beneath the surface mirrored above – thought 'branches' in one direction and is similarly 'rooted' oppositely. Although there is opportunity for thinking to divert and digress, it happens genealogically, through 'a logic of tracing and reproduction' (Deleuze & Guattari, 1987: 12). Tracing involves continuous repetitions of structural patterns already present (roots and branches), and reproduction is the continuous reconstitution of the closed structure or fixed entity (as the tree grows). Both tracing and reproduction produce more of the same by following a sequentially ordered process through specific points and positions that are restricted to a particular place and reach conventionally logical and coherent conclusions.

In contrast, heterogeneous connectivity characterizes the complexity of rhizome, such as the rhizo thinking and rhizo research methodology of the book~assemblage/research. A rhizome comprises ceaseless interrelational movements – flows of connectivity – among numerous possible assemblies of the disparate and the similar. Etymologically, *rhizo-* means 'combining' and in botanical terms a rhizome is a prostrate or subterranean root-like stem, which assumes diverse forms, from multidirectional surface extensions (kikuyu grass) to thick, swollen tuber-like masses (iris, root ginger). Because the botanical rhizome moves horizontally and expands multidimensionally, its points of regrowth, its shoots and roots, are chaotically a-centred, taking on a complex existence, as it spreads simultaneously outwards (extending), inwards (expanding), upwards (shoots), downwards (roots) (Figure 1.1a). In thought and thinking, a rhizome maps processes that are 'networked, relational and transversal' (Colman, 2005a: 231). A rhizome familiar in abstract or virtual terms, but also actual in the real world is the Internet, characterized by infinite connectivity (Figure 1.1b).

Together, these two images illuminate the complexity of working in rhizo ways. They open (to) a chaotic or differently ordered approach to thinking, writing and analysing research data, for example, as thoughts and ideas shift, (re)turn, (re)form (unlikely) connections, move in unexpected directions, perform surprises. Deleuze and Guattari (1987) say: 'A rhizome has no beginning or end; it is always in the middle, between things, interbeing, *intermezzo*…proceeding from the middle, through the middle, coming and going rather than starting and finishing' (p. 25, original italics). Simply put, 'the fabric of the rhizome is the conjunction, "and…and…and…"' (p. 25) so if a break occurs, the rhizome will start up again, travelling along an old line or generating a new one, these lines of flight becoming part of the rhizome. Ants are rhizome, defying destruction in this way; the rhizome may collapse but only momentarily, it never gives up, always restarting after a break occurs. Through such ruptures and irruptions, any part of a rhizome is always already connected to any other.

Thinking in rhizo ways thus opens (to) endless possibilities for approaching any thought, activity or concept, towards generating and assembling many and

Tangle of Rhizomes

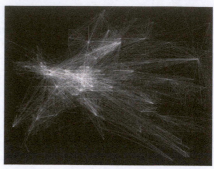

Figure 1.1a Rhizome~multidimensional and a-centred (drawing by Warren Sellers)

Figure 1.1b The internet ceaselessly establishes connections (drawing by Chris Harrison, http://www.chrisharrison. net/projects/Internetmap/ medium/euroblack.jpg)[6]

various ways of being and operating in the world. Diverging from the conventional and familiar can be challenging for both reader and writer as rhizo thought is concerned with flow and movement rather than with linearity, fixed endpoints or stable, specific conclusions. However, what matters to generating plateaus in this book~assemblage is connectivity, the in-between-ness of flow and movement, rather than points of connection or positions of their location. Recording this somewhat elusive flow calls on an amassing of open(ing) imaginaries, which in themselves defy discrete explanations; how they are understood is very much the reader's prerogative. Deleuze and Guattari avoid assigning any one meaning to their imaginaries, preferring they 'reverberate' through 'shifting contexts' (Lorraine, 2005a: 207), thereby generating non-totalizing fragmentary~wholes. Final definitions are beyond reach; expressing possibilities for future uses is what matters, such as: 'What new thoughts does it make it possible to think? What new emotions does it make it possible to feel? What new sensations and perceptions does it open to the body?' (Massumi, 1987a: xv). Thinking and writing with rhizome is, and performs, an open system that is ceaselessly converging and diverging as thoughts simultaneously (e)merge. For example, writing as a method of inquiry (Richardson, 2000a) or travelling as nomad, 'in the thinking that writing produces in search of the field' (St. Pierre, 2000: 258). Negotiating such rhizo nomadic moves I process[7] through (the) writing (of) this book~assemblage.

A rhizo approach to my writing, thinking and academic inquiry involves other Deleuzo-Guattarian imaginaries, thus explaining plateaus comes next. Plateaus disturb, disrupt, decentre, disperse, destabilize, and dispense with the linearity of conventional academic writing. Commingling the interplay among imaginaries, a rhizome generates plateaus and plateaus generate more of the rhizome. Generating plateaus becomes an intensifying endeavour, making more of the middle or milieu.

plateaus

Deleuze and Guattari (1987) consider a plateau as a 'continuous, self-vibrating region of intensities' (p. 22) constituted so as not to develop any external end or final climax. Rather, 'a plateau is reached when circumstances combine to bring an activity to a pitch of intensity that is not automatically dissipated in a climax' (Massumi, 1987a: xiv). A plateau is a never-ending assemblage; it is any multiplicity connected to any other multiplicities in ways that are non-constraining – intensities becoming rhizome becoming intensities and so on. As with rhizome, plateaus are always already a milieu of intensities, happenings rather than entities, fields of moving forces rather than things static and unchanging (Boundas, 2005); the plateau always already intensifying through/with/in *and...and...and...* Plateaus are thus open systems comprising dynamic spaces in flux, of in-between-ness – *intermezzo* – with/in which numerous possible pathways and connections (may) exist and (may) be explored. Marc Ngui, in his diagrammatic visualizations of passages from *A Thousand Plateaus*, depicts freely flowing plateaus (ovals) working in contrast to, while slip-sliding alongside, structured linear thinking and writing (boxes) (Map 1.2).

Working with rhizome, writing with/in plateaus means always already processing through middles, blurring any possible bounding of continually (e)merging plateaus. This disturbs any sense of culmination or end point; as with rhizome, a plateau is never a complete or definitive entity, both are always already ongoing happenings. Plateaus are never wholly formed, they are recursively (re)constitutive so that we can only ever talk about *some* of a rhizome or *some* of a plateau (Deleuze & Guattari, 1987: 9)[8] – rhizome is constituted of/by plateaus constituted of/by rhizome constituted of/by plateaus...spreading multidirectionally, intensifying multidimensionally. Always in the middle, amidst everything, generating and generated by circles of convergence. 'Each plateau can be read starting anywhere and can be related to any other plateau' (p. 22). There is an always already connectivity, with linkages forming, creating something anew, unpredictably and incipiently different. Other plateaus emerge through connections outside external constraints; plateaus becoming intensities that reverberate according to their unfolding rather than being determined by conventional boundaries (Lorraine, 2005a).

In this book~assemblage, although plateaus do not have to be read in any particular order, as each one works diffractively with/in the fragmentary~whole assemblage, the reading is likely eased by first engaging with this plateau that explains the opening imaginaries, through/with/in which budding ideas may unfold. Creating a book~assemblage, as a gathering of plateaus rather than a series of linearly ordered chapters, opens (to) (e)merging possibilities for thinking differently and

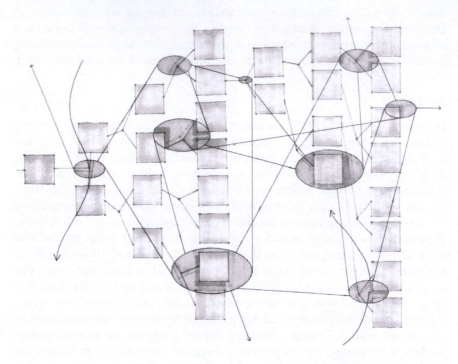

Map 1.2   Mapping openly connective plateaus and tracing structured linear thinking[9] (*1000 Plateaus Drawings: Intro Paragraph 15* by Marc Ngui, www.bumblenut.com)

(to) spaces for differing becomings, with plateaus diffracting as both expression and content. Becoming-plateaus becoming-assemblage; this assemblage of plateaus becomes the book~assemblage becomes (an) assemblage(s) of plateaus…

> *Becoming – an aside…* As stated above, discussing any one imaginary involves others. The notion of becoming for Deleuze and Guattari (1987) in not about serial progression or regression towards any anticipated state of being or future condition; it is *about* and *is* rhizome, producing nothing other than itself (pp. 238–9). Becoming involves dynamic processes, through/with/in which an assemblage is constantly changing through connections it is making. Becoming is thus characterized by mo(ve)ments of events, in which every instant is unique: 'a continual flow of changes…in an ongoing cycle of production…For Deleuze, the present is merely the productive moment of becoming' (Stagoll, 2005: 21–2). In this way becoming is always qualified as becoming-something different, such as in becoming-child, becoming-world, becoming-curriculum, becoming-imperceptible becoming-book~assemblage and so on. (Becoming is further elaborated in the *Children and childhood* plateau.)

In *A Thousand Plateaus* Deleuze and Guattari (1987) explain their writing as a circular exercise. Lines were written in a heterogeneous space~time, co-implicated in commingling, fluid mo(ve)ments of time and space, rather than through the reproduction and re/iteration of linear progression. In this way they generate an assemblage of plateaus that disrupt conventionally prescribed, sequential chaptering. They follow flows of ideas, moving freely in their thinking from one plateau to any other, processing without concern for completing the discussion in any moment before moving to any other. They say:

> *following is not at all the same thing as reproducing*, and one never follows in order to reproduce…Reproducing implies the permanence of a fixed point of *view* that is external to what is reproduced: watching the flow from the bank. But following is something different from the ideal of reproduction. Not better, just different. One is obliged to follow when one is in search of the 'singularities' of a matter, or rather of a material, and not out to discover a form…one engages in a continuous variation of variables…
>
> (Deleuze & Guattari, 1987: 372, original italics)

Through this ongoing engaging with a variation of variables, they generate circles of di/con/vergence so that reading the plateaus can start anywhere and be linked to any others – plateaus be(com)ing, (re)constituting an assemblage, connecting (within) multiplicities, interrupted and irrupting elsewhere. Similarly, the plateaus assemble in the multiplicity of this becoming-book.

assembling multiplicities ~ multiplicitous assemblages

For Deleuze and Guattari a multiplicity is not a multiple entity of discrete parts nor is it an unchanging collection of units (Colebrook, 2002). Rather, multiplicities involve continuous multidimensional expansion, generating and bringing together an infinite variety of thoughts, thinking and ideas, many times over – engaging with a variation of variables. An assemblage can then be considered as the ever intensifying dimensionality of a multiplicity generated from/through its connections with/in a multiplicity. In the mo(ve)ments in which a multiplicity emerges, it simultaneously irrupts into a web of proliferating fissures and converges in (another) space (Massumi, 1992). Multiplicities are thus rhizo, multidimensional intensities, transgressing, always already changing, attracting and repulsing connections with other multiplicities, altering through lines of flight and deterritorialization. In various movements diverse lines of flight cut across any assemblage, carrying it away, opening the territorial assemblage onto other assemblages (Deleuze & Guattari, 1987: 504–5). It is the territory *and* its connections that generate the multiplicitous assemblage as a complex array of happenings always already synergistic, a-centred and (e)merging.

The various texts deployed in this book then become a multiplicitous assemblage through heterogeneous processes of connectivity and intra-activity, changing in nature as linkages expand, working towards creating an ever growing fragmentary~whole. The assemblage works with re(con)ceiving young children's curricular performativity in one early childhood setting. The assemblage is constituted by and constitutes variously overlapping plateaus, which will likely (e)merge differently for different readers through/with/in differing readings. Commingling literature, data and rhizomethodology, the plateaus discuss (re)conceiving curriculum, various conceptions of children and childhood, children's curricular performativity and power-fullness, play(ing), rhizo-mapping, rhizomethodology and children's relations with matters of material worlds. So while any plateau generates an assemblage that slip-slides through various fragmentary intensities of the complex ~~whole~~, the gathering together of plateaus, related and disparate, generates more of the assemblage~multiplicity~rhizome. Plateaus (e)merge through/with/in a multiplicity recursively generating as the assemblage moves through/with/in the milieu, constantly changing. This then opens (to) unexpected, disparate, productive connections and possibilities towards nascent ways of thinking and learning~living...*and*...within this multiplicitous assemblage of rhizo plateaus nomad now (e)merges.

researching~thinking~reading~writing as nomad

Modernist thought presents as fixed, grounded and stable, with subject and object operating in a separated inside and outside. However, nomad thinking disturbs the linear rationale and logic of such essentialized thought, enabling open systems of thinking to come into play in productive ways, even and particularly when its object is open to destruction. There is no limit to what can be thought, at least for those willing 'to put their imaginations to work' (Gough, 2006a: xiv) as thoughts roam freely, wander, flow outside familiarity towards generating ever-expanding territories of difference and passages of thinking, opening (to) sites of emergence. Movement and territory being negotiated are entwined – each exists with/in the other, in open or smooth spaces as matter-flow. There is no anchoring or assignable reference point, nor are there confining boundaries. In nomadic mo(ve)ments, one can rise up, move to, and array oneself in any other space. When working nomadically to explore spaces for possible happenings of things incipiently different, questions about truth and meaning are cast aside in favour of 'How does it work?' and 'What new thoughts now become possible to think?' (Massumi, 1992). Flowing with St. Pierre (2004), within nomadic spaces of this rhizo research, other questions emerge: What exists here in the space of the play and in the play-space? What else might there be in these spaces? What other spaces might there be other than the physical surroundings and the enacted play? What might happen in those other interactive spaces?

Nomad thought rides difference (Massumi, 1987a); it works by 'travel[ling] in the thinking that writing produces' (St. Pierre, 2000: 258), processing from/through (the) middle(s), coming and going rather than starting and finishing, moving back and forth through a messy middle~muddle of ideas, through a complexly multidimensional milieu. Nomad thought~thinking opens (to) multidimensional readings of texts and data by skirting around the text, entering pleats, and folding one text on/in/to another (Richardson, 2000b). It resonates with laying-down-a-path-in-walking, mind-fully aware of negotiating enactive spaces of possibility through back-and-forth communication among inner and outside worlds of lived experience and knowing oneself (Varela, Thompson & Rosch, 1993). Nomad thought~thinking works to understand interrelationships of text, topic and writer (Richardson, 2000a) – what the writer brings to the topic, how the materiality of the text as it comes into being affects the writer, generating more thinking~thoughts and so on...

In the inquiry of this embodied thinking~reading~writing, St. Pierre (2000) talks about (re)turning to spaces already worked – mental spaces, textual spaces and theoretical spaces – that are always already challenging as inevitably with each engagement they become something different. However, continual (re)visiting and (re)turning to spaces of/within plateaus becomes a way of opening (to) hitherto unnoticed possibilities, such as in the *Matters of materiality* plateau; this plateau constituted by a later reading of data that illuminates relations among human and material worlds in a way different from with/in the plateaus generated earlier. As St. Pierre intimates, any concluding thoughts or after-wording turns out to be but a preface of preceding echoes as a desire or self-generated need to negotiate more (of the) middle(s) becomes apparent. Rhizo~nomadic inquiry of thought~thinking thus involves deterritorialization (continually (re)negotiating boundless spaces), destratification (generating undefined and indefinable smooth spaces from with/in linear spaces) and lines of flight composed of unlimited movement. It embodies notions of connectivity and heterogeneity, substantive multiplicity, nonsignifying rupture, and mapping and tracing (Deleuze & Guattari, 1987). It is about creating intensities of a-centred interconnections amassing as middles, clustering in plateaus, arraying through multidimensional movement, through ever (e)merging lines of flight.

de~territorializing lines of flight

Lines of flight are characterized as connectivity, forever (e)merging in 'creative mutations' (Lorraine, 2005b: 144) or mo(ve)ments of change. Deterritorialization is how the line of flight operates (Deleuze & Guattari, 1987); it is the 'creative potential of an assemblage' (Parr, 2005: 67). It is the movement of simultaneously leaving and (re)engaging with a territory. Like the singular and never ending surface of a Mobius strip,[10] these movements happen on the same plane, they are not polar opposites. Lines of flight are thus dynamic mo(ve)ments of de~re~territorialization that operate through/with/in creations, conquests and changes of territorialities, continually (dis)connecting. Deleuze and Guattari (1987) explain that it is movement not points, ends or destinations that matters in a rhizome~plateau~multiplicity~assemblage – 'the rhizome is made only with lines...[but not to be] confused with lineages of the arborescent type, which are merely localizable linkages between points and positions' (p. 21). While every assemblage is composed of connecting territories, it is also composed of lines of flight or lines of deterritorialization that cross through it and carry it away from its current form (p. 504).

However, Deleuze and Guattari do not believe that all lines of flight have productive potentially altering qualities; a line of flight can become a line of destruction, reconstructing rigid lines of segmentarity, reproducing linearity. For example, they consider the activity of interpretation as being a tracing through already established patterns of meaning. In contrast, maps work with connectivity, pursuing (im)perceptible lines of flight – perceptible to some, imperceptible to others (Lorraine, 2005b). As Lorraine elaborates, Deleuze and Guattari wrote their book as a map of plateaus, with the intention that readers would make more mappings in their reading, through continually following (dis)connecting lines of flight of thought and thinking. It is not about engaging in pure interpretation to establish what thoughts mean; it is about engaging with what thinking does; it is about how things work.

smooth nomadic spaces

Smooth spaces are open space throughout which 'things-flows are distributed' whereas striated spaces are closed; they are spaces plotted by points and positions and are concerned with enclosing things linear and solid (Deleuze & Guattari, 1987: 361). The nomad operates within smooth spaces and is oriented to an understanding of speed and movement rather than being confined in coded (striated) spaces. Smooth spaces are characterized by passages and passaging in-between, with points becoming relays to be passed through in mo(ve)ments of speed and slowness; the nomad is always already in the middle, in-between, with points passed through constituting a relay or trajectory (p. 380) – a line of flight. Nomadic movement is not so much about arriving in certain places or being positioned in one place and then another; it is about speeding~slowing through open spaces of shifting points. For example, in following the growth of 'rhizomatic vegetation' (p. 382) that appears in different places according to the rains, passages of crossings are constantly changing. The nomad arrays her/himself in smooth, open spaces, moving 'while seated...[and] only seated while moving' (p. 381) rather than being established in a fixed, closed, striated place. Operating in smooth spaces, the nomad 'can rise up at any point and move to any other' (Massumi, 1987a: xiii). However, smooth spaces operate in conjunction with striated spaces, each continually affected by and affecting passages of de~re~territorialization of the other – 'the nomad reterritorializes on deterritorialization itself' (Deleuze & Guattari, 1987: 381) so that smooth space is constantly 'translated, transversed into a striated space' and striated space is constantly 'reversed, returned to a smooth space' (p. 474). The smooth spaces of rhizo~poststructuralist thinking then can never be devoid of attention of/to modernist trappings always already lurking in the shadows. The tracing is always a palimpsest on the map; the map always a shadow on the tracing.

But, foregrounding a rhizo~poststructuralist approach, my passages of thought and thinking through this research become an embodied journey of travelling while seated. Explicating nomadic thought, St. Pierre (2000) points to the doubled activity of a nomad travelling on a camel being both mobile and sedentary, of travelling while seated. She explains this as a way of understanding the multidimensionality of processing through thought and thinking. Although seated at my computer writing via the attached keyboard, like a nomad travelling while seated I move through/with/in my thinking – movement of thought, sedentary body although outside movement affects the sedentariness. Nomad moves with the movement of the camel; my hands move in relation to the keyboard to record the thinking... *and*... the technology itself that I am operating through, both hardware and software, is likely influencing my thought patterns and my writing. In some mo(ve)ments I become lost in shifting space~times of a messy middle~muddle of the territory; in an endless desert of research and writing arrayed amongst shifting sands of data and rhizomethodology. Spaces of data, thinking~writing and text are continually shifting with/in various mo(ve)ments, generating imaginaries that are constantly (un)folding in an ever-growing textual milieu. The opening imaginaries of rhizome, plateaus and assemblage along with nomad, deterritorialization, lines of flight and smooth spaces explain some of my performativity of a rhizo approach to the research and its writing. More of this (un)folds through telling the rhizo research story – from/with/in the data, methodology and literature of the research project, and throughout the plateaus of writing here. Important to the telling are my subjective understandings.

my subjectivity ~ becoming-embodied-I

Subjectivity is commonly associated with reflection and reflexivity; however, I break with this to work with diffractive understandings. Barad (2007) explains diffraction in the physical world as having 'to do with the way waves combine when they overlap' and also with 'the apparent bending and spreading of waves that occurs when waves encounter an obstruction' (p. 74). Waves are thus disturbances, not specific entities or things. When a wave in the sea, for example, passes through a narrow opening, the wave as it was before encountering the obstruction, before being interfered with, is altered and an overlapping movement occurs. As well, diffractive patterns occur when waves of air (wind) interfere with waves of water (Figure 1.2).

The wave continues in its original pattern but it also combines with the activity of the disturbance from the interference; the wave may become larger or smaller as it continues to move as it was and as it has become. Diffraction unfolds the idea that, when different bodies meet, it is what happens in-between that matters for their ongoing engagement. It is relations of intra-activity in-between that intensify understandings rather than simply reflecting on the interactions that occur between separate bodies. It is looking at intra-active *movements* of the wave that (e)mergesthrough moments of interaction of sea and rock, for example, that

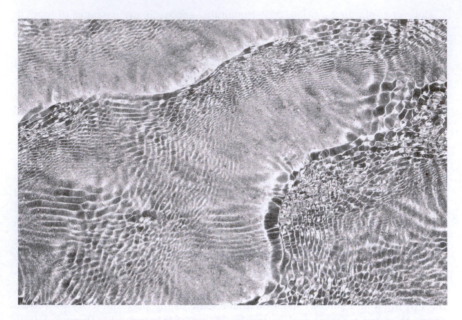

Figure 1.2. Diffractive patterns of sea waves disturbed by waves of wind (photograph by Paul Tricker, http://trickersinegypt.blogspot.com.au/2010_09_01_archive.html)

intensifies the understanding of waves materializing in relational mo(ve)ments; it is not about considering sea, rock and wind as separate bodies.

Bringing diffractive understandings to subjectivity thus becomes 'a way of understanding the world from within and as part of it' (Barad, 2007: 88) through critical, respectful practices of engagement. A diffractive approach works with embodiment or thinking from within various relational contact areas that are different but overlapping; in contrast a reflective approach is more of a 'distance-learning practice of reflecting from afar' (p. 90) in which interactions between separate bodies are the focus. Reflexivity attends to how my activity as researcher impacts on the children as participants; thinking diffractively engages with what happens in-between, within intra-active space-times of connectivity where children and adult commingle as participant-researchers. This connectivity, perceptible only as an entangled and embodied children~adult~participant~researcher~research~playground and so on, processes through becoming-something different. A diffractive approach considers from within the 'entangled effects differences make' (p. 73); it works to explore the folds of difference and how differences materialize; it works with difference not to reduce it but with understandings that difference(s) matter and are always already (im)perceptible. These understandings – of diffraction and difference – work with performativity, as do Deleuzian imaginaries (see *Preceding echoes*) and poiesis (see the *Play(ing)* plateau). Alternatively, reflection and reflexivity are about representationalism, as in metaphoric thinking, and about mimesis, which attempts sameness in terms of representation of the 'real' world and behaviours of/in specific social groups. Thus a diffractive, performative understanding opens (to) possibilities for different kinds of knowledge-making practices in which subjects/objects (e)merge through intra-active relations. A diffractive approach intensifies understandings of/through intra-activity, whereas a reflexive approach risks reducing bodies and their interactions by engaging with cause and corresponding effect analyses. In relational areas of intra-activity how this now embodied I~we perceive ourselves, singularly and severally, is an affect of and affected by interconnected human and material relations that I~we are operating with/in. I thus understand the 'I' of myself as embodied-I always already becoming-something different.

I speak and write as woman~Pākehā~Aotearoa New Zealander. Pākehā translates as 'non-Māori' – that is, all non-Indigenous New Zealanders. Although this includes people of all cultures that are not Māori, common usage positions Pākehā as the dominant, white majority of European origins. However, considering myself Pākehā, also foregrounds my lived relationship with Māori, the Indigenous people of my homeland. My feminist beliefs and poststructuralist thinking affect my living~learning, so in different space-times I am in continually diffractive, heterogeneous processes of woman~wife~grandmother~early childhood teacher~teacher educator~academic. In these I am both dominant and minority – dominant in my whiteness and as teacher but minority as woman and working in early childhood. In different moments, I negotiate diffractive possibilities of my subjectivity in this interconnecting milieu of complex, ambiguous and contradictory experiences characterized by overlapping (dis)continuities, always already rhizo and embodied. Subjectivity is always already in flux, it is provisional, (im)partial and in continuous conditions of becoming-something different. Thus, I am always already (in)variably, (im)partially, (im)perceptibly becoming-woman becoming-feminist becoming-poststructuralist thinker becoming-researcher becoming-writer…lack of commas signalling a complex refrain of rhizo flows of becoming-something different.

However, the Deleuzo-Guattarian notion of becoming-woman is controversial among feminist scholars. Although my attention in this book~assemblage is with becoming-child(ren), my thinking as becoming-woman inevitably affects the discourse – Deleuze and Guattari (1987) say that becomings 'always pass through a becoming-woman' (p. 291). However, Braidotti (1994b) expresses ambivalence to this idea, which she ascertains neutralizes gender dichotomies to overcome sexual difference; by dissolving the subject 'woman' towards transformatively processing 'becoming-woman' – a gender-free becoming – 'woman' disappears into the forces that structure her. Similarly, Grosz (1994a) says Deleuze and Guattari 'fail to notice that the process of becoming-marginal or becoming-woman means nothing as a strategy if one is already marginal or a woman' (p.188). Citing Irigaray (1985), Grosz also says that becoming-woman, paradoxically, 'prevents women from exploring and interrogating their own specific, and nongeneralizable, forms of becoming, desiring-production, and being' (Grosz, 1994a: 189).

More recently, Braidotti (2001) admits to bending Deleuze for her own needs, working with the 'subject as the plane of composition for multiple becomings' (p. 410). She approaches subjectivity in terms of a 'constructive paradox', in which the processual becoming is central to the project (p. 395). Working with this idea I perceive myself as always in process of producing (my, singularly) becoming-woman and forever becoming-something different. I am freed from marginalized woman and not immobilized in past, present or future moments. As Dosse (2010) says: 'Becoming breaks out of time and is never reduced to it' (p. 323). For Deleuze and Guattari, becoming-something different cannot be conceptualized historically – that is, linearly as past, present, future; neither is it about becoming different from someone else. Becoming is beyond before[11] – it is outside time and what I might have been. Rather, there are only de~territorializing space~times of becoming-something different; 'We can be thrown into a becoming by anything at all, by the most unexpected, most insignificant of things' (Deleuze & Guattari, 1987: 292). My subjectively singular reading of Deleuzo-Guattarian becoming, casts aside any sense of umbrage to literally bring remnants of the marginalized becoming-woman out of the shadows and flaunt the becoming-woman that constitutes my every other becoming. Despite critiques by Irigaray, Grosz and Braidotti of Deleuze and Guattari's elucidation of becoming-woman, *my* primal becoming-woman is inseparable from all other becomings that I produce. It is not so much that, for me, becomings pass through becoming-woman; it is that becoming-woman is always already (im)partially and diffractively all other becomings. As I try to pare them all back towards understandings of becoming-human, becoming-woman refuses reductionism; 'becoming-woman is always a function of something else' (Deleuze & Guattari, 1987: 275) and not anathema to my becoming. Contrary to feeling neutralized as woman or that I have disappeared, the woman of my becoming-woman always already diffracts in (re)production of becoming-woman.

But, while writing as becoming-woman embodied with/in various other becomings, the site from which I speak in this research remains dubious, that of speaking *for* young children. As adult articulator of the project, I work to present children and their childhood(s) and the understandings they communicate through their curricular performativity; also to illuminate their becomings through/with/in all of these. However, in attempting to move outside speaking *about* them, in thinking I can speak *for* them I am by extension co-opting their 'voice' and risking (mis)appropriation. But, to say nothing forecloses the project – the research and becoming-book~assemblage – and so I work to write the children in, generating a multiplicity of texts that open (to) possibilities for expressing their words and play(ing) through the actual telling. This seems an impossible task and I wonder if a study over a longer period of time may have opened more authentic ways for this to happen – the children telling their stories – if I could have returned to talk more with them about their play(ing). Yet no matter how often I returned, each engagement may be like stepping into the same stream although into a different flow of their thinking and doing, so the conversation would continue to open (to) more possibilities rather than answer specific queries around their conversations...

and...no amount of time will ever put an end to my thinking differently about their play(ing), the territory continually de~territorialized...

plan(e)s of encounters

In attempting to rethink my thinking, in particular thinking differently and diffractively outside the dominating persistence with developmentally appropriate practice, for example (discussed in the *Reconceiving curriculum* plateau) in regard to children, childhood and curriculum, I work through an array of connectivity among a multiplicity of (im)personal force-affects embodied with/in the plateaus. Disrupting the pervasive scientific orientation of developmental influences opens (to) possibilities for presenting young children as equitably power-full players in curricular performativity, as equitably knowledgeable theorists of adult conceptions of curriculum. Similarly, Olsson (2009) puts Deleuzo-Guattarian philosophy to work in early childhood education towards generating collectively agential and power-fully productive processual spaces. These spaces operate as a relational plane of encounters, sometimes transforming and connecting, sometimes not; it is a milieu in which there is no stability of ground, subject(s) or object(s) – children's subjectivity, processes of learning, teachers and the materiality of the milieu itself collide. Exploring ways of thinking differently about the complex relation of research to practice, she uses Deleuzian notions of immanence and transcendental empiricism to disrupt a binarial research|practice divide. In this, theories and practices of both research and practice are considered not 'to explain, contain or be the cause of the other...[rather it is] the question of an encounter, a speaking with, that forces both theory and practices to *experiment* and *do* new things' (Olsson, 2009: 208, original italics).

Throughout her research, Olsson presents subjectivity and learning as a relational field of children, teachers and materiality, inseparable from the research and its undertaking. Her attention is with processual conditions of negotiating learning spaces, with/in which the (re)constitution of subjectivity and learning starts up 'from *flows* of belief and desire' (p. 49, italics added), that is, the *movement* of the flows becoming the expressions of subjectivity and learning. Foregrounding processes of children's desires for their learning, she condemns any attempt to plan, control and evaluate according to prescribed standards, these disrupting flows of learning mo(ve)ments. She promotes the need to 'find another logic for how to treat what takes place *in between* constructed and imagined entities such as individuals and societies' (p. 31, italics in original) so that the collective desires of children are accepted as an important contribution to the classroom and the school system (p. 186). Confronting the individual|society binary, which she contends immobilizes subjectivity and learning, resonates with my challenge to the adult|child binary as blocking children's expressions of curricular performativity.

This works towards collapsing modernist univocal discourses that oppress children and childhood, opening (to) possibilities for affirming a multiplicity of differences among child(ren), childhood(s) and conceptions of adulthood, for riding a 'positivity of differences' (Braidotti, 1994b: 164). Emerging from the shadows come ideas of 'performative utterances', ideas of young children's expressions of 'rhizovocality' (Jackson, 2003: 707). Momentarily this seems to open (to) possibilities for problematizing a dilemma within this research of needing to articulate the children's expressions of their understandings within their childhood(s) – essentially to speak for children. But, inevitably the thinking~writing here is situated with/in my adult understandings, through a becoming-embodied-I, using my adult(erated) perceptions. From Foucault (in conversation with Deleuze) I infer that it is not about situating myself ahead of, outside or even beside the children in an effort to 'speak the silent truth of each and all' (Deleuze, 2004: 207), rather through relations of intra-activity I may negotiate an (un)acceptable way through 'the indignity of speaking for others' (p. 208). As my words inevitably are speaking for the children, more and more the task of writing becomes problematic – how to disrupt the 'traditional ethnographic, even confessional 'I' that haunts…critical qualitative research traditions' (Jackson, 2010: 583–4); how to embody (a) becoming-I.

reading~writing the book~assemblage rhizo-nomadically with/in/through plateaus

Generating plateaus with rhizome, rather then developing chapters linearly, is the methodological work of the research~writing~reading of this book~assemblage. Through embodied processes of rhizo writing and writing the rhizome, becoming-embodied-I of writer~reader~text generates a continually changing assemblage or multiplicity of passages for negotiating the space-times of ideas, thoughts and concepts. These are always already in flux, in constant processes of becoming, opening (to) a collection of (in)discrete plateau-like (non)-entities connected temporally and spatially, forming (an) always already (e)merging fragmentary~whole(s). This is not only about adding things at the boundaries of the thinking~conversation~discussion~writing, it is also about writing (from) with/in (a) middle(s) always already generating plateaus of intensities and intensities of plateaus – slip-sliding through the exterior and interior as insider~outsider. Gathering this assemblage together is about writing as I negotiate a becoming-embodied-I of thinker~reader~researcher – not always flowing through any space-time without interruption but attending to ir/dis/e/ruptions. All these ruptures provoke a following as plateaus (e)merge to be negotiated. Particular ideas do not necessarily claim any hierarchy in the relations of thinking, they merely move from the shadows and are illuminated alongside/with/in the always already changing reading~writing~thinking journey. Following lines of flight, I flow in and out of boundless territorial spaces, cutting across and carrying away rhizo thought and thinking, exploring 'spaces in which something different might happen' (St. Pierre, 2004: 287). This book~assemblage and the research stories it tells are but di/con/vergences accumulating as a-centred masses of (mis)understandings.

Having opened possibilities with/in/for the writing~reading of this slip-sliding research journey, the option is now open for negotiating the plateaus as they are written here or following other lines of flight. In this processual becoming-I (ad)venture, I anticipate reader and writer flowing through the plateaus, journeying as an intermingling becoming-embodied-I, commingling with/in/through a reading~writing~thinking assemblage of multidimensional extra/inter/textual experiences, co-implicated in dynamically changing conversational space-times, everyone and everything alluded to here always already (im)perceptibly in flux…

> *Allusion – an aside…* 'allude' signals the play-full life that the writing takes on here: from L. *alludere*, from ad- 'towards' + ludere 'to play' (*Concise Oxford Dictionary*, 1999).[12]

Notes

1 Commonly called *Te Whāriki*, the full title is *Te Whāriki: He Whāriki Mātauranga mō ngā Mokopuna o Aotearoa: Early childhood curriculum* (Ministry of Education, 1996). Note: Excluding titles, Māori words are not italicized throughout, Te Reo Māori being an official language of Aotearoa New Zealand.

2 The expression 'opens (to) possibilities' signals the activity of opening to possibilities *and* that there are, potentially, possibilities to be engaged with.

3 (E)merges, emerges from and merges with.

4 Words joined by a tilde signal conditions and matters of expression that are always already co-implicated, embodied, each merging with and emerging from the other.

5 Mo(ve)ments, an elision of moments and movements.

6 Chris Harrison, Carnegie Mellon University, is the creator of this social networking image, *Internet Map: City-to-City Connections*.

7 In working generatively *processing*, as in to go along or through, is more appropriate than *progressing* to arhizo book~assemblage. I understand progress as sequentially additive forward movement and advancement towards a specific destination or more complete condition, whereas working processually signals non-hierarchical multidimensional movement.

8 Thus, both notions of 'the' (definitive) rhizome or 'a' (as in indefinite article) rhizome are arguably redundant and should be *sous rature*. However, there are moments when using 'a' or 'the' eases the reading and as in Massumi's translation of Deleuze and Guattari (1987) I concede to use of the article.

9 Marc Ngui, Toronto, Canada, is the creator of this drawing from *1000 Plateaus Drawings: Intro Paragraph 15* (www.bumblenut.com).

10 A Mobius strip is 'a surface having only one side…formed by twisting one end of a rectangular strip through 180 degrees and joining it to the other end' (*Oxford English Dictionary*).

11 This phrase coined by Warren Sellers (personal conversation, January 2012).

12 See Pearsall (1999).

Reconceiving curriculum ~ mapping (a) milieu(s) of becoming

opening this reconceiving curriculum plateau

In this plateau the notion of (re)conceiving is brought into play, for thinking differently about conventional curriculum conceptions towards generating a way of conceiving curriculum as (a) milieu(s) of becoming. To disturb technicist views of 'the' curriculum, commonly viewed as a specific object or thing, in the following conversation the definitive 'the' is discarded in the understanding that 'curriculum' is a complex array of matters rather than a singular object (syllabus) comprises things (subject or content knowledge). Casting 'the' aside illuminates an holistic approach to curriculum, such as an autobiographical approach, which is embodied in processes of living, that is, singularly contextualized experiences of learning~living. Using the notion of autobiography to reconceptualize curriculum, Pinar (1974) foregrounds the significance of understanding the nature of personal educational experiences; alongside this, Apple's (1979) ideological critique also works to reconceptualize curriculum, by confronting ramifications of power embedded in education, schools and texts. Commingling with these notions of autobiography and power, I deploy Deleuzo-Guattarian imaginaries towards transgressing the scientistic orientation of developmental influences on early childhood curriculum.

From/with/in a processual, lived understanding curriculum is thus problematized, as matters of speculation and inquiry rather than an object to be fixed, stabilized, corrected or repaired. However, in the recursivity of *reconceptualizing* curriculum where *re* implies ongoing processes at work, a modernistic, structural expectation lingers, suggestive of a new concept being eventually arrived at. But my (re)conceiving endeavour is neither a corrective mechanism nor a reconceptualizing exercise *per se*. It avoids developing a potentially concretizing concept, instead working (with) thinking processes for imagining things differently, towards understanding how it works, that is, how curriculum works and how thinking differently might work. So, I work towards al(l)ways thinking differently about curriculum, in particular flattening the adult|child hierarchy that valorizes conceptions of the mature adult by receiving understandings of young children as equitable play(ers) in/of curriculum, and by (re)conceiving curriculum as a milieu of curricular performativity.

Negotiating the milieu of early childhood curriculum in this plateau involves conversational encounters with historical philosophies affecting early childhood curriculum; a genealogy of reconceptualizing early childhood curriculum; influences of developmental psychology and sociocultural approaches on early childhood curriculum; and unravelling the woven mat of *Te Whāriki* (Ministry of Education, 1996), the Aotearoa New Zealand national early childhood curriculum statement. Other linking plateaus – *Rhizo-mapping* and *Children performing curriculum complexly* – present interconnecting ideas of mapping as a way of making sense of children enacting learning and complex matters of their curricular performativity from the data of the research project drawn upon here.

once upon a time, curriculum was...and is becoming...

Two thousand years ago, Cicero (the Roman philosopher, statesman, lawyer, orator, political theorist and consul from the first century BC) used *curriculum* to mean a relatively contextualized living and learning process, viewing the temporal space in which people lived as a container within which things are studied (the *what* of curriculum); however, pedagogical issues of method and instruction (the *how*) were not questioned. Centuries later in the pre-print medieval world it remained a given that the master taught the novice, and by the end of the nineteenth century, curriculum was still understood simply as content – the syllabus. The *what* of curriculum was the focus, pedagogical processes of *how* receiving less attention. But, questions about pedagogical processes were evolving, evidenced in the theoretical and practical work of Rousseau, Itard, Seguin, Montessori and Dewey, for example. These educationists developed methods and procedures for educating 'abnormal' and disadvantaged children, these developments then informing teaching within 'normal' schooling. To make a point, I use 'abnormal' and 'normal' as in the times and work of these well-meaning educationists. Contemporarily, these terms are contestable, challenging an inherent deficit of children and raising ideological questions such as: Who decides what is 'ab/normal' and for what reasons? Which children are perceived in 'need' of educational intervention? How will this intervention be organized? How will these children be managed?

As schooling became more universal, it became a political necessity and economic concern to question the fundamentals of curriculum around what is important and worthwhile knowledge. *What* children should be taught and *how* things should be taught have thus become contested issues for practitioners, policy-makers and academics, the discussion involving disciplinary understandings of psychology, philosophy, sociology and political studies. Significantly, Egan (2003) is bold enough to say that despite extensive questioning of curriculum through the past two thousand years, nothing much has changed in how curriculum is understood. Historical tracings of *what* and *how* are pervasive in westernized understandings.

During the twentieth century three models of education dominated, with differing interpretations of curriculum. One requires a passive child, socialized in a uniform school culture through indoctrinating her/him with a standardized and lock-stepped curriculum. Another assumes a biologically driven child doing what comes naturally, with biological readiness determining curriculum goals and methods. A third promotes education as progressive, as a transforming experience in which learner and teacher share control of the process in working together. Somewhat ambiguously aspects of all these pervade, although over the past 50 years or so, the conversation about curriculum has turned from a reliance on understandings of the major technical paradigm towards critically questioning *what* curriculum is and *how* it is enacted. Pinar (1975a) notes that the *what* and *how* of curriculum has been traditionally understood in many ways: as a course of study; as material or artefacts used in a course of study; as intended learning outcomes; with a focus on process; as being synonymous with education; about design and planning; about development of materials; about instructional strategies and saleable packages; about instruction and evaluation. Curriculum is this imbued with shifting meanings.

In recent decades, an extensive body of multidisciplinary scholarship has emerged generating diverse possibilities for a more organic reconceptualizing of early childhood curriculum, away from a technicist focus on *the* curriculum. This has been influenced by work from poststructuralist, feminist and postcolonial perspectives within sociological, psychological and critical theories in particular. Works that mark significant turns include: Silin's (1987, 1995) philosophical perspective explores the predominant knowledge base that has historically informed early childhood curriculum, challenging the recent reliance on psychological considerations, which are commonly misconstrued for educational goals; Kessler and Swadener (1992) situate their queries about early childhood curriculum as sociology of curriculum; Bloch's (1992) critical feminist perspective queries the emphasis of positivist traditions of developmental psychology on early childhood research and practice; Miller (1992) brings a feminist autobiographical understanding to the conversation; Jipson (1992) enacts a feminist form of pedagogy; Cannella's (1997) critical perspective deconstructs economic and political concerns and promotes social justice for young children, and with Viruru opens a postcolonial critique (Viruru & Cannella, 2001). As anthropologists, sociologists, feminists, historians and early childhood educationists, these scholars and others illuminate the ongoing critique of developmental approaches to understanding children's growth and learning and curricular practices. Conditions and matters of *what* children should be taught and *how* they should be taught are thus contested issues involving practitioner, policy-maker and interdisciplinary academic perspectives.

introducing reconceptualizing

The 1970s marked a significant turning point in the characterization of curriculum, both conceptually and methodologically as supporting structures were turned back on themselves, revealing an abundance of rich experiences previously concealed (Grumet, 1999). This work represented a reaction to the Tylerian tradition, which promoted a technicist model with clearly defined subject areas, and limited curriculum to overt behavioural objectives. Scholars dedicated to reconceptualizing curriculum understood curriculum as complex, in contrast to Tyler's linearly structured rationale. They worked to (re)shape the curriculum field through philosophical, historical and political dimensions of learning~teaching, promoting curriculum not as a sequence chart or a list of objectives, but as processual, interdisciplinary experience involving theoretical, social and cultural phenomena, through which 'all life experiences are valued for their potential to inform and inspire learning' (Kincheloe, Slattery & Steinberg, 2000: 325). Pinar (1974) and Apple (1979) provided significant challenges to conventional approaches to curriculum and, within Grumet's (1976b) autobiographical perspective, reconceptualizing became a reflexive project, placing conceptual understandings alongside lived experience. This exemplifies the shift from practical interests in the development of curriculum (as thing) to a theoretical/ practical interest in understanding processes of curriculum (Pinar, Reynolds, Slattery & Taubman, 1995), which was about not only developing alternatives to 'the' curriculum, but also reconceiving ideas about mapping the field of curriculum. As Marshall, Sears and Schubert (2000) explain, reconceptualizing is not so much a paradigm shift but more about shifting ground.

This philosophical shift in reconceptualizing curriculum – from a focus on a technicist development of 'the' curriculum towards developing philosophical understandings of what curriculum means in practical and theoretical terms – was also attended to by early childhood educationists as they reconsidered and re-imagined (other) ways of thinking about early childhood curriculum. From the early 1980s, critical theories of curriculum addressing ideology, power and knowledge in curriculum, as well as historical questions about curriculum formation and the inherent power relations, appear in early childhood research and literature. From the UK, contributions included: David's (1980) radical social ideas that questioned teacher–student relationships and foregrounded links between home and school, and Walkerdine's (1998/1984) critique of developmental psychology and its emphasis on child-centred pedagogy. As well, contributions from the USA included: Suransky's (1982) dissertation on the erosion of childhood; King's (1992) work foregrounding the significance of context in children's play, disrupting dominating developmental analyses; and Ayers' (1992) contribution in bringing teachers' autobiographical accounts of their teaching experiences into scholarly conversations of researchers and policy-makers. Annual curriculum theory conferences from 1983 through the early 1990s were a prime forum for reconceptualist work in the USA and discussions that took place there were significant to reconceptualizing early childhood education.

From within this reconceptualizing project, many early childhood curricularists, practitioners and researchers confronted the reliance on psychological considerations as educational goals, which silence sociological and philosophical perspectives (Silin, 1995). While developmentalism loses some of its hold, governmental economic and political agenda override critical concerns (Cannella, 2005), concerns all too frequently left in the shadows by (pre-1970s) dominant bodies of thought. Contributions to the curricular conversation from critical sociological and feminist perspectives include the works of Miller (1982, 1999), Davies (1989) and Silin (1995). Critical decolonizing research that works to make audible all voices has also informed the endeavour (Smith, 1999; Swadener & Mutua, 2007; Bishop, 2008). Issues of power, diverse lived experiences of children and Indigenous knowledges are brought into the curriculum conversation (Grieshaber & Cannella, 2001; Ritchie, 2001; Reedy, 2003; Quintero, 2007). Throughout, the perpetual question resounds: Whose knowledge is privileged (Bloch, 2007)? Also: Who chooses what research methodology (Rhedding-Jones, 2007)?

Reconceptualist work has revealed that what we think we know about children and curriculum is affected by the values and biases of those who dare to speak and theorize the issues, this being a somewhat risky enterprise. As Lubeck (1991) says: 'To reconceptualize is to be angry and to dream' (p. 168). More pragmatically, Cannella (2005) considers that reconceptualist work questions overt and hidden agenda of particular knowledges, circumstances under which certain beliefs evolved, how 'truths' have been constructed, and who has been/is supported, hurt, privileged, disqualified. In questioning what we do, why we do it, whose interests are served, and the (un)intended consequences of these, we begin to understand what is missing and what could be. Critiquing such ideological assumptions is intermingled through this book~assemblage, in conversations about desiring change (supposedly for a greater good – whose? why?), unravelling (a misfit of?) educational curriculum with processes of living (which ones matter?), imagining difference (as meaning what?) and responding passionately and creatively (who says that these matter? why?) to personal ideals (in whose terms?). Such political agenda – personal and/or societal – about curriculum do not, however, deter an ongoing general curricular focus on *how* and *what* but they are an undeniable affect; what happens in-between in political terms is always already (im)perceptible. Co-implicated with political issues of what matters to whom and why, a philosophical challenge arises in considering the *how*, that is, issues of method and procedure:

> The difficulty in admitting the question, *how*, into curriculum matters is that there becomes little of educational relevance that can be excluded from the curriculum field. This means that one can do almost anything in education and claim plausibly to be working in 'curriculum'.
>
> (Egan, 2003: 69, italics added)

Yet, should this be as problematic as Egan implies, given the complexity of the world we live in? For example, using the concept of *currere*, Pinar (1974; Pinar & Grumet, 1976) complexifies curriculum through an autobiographical experiencing that includes the contextual as relevant to the postmodern condition with/in which we live...*and*...Grumet and Stone (2000) characterize the nature of curriculum as inextricably entwined relationships of living and learning – 'curriculum *is* everyday life. It is a gathering of social practices, of relationships, events, coming and goings, inscriptions and erasures. It is politics, funding, certifications, and social mobility' (p. 191, emphasis in original)...*and*...Warren Sellers (2008) invents *c u r a* to explicate this contextual inclusiveness in a performative merging of living and learning – living~learning – embodying 'continuous~various~diverse~ learning experiences that are always-already occurring' (p. 207)...*and*...this embodied autobiographical living~learning of *c u r a* emerges here in the writing of this plateau as I struggle with the presence of many lines of flight. I have long since lost sight of the space-times of their emergence and have re-ordered the ideas many times over in my desire to make sense of it all. If there was some logic to it, it is lost in this a-logical rhizo milieu. I know that rhizome defies arborescent linearity, yet I persist, with scissors, tape and pages spread over the living room floor...*and*...time and time again; when compiling my doctoral thesis and again in the here and now of this book~assemblage...*and*...I know in another time the text may demand a different (re)ordering in my thinking according to my differently emerging autobiographical experiencing of these curriculum wor(l)ds. Curriculum is undoubtedly a shifting enterprise imbued with shifting understandings; curriculum-ing, perhaps.

(re)thinking 'curriculum'...reconceiving through *currere*

The concept of 'curriculum' derives from the Latin infinitive *currere*, meaning 'to run', which Egan (2003) explains as 'a running, a race, a course' (p. 10); similarly, Kincheloe *et al.* (2000) foreground the activity of the process, as in to 'run the racecourse' (p. 329). In the mid-1970s, in a critical response to artefact-oriented approaches, which consider courses as entities rather than as a coursing activity, Pinar and Grumet (Pinar, 1974, 1975b; Pinar & Grumet, 1976) called on the notion of *currere* to bring together the lived experiences of the learner and the context of learning. They use *currere* to refer to a method and theory of reconceptualizing curriculum as educational experience:

> [*Currere*] describes the race not only in terms of the course, the readiness of the runner, but seeks to know the *experience of the running of one particular runner, on one particular track, on one particular day, in one particular wind*...Educational experience is a process that takes on the world without appropriating that world, that projects the self into that world without dismembering that self...
>
> (Grumet, 1976a: 36, italics added)

This autobiographical approach foregrounds the significance of understanding matters of personal educational experiences and that these living~learning experiences matter. *Currere* breathes life back into traditional views of curriculum by considering curriculum as living and lived experience with/in which learners~teachers are embodied. In reciprocal relationships, both learners and teachers move backwards and forwards, simultaneously, through learning experiences towards enhancing the knowing and knowledge of their inner and personal worlds. But, exploring matters of these experiences is not about content (the *what*) and differs from process (the *how*). Rather, it is about being embodied in educational contexts, which involves a shift in cognitive and affective insight (Pinar, 1974) – teachers must also become students of *currere*, to learn to become students of them/our/selves. This also means seamlessly learning alongside young children…as we seek to understand our own learning…as we come to understand something of young children's understandings about their learning…

The significance of the educational journey is with engaging with conditions and matters of the experience. For example, we might ask of ourselves as teachers~students – at the same time considering how it might be for young children – questions adapted from Pinar (1974: 152–3): How does it feel to be uprooted from my daily life, geographically, socially, psychologically? What is my experience of this place, its people, of other children~learners~teachers? What emotions are evoked? When? Why? How do I respond? What do my responses tell me? Do I actually want to make this particular learning journey? Do I have a choice? What about my peers~teachers~students~colleagues, their motives and interest in me? What can we learn from one another? These kinds of questions require a diffractive methodological response that intra-actively engages with autobiographical experiences of *currere*, moving away from a purely *what–how* agenda, instead foregrounding how things work for an embodied children~teacher~you~me~learning journey within any educational context. Pinar maintains that this approach – of studying the experience of the educational journey and the journey of the educational experience – is a more apt interpretation of curriculum when considering its derivation, *currere*. This to-ing and fro-ing through the interconnectivity of education, experience and journeying links to Deleuze and Guattari's urge to work in rhizo ways and mapping becomes a way of thinking that disrupts a linearly ordered, rational approach.

> The map is open and connectable in all of its dimensions; it is detachable, reversible, susceptible to constant modification. It can be torn, reversed… reworked by an individual, group, or social formation…it always has multipleentry ways…The map has to do with performance…
>
> (Deleuze & Guattari, 1987: 12)

Interestingly, *currere* as a way of reconceptualizing curriculum, emerges in 1974 only a moment before Deleuze and Guattari's (1976) imaginary of rhizome, with both opening (to) possibilities for thinking differently about curriculum. In presenting a learning~teaching~curriculum assemblage as contextual, with complex and generative possibilities, Pinar's autobiographical approach critiques the dominating scientist, technicist conceptions of curriculum. Deleuze and Guattari's phil-

osophical discourse around the activity of thinking differently perturbs
and rationale of modernity's arborescent thought and opens (to) (postst
ist) possibilities for thinking curriculum otherwise/other ways, although
and Guattari refuse the label 'poststructuralist'. However, Pinar was a dedicated
reconceptualist and the reconceptualist project can be read alongside the Deleuzo-
Guattarian project of thinking differently – 'Reconceptualization is never finished;
it is not a doctrine or an end point, but constant critique from which new constructions emerge' (Cannella, 1997: 161).

Currere opens rhizo possibilities for reconceiving a different kind of curricular
performativity, commingling *what* and *how*. Curricular performativity of *currere*
works alongside Deleuzo-Guattarian understandings of becoming-curriculum…
alongside Dewey's understandings of learning as experience…

linking Dewey and Deleuze

Dewey's (1943) was not a traditional content-oriented curriculum; he conceived curriculum as both content and process, the *what* and *how* integrated in
ways that matter to the student, knowledge being a by-product of processes
of learning, inseparable from the activity that produced it. Curriculum is thus
perceived as experience *and* subject matter *and* interactions with people *and*
the environment; there was no place for rote learning. Also, play is central to
this process of learning by doing, requiring children to think about actions and
processes of the world they live in. Dewey's view of curriculum is that activity
(the *how*) and subject matter (the *what*) need to be considered equally, to avoid
a false dualism. For Dewey, subject matter is neither stable nor prescriptive; he
perceives content (the *what*) as being in flux, constantly changing and contextually situated:

> Abandon the notion of subject-matter as something fixed and ready-made in
> itself, outside the child's experience; cease thinking of the child's experience
> as also something hard and fast; see it as something fluent, embryonic, vital;
> and we realize that the child and the curriculum are simply two limits which
> define a single process.
>
> (Dewey, 1943: 11)

In this, curriculum emerges from experiences of the child, the child's experiences
becoming curriculum. This converges with the Deleuzo-Guattarian notion of
becoming – as the child becomes curriculum, curriculum becomes the child so that
curriculum and child are always already in conditions of becoming; becoming-
curriculum, becoming-child recursively changing and embodied with/in the other.
How the *what* manifests and what the *how* is, or how they both work, blurs in/to/
with/in territories of child and curriculum. Both curriculum and child (e)merge
as fluid and diverse, intensifying through/with/in processes of (dis)continuities
– through de~territorializing lines of flight.

Dewey's work is not only understood as a series of related projects of logical, progressive development but also as the whole experiential situation preceding the process of knowing (Semetsky, 2006). In encouraging teachers to connect the interests of children to everyday activities in the adult world, Dewey's project approach becomes less a linear exercise and more like 'laying down a path in walking' (Varela, 1987: 48). For example, Mayhew and Edwards (1966/1936) tell the story of a learning journey of a group of six-year-old children in the Laboratory School, run by John Dewey at the University of Chicago. The children negotiate a (rhizo) pathway through subjects related to curriculum areas of the natural/living world and technology (woodwork, cooking) and through social world interrelations among peers, teachers, the school community and the community outside. In this, the complexity of curriculum in action and children's curricular performativity is perceptible. For more than a year this particular group of children moved through an array of connected topics that grew out of a farm project, although as Mayhew and Edwards' narrative closes, there is a sense that the extensive sheep/wool exploration that it had become was barely beginning.

As well as the extent of the topics (the *what*) investigated and *how* the above project evolved through the children's desires and explorations, what is inspiring is how it worked. The project grew through time and it had grown out of earlier projects, suggesting there was no actual beginning or ending, rather that the project described was part of an ever growing, multidimensional, middle of curricular intensities – a milieu of becoming-something different. There was no attempt to curb the direction or extent of the children's learning desires or to take over in any way and the narrative suggests that the teachers were as engaged in the project as the children, quietly waiting for moments when their adult knowledge might enhance what was already happening…embodied learning of works in progress… and Dewey's legacy lives on: 'The curriculum of the Laboratory Schools is by no means set in stone. It changes. It evolves. It is a work in progress…' (University of Chicago Laboratory Schools, 2012).

Semetsky (2006) identifies this affinity between Dewey and Deleuze's work, bringing Dewey's 'naturalistic epistemology and aesthetics' and Deleuze's 'conceptual space' of becoming together to address the relevance of one to the other in education (p. xxi). She demonstrates the continuity of thought in relation to the experiential and experimental nature of their respective philosophical inquiry, such as common understandings of teaching and learning as a 'research laboratory' (p. 119). The virtual interaction that she opens illuminates 'the presence of an organizing vital force which is *"free, moving and operative"*' (Dewey, 1925/58, quoted in Semetsky, 2006: xxiv, italics added), this kind of activity similarly characterized within the Deleuzo-Guattarian nomad, rhizome, de~territorializing lines of flight and smooth spaces of assemblage~multiplicities. Semetsky recognizes 'a living spirit' in the works of Dewey and Deleuze – each lives in their own works and in the works of others.

developmental psychology impacts early childhood curriculum

Psychological interpretations of early childhood curriculum evolved through the study of child development. These psychological influences, although supposedly fading (Prout, 2005), are nonetheless pervasive in early childhood curricular theorizing and practice, promoting western perspectives of a universalized, individualized, normalized child. Informed by the direct observation of children, the child study movement that emerged in the 1890s aimed to utilize scientific findings on what children know and when they should learn it, as a way of understanding the means of progress in human life. 'Normal' developmental stages were thus universalized in child development studies, this positivist world-view legitimizing a predetermined sequence of experiences with which early childhood education could work. Information gained from observing this supposedly 'normalized' child could then be used to structure appropriate educational environments, providing for developmentally determined interests of individualized children. But these views overlook the fact that valorizing normalcy limits possibilities for children, and positions those who define what is 'normal' – adult experts, most likely white, middle class – at the top of a hierarchy of power.

Early childhood education thus became conflated with child development, and learning with development. Child study morphed into the new science of child development, which required positivist methodology that was experimental, deemed to be rigorous, objective and quantitatively measurable. Kessler (1991) contends that the qualities of the subsidiary concept of development became exaggerated to the extent that it replaced education as a lens through which to view early childhood programmes. Walkerdine (1998/1984) claims the psychological perspective of child development was constructed to privilege objectivist, scientific approaches and individualism. For example, Piaget's maturationist view – alongside the theories of Freud, Gesell and Erikson – of children developing through predictable and sequential stages was in opposition to a naturalistic view of inherited or pre-given intelligence associated with a Social Darwinism perspective. Thus, Piaget's theory evolved through the 1950s when the emerging technocratic ideology optimistically valorized the scientific method of behaviourism. Psychoanalysis thrived at this time, and alongside these the pedagogy of child-centredness evolved in the 1960s from within the child study approach. Then, learning theory (Bruner, 1986) emerged, similarly describing development in universal terms, as an individualized and individualizing process, ignoring the cultural nature of human development (Rogoff, 2003). Walsh (1991) attributes the widespread acceptance of developmental theory in early childhood education to a comfortable blend of Piagetian stages of development with the romantic maturationism of early twentieth-century theorists. As he notes, it is curious that allegiance to Piaget – who was neither educationist nor psychologist – remains strong despite weaknesses in the individualistic perspective, as Vygotsky's sociocultural approach to development reveals.

Vygotsky's (1978) social constructivist perspective on development and learning posits that individualized psychology is culturally mediated; we learn that through interaction with others, thought develops socially and we are who we are because of others. Through social interactions, children learn the habits of mind of their culture, through which they derive meaning and this affects the construction of their knowledge, the specific knowledge acquired by children through these interactions representing the shared knowledge of a culture. But, as Cole and Wertsch (1996) suggest, the strengths of both Piaget and Vygotsky's theories complement their respective weaknesses and to debate the primacy of the individual or the social serves no useful purpose. A more recent sociocultural response to young children's growth and learning is Rogoff's (1998) personal, interpersonal and community/institutional planes of analysis, which adopts these three lenses for viewing the sociocultural complexity involved. 'Using personal, interpersonal and community/institutional planes of analysis involves focusing on one plane, but still using background information from the other planes' (p. 688), thus engaging more authentically with the complexity of cultural contexts of human development.

However, despite these movements to engage with sociocultural contexts, the contemporary discourse of developmentally appropriate practice [DAP] continues to work with individuality (Bredekamp, 1987; Bredekamp & Copple, 1997). DAP reflects universalism, assuming that knowledge of children's development determines what makes worthy practice, but Damon (1998) argues that such grand, universalizing systems are no longer viable. Similarly, Soto (in Hatch, Bowman, Jor'dan, Morgan, Hart, Soto, Lubeck & Hyson, 2002) recommends researchers and practitioners 'pursue more liberal, liberating, democratic, humanizing, participatory, action driven, political, feminist, critically multicultural, decolonizing perspectives' (p. 450). Working with/in an accumulation of diverse values, beliefs and expectations in immediate and larger cultural contexts (Walsh, 2005) acknowledges the function of a multiplicity of cultural~contextual perspectives (Bruner, 1996; Rogoff, 2003) and promotes the understanding that human existence does not conform to one predetermined reality. That psychology promotes the primacy of individual cognition, in the process sidelining the complexity of sociocultural contexts for understanding ourselves in our becomings, is an ongoing challenge (Henriques, Hollway, Urwin, Venn & Walkerdine, 1998/1984).

Privileging cognitive developmental theory privileges the construct of the individual over collective orientations, and privileges stereotypically male, deterministic assumptions that presume to know the mind of the child (Cannella, 2005). Henriques *et al*. (1998/1984) disturb psychologically based assumptions and associated self-understanding, challenging normative understandings of subjectivity through the notion of embodied subjects. They claim that psychology can renew itself only by engaging with 'a multiple, relational subject not bounded by reason' (p. xviii). However, despite the theoretical critique, several doctoral studies out of Aotearoa New Zealand, for example, suggest that teaching practices are resistant to change, with developmental traditions remaining strongly influential (Dalli, 1999; McLeod, 2002; Jordan, 2003; Nuttall, 2004).

a reconceptualizing project ~ Te Whāriki: He Whāriki Mātauranga mō ngā Mokopuna o Aotearoa

In Aotearoa New Zealand in the early 1990s, in a political move to bring early childhood practice closer to compulsory schooling, early childhood curriculum was brought to the table, by extension contributing to reconceptualist theorizing worldwide. With a somewhat different agenda, the early childhood curriculum national statement was developed – *Te Whāriki: He Whāriki Mātauranga mō ngā Mokopuna o Aotearoa*[1] (Ministry of Education, 1996) – through a governmental initiative of the education reforms of the late 1980s that saw new legislation introduced to replace the 1877 Education Act. Significantly, these reforms integrated early childhood education and care, bringing the whole early childhood sector, *from birth* to six years, under the auspices of the Department of Education – previous education policies had considered preschool to involve three and four year olds only. In 1988, the Department of Education established a working group to investigate the mission of early childhood education, and in 1990 a tender went out inviting proposals for the development of curriculum guidelines for developmentally appropriate programmes. However, in 1991 Helen May and Margaret Carr were contracted to co-ordinate the development of a curriculum that embraced diversity of early childhood services and cultural perspectives as well as quality early childhood practice that went beyond a purely developmental approach. Their proposal represented a re-conceptualization of the previously dominant westernized approach to early childhood curriculum development, considering content, process, context and evaluation as interdependent (May, 2002; Te One, 2003).

In extensive consultation with the early childhood sector, and informed by Māori understandings of development and pedagogy gifted by Te Kōhanga Reo, a bicultural curriculum model – *Te Whāriki* – was developed, linking Māori and western understandings of young children's learning. Te Kōhanga Reo, established in 1984, are early childhood centres that work with Māori immersion programmes to promote and nurture Māori language (Te Reo Māori) and culture (tikanga Māori). Reflecting the Treaty of Waitangi partnership of Māori and Pākehā, Aotearoa New Zealand's cultural aspirations are with biculturalism in the understanding that strengthening relationships between Māori and Pākehā[2] honours Māori as tangata whenua, the Indigenous people of the land, with benefits potentially extending across all cultural relations. However, Durie (1998) cautions against the use of the westernized term, biculturalism, instead preferring tino rangatiratanga – that is, self-determination for all cultures working together to honour an array of values and beliefs – as discussed further on, *Te Whāriki* embodies tino rangatiratanga in its sociocultural, contextually appropriate approach.

Despite the contract brief from the government for an early childhood curriculum statement requiring developmentally appropriate guidelines as a feature, specifics of these were essentially sidelined and the westernized brief essentially displaced. Honouring the Treaty of Waitangi,[3] *Te Whāriki* embodies a traditional Māori philosophical approach and opens (to) possibilities for diverse cultural understandings and contextually appropriate practice, similar to the critical sociological, reconceptualist concerns emerging at the time in the UK and USA. Philosophical principles underpinning the model, namely empowerment~whakamana, holistic development~kotahitanga, family and community~whānau tangata and relationships~ngā hononga, represent parallel, complementary Māori and Pākehā/western understandings. In the same way, the interwoven strands of well-being~mana atua, belonging~mana whenua, contribution~mana tangata, communication~mana reo and exploration~mana aotūroa depict shared, desired attributes (Figure 2.1).

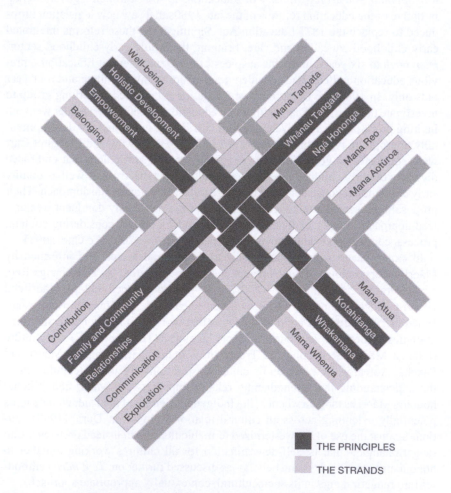

THE PRINCIPLES

THE STRANDS

Figure 2.1 Te Whāriki woven mat of principles and strands (Ministry of Education, 1996: 13)[4]

In this context *Te Whāriki* translates as 'a woven mat for all to stand on', presenting curriculum as a weaving of parallel Māori and Pākehā educational ideals and aspirations for young children and their education. Philosophical principles and strands, which arise from the principles, are depicted as the warp and weft of the woven mat. The strands, originally called 'aims for children' (May, 2002), tease out the fundamental principle of empowerment through concepts that weave through cultural difference. The shared conceptual strands are considered as equivalent domains representing desirable attributes embodied in healthy communities, not as direct translations between Māori and English concepts. This complexly bicultural weaving mat connects cultural aspirations for young children along each thread or strand of the weave, these also interconnecting as the strands and principles weave through one another.

Supporting *Te Whāriki* as a woven mat, the subtitle *He Whāriki Mātauranga mō ngā Mokopuna o Aotearoa* adds to the translation: 'the strands of the woven web of knowledge for the children of Aotearoa New Zealand'. However, a Māori perspective works not so much with a literal understanding of the words, but more with whāriki as a metaphor for bringing together or interweaving various topics and issues around the scope for education of young children in Aotearoa New Zealand.[5] *Te Whāriki* thus provides a metaphorical mat for all to stand on, a mat of interwoven principles and strands for diverse early childhood programmes to work with. It opens (to) possibilities for different weavings as early childhood centres work with their cultural communities and differing perceptions of children and childhood in ways that weave their own desires for early childhood curriculum into the fabric of the mat (Podmore & May, 2003). This approach considers learning as complex and having functional understandings of knowledge and skills attached to specific sociocultural contexts, rather than thinking of learning as a universally prescribed 'staircase of individually acquired skills' (May & Carr, 2000: 163), the latter all too frequently considered primarily in terms of preparation for schooling. The underpinning philosophy of *Te Whāriki* values early childhood learning as learning for/with/in early childhood and foregrounds formative assessment procedures. *Te Whāriki* thus becomes a curriculum space within which all languages and cultures can thrive authentically, not as add-ons to mainstream ways of operating (Mara, 1998). The weaving of principles and strands together expresses ideals and aspirations for young children, and possibilities for working respectfully across cultures, weaving people and cultural values, beliefs and traditions together. However, scholars argue that there is an ongoing need for critical engagement with implications of the sociocultural ideals for teaching practice (Cullen, 2003; Edwards & Nuttall, 2005; Duhn, 2006), towards furthering possibilities for *Te Whāriki* as a catalyst for change.

In the presentation of curriculum as a weaving of principles and strands, *Te Whāriki* is not a prescriptive, definitive document. Rather, it provides direction; content is not specified and proposed learning outcomes are presented as indicative. It is curriculum without 'recipes'; it is a 'dictionary' of possibilities (May & Carr, 2000). However, the articulation of learning outcomes, including examples of learning experiences for meeting these outcomes, as well as key curriculum requirements for infants, toddlers and young children, slip into western developmental theory and achievement expectations; and these learning outcomes in particular are frequently diligently adhered to, without critiquing their relevance to all cultures. As Cullen (2003) notes, the programmes of many early learning services reflect those of the 1980s and early 1990s when the developmental discourse flourished. So while *Te Whāriki* opens possibilities for significant changes in thinking about curriculum and ways in which it matters for children and their childhoods, it also makes perceptible difficulties of trying to think and speak differently within the worlds of educational theory and practice, in which modernist, hegemonic concepts and language pervade. A problematic then arises of how to articulate these possibilities in ways appropriate to the differing cultural worlds of teachers, children, families and communities they are part of. Possible openings are offered by trying to work other ways of thinking into our repertoire.

Ongoing reconceptualizing of curriculum works to disrupt the pervasiveness of modernist, developmental modes of thinking within early childhood curriculum (see, for example, Cannella, 1997, 1998; Kincheloe, 1997; Grieshaber & Cannella, 2001; Jipson & Johnson, 2001; Cannella & Kincheloe, 2002; Cannella & Viruru, 2004; Yelland, 2005). However, there is no one way towards reconceiving curriculum by way of this reconceptualist task. Rather it is multidirectional and multidimensional, open to continual critique and revision, emerging from collective conversations, and using new inventions and new languages (Cannella, 1997: 160–1). Such spaces open (to) possibilities through a Deleuzo-Guattarian reading alongside.

(re)turning to 'what' and 'how'

While the historic undermining of the centrality of content may be conceived as potentially problematic to traditionally modernistic views of curriculum, it is worth noting that the *Te Whāriki* (Ministry of Education, 1996) definition of curriculum for early childhood education in Aotearoa New Zealand contextualizes Egan's (2003) almost-anything-goes-claim-to-plausibility. *Te Whāriki* opens a multiplicity, stating that everything surrounding learners and learning matters, simultaneously avoiding specifics of *what* and *how*. Curriculum is described as:

> the sum total of the experiences, activities, and events, whether direct or indirect, which occur within an environment designed to foster children's learning and development...curriculum is provided by the people, places, and things in the child's environment; the adults, the other children, the physical environment, and the resources.
>
> (Ministry of Education, 1996: 10–11)

This inclusive understanding of curriculum as experiential is a commonly accepted, albeit variably practiced, characteristic of early childhood curriculum in Aotearoa

New Zealand. It is a working and pertinent response to Egan's (1978) philosophical challenge to curriculum, in which he posits a (supposed) general failure of nerve, vision and direction by contemporary educationists:

> To know *what* the curriculum should contain requires a sense of what the contents are for. If one lacks a clear sense of the purpose of education, then one is deprived of an essential means of specifying what the curriculum should contain. More commonly now, this problem is stated in terms of the accumulating pace of change, making decisions about a content-based curriculum meaningless. Who can specify what skills will be needed in the future? This manner of stating the problem *exemplifies* the failure of nerve: it suggests we have no control over the future; we cannot make of it what seems best to us.
>
> (Egan, 1978: 70, original italics)

Curriculum thus ought to respond to complex and ecologically sustainable issues of living~learning; to do otherwise lacks the nerve, vision and direction that Egan elucidates. We demonstrate considerable nerve and vision when we are willing to say 'no' to prescribing curriculum and 'yes' to opening (to) possibilities for rethinking what curriculum might mean, to changing our perspective(s), to opening to incipiently different ways of thinking about curriculum(ing), to (re)visiting the (ongoing) (re)conceptualizing curriculum endeavour. So, as Egan (un)intentionally points out, making content-based decisions about curriculum as it relates to the learning of young children in particular appears redundant. Querying how curriculum works for young children and how young children make curriculum work opens (to) ongoing curricular possibilities.

Egan (2003) does allude to curriculum being understood as functional, in saying that 'knowing *what* the curriculum should contain requires a sense of what the contents are *for*' (p. 14, original italics, underline added), or what do children want to do with the *what*? To take this part of the challenge seriously, we need to take young children seriously and openly receive their curricula performativity as expressions of their understandings. In posing the rhetorical question about who can say what skills will be needed in the future Egan implies that adults may *not* know best. Thus, considering what young children (may) do with/in curriculum is not only significant to understanding how it (may) work(s) for them, not bringing young children's understandings into the conversation is not an option, it is paramount.

Young children's ideas about the *what/how* needs of their *own* learning is as relevant and appropriate to their future living~learning as any adult predictions from educationists, politicians or parents. Young children's conceptions of curriculum may constitute a more visionary approach. Schubert (1986) states that 'every individual in the final analysis must direct his or her own learning. Thus, every person, regardless of his or her age, is in charge of his or her own self-education...be they children, adults, or entire communities' (p. 6). Assuming 'every person' includes young children, including infants and toddlers, this means welcoming young children's desires for growing their learning in ways they consider appropriate, for receiving expressions of their curricular understandings. All this, without prescriptive constraints imposed by adults – curricularists, policy-makers, educationists, parents – who commonly claim to know what young children's learning should comprise and how they should go about it. The adult world most often sees no need to question whether mature, rational adults do indeed know 'best', oblivious to younger human beings' capacity to participate in curriculum in a critically aware manner.

Deleuze (Foucault & Deleuze, 1980) adds credence to the above proposition. He believes that young children's verbal and non-verbal expressions about their learning are not listened to and the potential impact on the educational system of their expressions is not acknowledged. In a conversation about the nature of power-imbued reforms, he states that reforms are frequently 'designed by people who claim to be representative, who make a profession of speaking for others…' (pp. 208–9). He asserts that if the 'protests of children were heard in kindergarten, if their questions were attended to, it would be enough to explode the entire educational system' (p. 209). This is a power-full statement... and... I am reminded that I presume to speak for young children... and... although ever-mindful of not (mis)appropriating their intellectual space-times, I am an agent of this adult(erated) system of power... and... from a Foucaultian perspective, (re)conceptualizing curriculum is inevitably part of this system of power... and... while I admit responsibility for engaging diffractively with the discourse, my responses inevitably form part of the power-imbued system of reform. Aware that the/my embodied-I is continually foreshadowed by power-full systems, I am sensitive to 'slip[ping] inadvertently into constituting the very self that seems to contradict a focus on the constitutive power of discourse' (Davies, Browne, Gannon, Honan, Laws, Muel-ler-Rockstroh & Petersen, 2004: 360), and of attempting not to inasmuch as it is (im)possible to do so. The conversation is thus always already (im)perceptibly (im)partial.

In a study exploring how a group of children aged six to eight years were making meaning and expressing their understandings of their worlds through graphic-narrative play, Wright (2007) reports that 'many of their abstract concepts demonstrated wisdom which *seemed*…well beyond their years' (p. 24, italics added). Even in promoting young children's wisdom, when we exhibit surprise that children are performing 'well beyond their years', are we under-rating and under-valuing their capacity as young human beings? Arguably, we are reducing them to an immature, incompetent other. Tapping into such wisdom requires reciprocal relations of telling and listening, this also requiring that we operate with considerable openness in order to hear and make sense of children's wisdom.

Making sense of the expressions of curricular performativity of the four and a half year olds of the doctoral research drawn upon here is similarly challenging. Even though, in scholarly terms, young children have no formalized theoretical understandings of curriculum, they often communicate what works in regard to learning~teaching by their willingness to participate – or not. For example, Marcy,[6] aged two, makes perceptible, forcefully and confidently, what matters for her learning in the moment she resists leaving her puzzle unfinished just because it is time to sit at a table and listen to a story; she even attempts a compromise by planting herself firmly on my knee as I sit nearby. Both actions are to no avail – her teachers inform me that this is typical of her 'disruptive' behaviour. More to the point, Marcy is demonstrating her understanding of doing learning, with wisdom appropriate to her years not beyond them, yet beyond the comprehension of her teachers. Not uncommonly, psychological developmentalist interpretations prevail.

(un)ravelling the weaving of *Te Whāriki* ~ generating matting and mapping

While *Te Whāriki* is presented as regular, linearly ordered weaving in 1996, May and Carr's (2000) more recent metaphorical explanation of the whāriki alludes to complexity. In contrast to the stepped model of the traditional developmental curriculum based on physical, intellectual, emotional and social skills, which dominated western curriculum models in the past but remains pervasive in early childhood practice, May and Carr say that as centres weave their own curriculum within conversational and planning spaces, a curricular spider web is created. Merging the organization suggested in this spider web imagery with the differently ordered woven mat opens a 'tapestry of increasing intricacy, complexity and richness' (Smith, 2003: 7) and opens rhizo mapping. In a move that resonates with putting the tracing back on the map, the woven mat (e)merges as a matting of complex possibilities, a curricular multiplicityal ways already working to enrich children's emerging understandings and intensities of (their) learning; rhizo mapping of rhizo matting.

In an earlier exploration (Sellers, 2005), I brought the idea of matting alongside Deleuzo-Guattarian mapping as a way of interrupting the orderliness of the conventional weaving that *Te Whāriki* represents. This idea of matting resonates with the metaphorical image Surtees (2003) presents of unruly paniculata, such as puawānanga,[7] the Aotearoa New Zealand native clematis (Figure 2.2a), and with the tangled threads of felted fabric (Figure 2.2b). The artist who created this felted piece comments that it looks like cobwebs,[8] this aptly expressing the contrast between woven mat and matting, tracing and mapping. A cobweb is more than just the woven web of a spider, a cobweb is also an accumulation of dust and debris characterized as the 'unsubstantial texture' of a 'musty accumulation' and 'accretion' of a 'subtly woven', 'entangling mesh' (*Oxford English Dictionary*, online).[9] Cobweb, matting and mapping generate and are generative of rhizo intensities – tracing and map always already operating in de~territorializing mo(ve)ments.

Surtees (2003) unravels the woven mat as she shifts possibilities for *Te Whāriki*, que(e)ring the principle of holistic development when the 'weft that weaves' (p. 146) the whāriki includes cognitive, social, physical, cultural and spiritual dimensions but excludes children's developing sexuality. Without arguing with Carr and May's (1993) metaphor of the four kauri trees used in the development of *Te*

 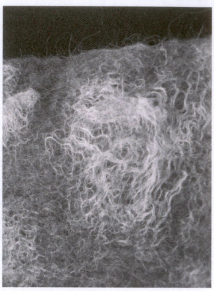

Figure 2.2a Puawānanga (Aotearoa New Zealand native clematis) (author photograph)

Figure 2.2b Felted fabric: *Grey Suffolk and Banana Fibre,* by Z. Vrkast, fibre artist (http://www.flickr.com/photos/zedster01/7031516503/in/pool-1654385@N23)

Whāriki – the four kauri trees being the guiding theorists Piaget, Erikson, Vygotsky and Bruner – or the rationale for using them to find a path through the forest of curriculum development, Surtees notes that the over-reliance on developmental, structuralist and biologically based theories at the expense of poststructuralist and humanities-based perspectives distorts our thinking about young children's growth and learning. Using queer theory, she says that there is space in the whāriki for the weaving of alternative threads and suggests adding puawānanga to the forest to include the contribution of queer theorists: 'Queering the whāriki in this way gives rise to endless possibilities as the previously unquestioned dominance of the kauri is disrupted and troubled by the unruly [puawānanga] weaving under, over and through the forest' (Surtees, 2003: 150). The tangled network of puawānanga provides a visible, above ground image not unlike the interconnecting lines of flight of a biological rhizome that often exists out of sight underground although sometimes in tangled matting above ground (e.g. kikuyu grass), so entangled that it is hard to see what is happening. The unruly puawānanga makes perceptible similar imag(in)ing.

Te Whāriki, as a metaphorical woven mat, depicts the orderly weaving of principles and strands into an objective construct, but it is possible to extend our reading of this complicated order (Deleuzo-Guattarian tracing) to include complex rhizo concepts (Deleuzo-Guattarian mapping). (Re)conceptualizing early childhood curriculum as complex matting, as a milieu of becoming, chaotically a-centred traversed by processual lines of flight, opens possibilities for uncovering interwoven systems that map unanticipated connections and enable a rhizo exploration of ways – including those not yet thought of – for (re)conceiving early childhood. Thinking of *Te Whāriki* as rhizo matting becomes a way for teachers, children and researchers to appear in different curricular space-times, unconstrained by conventional linear ways of thinking and operating. We can process through learning by continuously asking: What else exists in these spaces of learning? In such spaces we open (to) possibilities for complex curricular understandings, particularly children's, to become perceptible.

With their roots in one place and their stems wandering through the foliage of other plants, puawānanga is indicative of a liminal, in-between space between arborescence and rhizo growth, between the firmly rooted tree (curriculum as content only) and wandering~rooting~shooting~amassing rhizo systems that matting presents (curriculum as a milieu of becoming). Although rooted in one spot, puawānanga illuminates rhizo matting at work; its tangled web of lines of flight opens (to) a multiplicity of possibilities. Thinking of *Te Whāriki* as entangled matting and curriculum as mapping a milieu of becoming are such possibilities.

~curriculum as (a) milieu(s)~

From chaos, Milieus and Rhythms are born.

(Deleuze & Guattari, 1987: 313)

In rhizo thinking, the Deleuzo-Guattarian philosophical *milieu* embodies all three translations of 'surroundings', 'medium (substance)' and 'middle' (Massumi, 1987b: xvii). In (a) milieu(s), there are no beginnings or endings from which linear sequences derive; rather, middles or milieus work to intensify the embodied multidimensionality of thought and thinking. A milieu grows and overspills through flows that constantly radiate both outwards and inwards. 'Nomadic waves or flows of deterritorialization' (Deleuze & Guattari, 1987: 53) go from centre to periphery and all at once the periphery falls back upon the centre, moving towards a new centre in relation to a new periphery. In this way a milieu is continuously (re)constituting, oscillating through a multiplicity of interior elements, exterior milieus, differential relations of intermediate milieus, between conditions of the interior and exterior and through associated milieus of energy sources. As children play – a curricular performance perceptible as curricular performativity – their singular interiority operates with/in an exteriority of their games, with interior and exterior forever exchanging places and existing only in relation to the other. Constantly, there is a (re)negotiating of storylines of intermediate milieus, always in relation to other children playing games nearby, these other children and games always already constituting energy of and through an associated milieu – of children, storylines, games…and so on…

In this intensifying activity, there is a complex interweaving of 'active, percep-tive, and energetic characteristics' (Deleuze & Guattari, 1987: 51) as all kinds of milieus slip and slide in relation to, and over others. Relative to curriculum, these rhizo milieus can be understood as slip-sliding among: children and adults in recip-rocal relations; theories of play and children's spontaneous games; discourses of learning and teaching; children's social(izing) performativity; children and adults negotiating their power-fullness; children mapping their playing and playing their learning; historic curriculum theory and contemporary discourses represented in/as *Te Whāriki*; and, discourses of children and childhood of various era. Through transcoding or transduction one milieu is constituted or dissipated in another, one atop the other, one alongside the other. The work of the kinds of milieu listed above does not stay within specific boundaries; any one is likely to (e)merge from/with (any of) the others. For example, as historic discourses of childhood affect children's expressions of power-fullness, and adult interpretations of these, or, as theories of play affect understandings of children's spontaneous games. Percep-tible in children's playing of games is a commingling, interweaving embodiment of activity as children, games and play continually (re)constitute chaotically com-plex milieus.

From psychological and sociological perspectives, a game could be interpreted as a platform for individual children to develop skills for operating in the wider social world, but rhizo thinking works to illuminate it as a milieu of interiority, exteriority, intermediary spaces and associated energy sources. These interlac-ing characteristics of children's games include the storylines narrated by the children as they play (children often talk about what they are doing), the spaces of (mis)understandings among players about the game, which on one plane are circumscribed by the proposed but contingent storyline and on another plane are reflected in a liminal space with/in/through which characters emerge or fade away. More of the milieu of the game includes the players, their play-full activity and their energy forces, the physical territory of the game and the surrounding environment, including natural resources and material artefacts. There is also the imaginative territory of the game, the teachers and children nearby, and, possibly more. All this, remembering that expressions and movement of the milieu are irre-ducible, as everything is always already chaotically becoming with/in/of/through the children's playing of games. Deleuze and Guattari (1987) say that chaos is the 'milieu of all milieus' (p. 313), and while milieus are open to chaos, it is a relation-ship with rhythm that subverts any risk of collapse: rhythm of the liminal spaces between milieus; rhythm that brings together critical moments of heterogeneous space-times. In this understanding, rhythm is difference, not repetition; rhythm is the continual and continuous mo(ve)ments *between* – 'between things, interbeing, *intermezzo*' (p. 25). What is often perceived negatively as chaos is imbued with rhythm, such as rhythms of children constantly negotiating storylines and play spaces of the game, coming and going through interiors of the game and exteriori-ties of other games being played nearby and other play spaces occupied by other children's play(ing).

Thinking 'milieu' and 'rhythm' opens understandings of curriculum and opens possibilities for understanding young children's workings of curriculum. The imaginary games children play happen *within* milieus, *are* milieus and *illuminate* milieus at work, a becoming-curricular performativity. They weave strands of storylines through their games and games of others, commingling in a productively chaotic milieu (re)constituted as spaces opening with/in/through/among a rhizo tangle of characters and roles as they play out the storyline and explore spatial and temporal interconnections. Sometimes the play(ing) is subverted, dying in one place but irrupting elsewhere. The children work with their collective imaginings and those of games and children nearby. The forces of the play(ing), the games and their interrelationships affect and are affected by other play and relationships around them, also the programme and their physical territory of the setting and its culture of operating. The milieu of curricular performativity becomes the curricular performativity of the milieu.

In a linking plateau of *Children performing curriculum complexly*, three games illuminate the complex interrelations of the milieu(s), of the storylines of the games, the play activity, the relationships among the children and their curricular performativity. In another linking plateau, *Rhizo~mapping* furthers this idea of curriculum as milieu. (Re)conceiving curriculum thus is always already a continuous, never-ending process, never complete, with questions never fully answered, working with incipiently different thinking to think differently about other ways of thinking differently, and so on…generating a multiplicity of multidirectional and multidimensional movement of/through various space-times, with/in which an openness of reconceptualizing work continues to move. These space-times are characterized, (im)partially, (im)perceptibly by the subjectivities we lay open as we admit our own histories, culture, contextual and temporal experiences to the conversation, in the process, (re)opening (to) a milieu of diverse and diffractive realities and possibilities…

Notes

1 Commonly referred to as *Te Whāriki*. As with other Māori terms used here, it is not italicized as Te Reo Māori is an official language of Aotearoa New Zealand. http://nzcurriculum.tki.org.nz/Curriculum-documents/The-New-Zealand-Curriculum/Official-languages.

2 Although Pākehā commonly refers to white New Zealanders of European extraction, linguistically it encompasses all who are 'non-Māori'.

3 The Treaty of Waitangi (Te Tiriti o Waitangi), the founding document of Aotearoa New Zealand, was signed in 1840 by Māori and the British Crown to protect tino rangatiratanga (governance), taonga (treasured sites and objects) and land for Māori; also to establish British rule for the settlers. The articles of the Treaty ensure ongoing relationships of partnership, protection and participation for Māori within the British-based New Zealand legal system.

4 The *Te Whāriki* diagram is reproduced by permission of the New Zealand Ministry of Education, published in *Te Whāriki* by Learning Media Limited. Crown Copyright 1996.

5 Thomas Tawhiri (Te Whakatōhea, Ngāti Raukawa), personal communication, 22 December 2008.

6 See *Letter to Marcy* in the *Preceding echoes* plateau.
7 Puawānanga (flower of the skies), one of Aotearoa New Zealand's native clematis species, adorns the upper layer of the native bush, trailing up forest trees.
8 Z. Vrkast, fibre artist known as Zed, can be found at: http://feltbyzed.blogspot.co.uk/ and http://feltingandfiberstudio.com/.
9 See 'cobweb' in References.

Children performing curriculum complexly

...we live curriculum before we describe it. The event and the thought about the event are never simultaneous, never identical...Curriculum as lived and curriculum as described amble along, their paths sometimes parallel, often not, occasionally in moments of insight intersecting.

(Grumet, 1999: 24)

opening the plateau

How do young children make curriculum work? In this plateau I explore children's curricular performativity within the spontaneous games they play, towards opening (to) possibilities for envisaging and envisioning curriculum differently. Resonating with Grumet's (1999) living curriculum, I work towards incipiently different 'possibilities for imaginative thought' to provoke 'ethical action' (Gough, 2006a: xiv) in respect of young children's understandings of themselves and their learning. Thus, by moving outside the conventional conversations about the *what* (content) and the *how* (processes) of curriculum I attempt to make perceptible children's curricular performativity as they *do* their learning in an early childhood setting. Expressions of the children themselves that illuminate a Deleuzo-Guattarian (1987) machinic assemblage of children~curriculum~games become a way of receiving the play(ing) of their curricular performativity into the reconceiving curriculum conversation.

complexity of curricular performativity

Complex interrelationships around play and curriculum that are made perceptible through the spontaneous games that children play come alive within the data of this research. As children perform their understandings of curriculum they open possibilities for enhancing adult views of curriculum, for re(con)ceiving children in curriculum. To illuminate the complexity at play in the children's play and their playing of their curricular understandings, I use images from a four-minute snippet of data to present the stories of each of three games that are happening simultaneously and discuss intersecting lines of flight within the curricular performativity.

The three games referred to as Goldilocks, the chocolate factory and muddy monsters, each influenced by children's popular culture, are being played out in close proximity in the sandpit. A group of five boys – Kane, Rylie, Callum, Alec and Nic – are engaged in a chocolate factory game, busily mixing sand and water in various containers including the water trough and a bucket/pulley arrangement nearby. Amidst this, Nic, Alec, Kane and Josh are playing a monster game, which involves sandy hands and chasing. Close by, Libby, Lee and Alice are playing Goldilocks, mixing sand and water to make cake then porridge. Image 2 of Storyboard 3.1 shows where the children are positioned in relation to one another and to the equipment in the opening moments of this data snippet. Rylie is at the water trough (blue); about three metres away the red bucket is suspended from the end of the pulley nearest the water trough; a couple more metres away Libby and Lee are digging in the sand close to the bucket with Alice (in red) standing to the right; Kane is parading through the space within which the games are all happening.

These games, singularly and severally, ebb and flow, with pauses and forward rushes, 'proceeding from the middle, through the middle, coming and going rather than starting and finishing' (Deleuze & Guattari, 1987: 25) sometimes blocking and sometimes being blocked, all (re)constituting an intensity of the play(ing). Linkages appear as lines of flight intersect, as the play(ing) traverses the plateau of each and every game through smooth moments, through dis/inter/ruptions, through irruptions. However, in an untwisting move, the threads of games are discussed separately, but only for ease of understanding the inherent complexity. The games are only momentarily untwisted; as with applying a backwards force to the threads in the middle of a strand of rope, for example, when the force is relinquished the rope returns to its entwined condition. This is not an untangling as such; rather, it is an attempt to explain the twisting backwards – backwording the twisting – that needed to happen to negotiate the complexity of the play space. It functions as an opening of the in-between space-times or liminal spaces of the backwards~twisting of the entanglement. Through negotiating these in-between spaces between the threads of the games the synchronistic relations of the games and complexity of the children's curricular performativity generated become apparent.

A Deleuzo-Guattarian reading of the backwards~twisting generates a collective mapping, illuminating the complexity of de-territorializing lines of flight of the monster game, the flowing activity of leading flows that disrupt any fixed leadership within the chocolate factory game and a rhizoanalysis of conventional notions of gendered-ness in the Goldilocks game. It is an amassing of... *and... and... and...* as the three games work to singularly produce more of themselves *and* severally to make more of a rhizome. Mapping the movement and gestures of both games and players, I combine several maps, putting tracings of all three games onto the map, bringing one into several into one again, generating through intersecting lines of flight 'diverse map-tracing, rhizome-root assemblages, with variable coefficients of deterritorialization' (Deleuze & Guattari, 1987: 15).

introducing the chocolate factory[1]

The opening set of storyboards (Storyboards 3.1–3.6) illuminates the activity of five boys playing a game of *Charlie and the Chocolate Factory*, noting that the four-minute snippet is from a game that lasted more than 90 minutes. This game presents as the dominating activity in the sandpit, with a changing group of boys variously involved in making chocolate in Willy Wonka's factory. The water trough is in the sandpit and contains a muddy sand-water mix (chocolate), and currently Callum, Rylie and Nic are working with a tray and buckets of muddy sand (more chocolate) positioned on a low wall nearby. Kane, as Willy Wonka, is attempting to manage the chocolate-making enterprise, and it is his desired and supposed leadership, referred to as ~~leadership~~ because it both is and is not, that I work with here.

the chocolate factory ~ 'We're making chocolatey yes yes yes yes yes'

Typical of the spontaneous games the children play, the children are operating in rhizo flows, flowing with their own and the collective understandings of how the game should progress. Such rhizo flow makes any ~~leadership~~ role – assumed, claimed or elected – a challenging and contestable activity. The rhizo leading flows make perceptible children's ways of disrupting authoritarian modernist views that consider leadership as absolute. Although Kane may have desired total control, he manages the fluctuating interest of his being in charge in a particular style of his own. He works the role to suit his interpretation of the game and to optimize its continuity. For example, when Rylie and Callum tussle over the use of a particular trowel, Kane moves to maintain the focus on the collective chocolate making (images 4 and 5).

With the back of his rounded trowel, Callum is smoothing the top of the sand in the tray.

> Rylie shouts: *No! This is the flattening out thing!*
> Callum grabs at Rylie's flat trowel: *I need the flattening out thing for a minute.*
> Rylie: *No-o!*
> Callum: *I need it!*
> Rylie: *No!*
> Kane walks up behind them: *C'mon, let's see about that chocolate... akkagagga...*

Apparently satisfied that they are on task, Kane returns to making odd noises. Unsurprisingly, there is a need for some kind of consensus throughout children's games to ensure the game continues. Achieving this may involve dispute and Kane's approach seems to be as much about progressing the game as mediating the activity of the players. As unprofessed but seemingly acknowledged leader, Kane assures himself everything is under (his) control, through his tone of *C'mon* and through drawing attention to the task of seeing to the chocolate. This seems to be a (not so) subtle way of assuring himself of his control, ensuring the chocolate makers stay focused and keeping the plot on (his) track. However, any control he may desire is immediately mediated by deferring to the plot, it is de~territorialized by his own understandings of the game as he promotes his supervisory role by turning attention to the chocolate. In this moment it seems that 'it is no longer of any importance whether one says I. [He is] no longer [himself]' (Deleuze & Guattari, 1987: 3). As ~~leader~~ his leading flows (e)merge from/with/in the game. Evident also is the change of leading flows. While the dispute over the flat trowel does not disrupt the game, it does signal Rylie's input into progressing the game, perhaps reminding Kane that, while he may be Willy Wonka, the chocolate makers are also concerned with how this should happen. Any perceived ~~leadership~~ is likely to change without warning and becomes easier to resolve when a line of flight is flowed with, as appears here.

While Kane is forthcoming in exercising his leading flow, he is unperturbed about the mixed responses when he calls for the chocolate makers to grab sand from his bucket (images 6 and 7). Callum and Rylie continue with their mixing; only Nic does as Kane requests. Unfazed, Kane acknowledges neither response, both Callum and Rylie's ignoring him and Nick's acquiescence. He shifts from his overseeing position on the sandpit edging (image 8), gathering sand and checking if anyone else wants chocolate (image 14). There is no direct reply, although Callum intersperses Kane's movements with affirmations of Kane's pronounced ~~leadership~~ of the chocolate-making enterprise. Callum supports the storyline as Kane has announced it (image 10), simultaneously, taking the leading flow for a moment by announcing his input into progressing the game, as Rylie had earlier in the trowel disagreement. Callum now looks at Josh, new to the scene, and shouts at the top of his voice (images 9 and 10). The leading flows through Kane and Callum (images 14 and 15), also through Rylie, each claiming and conceding leading in a changing rhizo flow.

In the conversational interchange of leading flows between Callum and Kane, it is impossible to tell from Kane's intonation (on the soundtrack of the videorecording, affected by general playground noise) whether his yelling is intended as statement or inquiry (image 15), but there is a sense that it is both – he is sending out a query while simultaneously demanding acquiescence. In this sense, he is playing with differing flows of leading, suggesting, as well as his (non)resistance to the ~~leadership~~ flow, an understanding that ~~leadership~~ is not fixed or linearly progressive; rather, leading circulates, in ebbs and flows. 'What is important is not whether the flows are "One or multiple"…[rather] there is a collective assemblage…one inside the other and both plugged into an immense outside that is a multiplicity' (Deleuze & Guattari, 1987: 23) – a multiplicity of rhizo leading flows. Kane's leading is all at once acknowledged, supported and challenged, (un)intentionally given over to and shared in all its complexity with Callum and Rylie.

However, Kane's ~~leadership~~ becomes an activity of protecting his territory from outsiders. The girls, who have been playing nearby throughout (images 2, 12, 14 and 16), are now apparently too close to Kane for his liking (image 17). Two seconds later, the soundtrack records Kane growling loudly at the girls before chasing after them as they flee the territory of their game and the sandpit (images 20 and 21). As Kane stumbles~waddles after the girls, flopping his head from side-to-side (images 21–27), his gait evokes images of Willy Wonka from Tim Burton's movie, *Charlie and the Chocolate Factory* (2005), in which Willy Wonka walked with a stick and an odd bouncy stride. Was it that Kane's announcement of an idea was a Willy Wonka-type way of chasing the girls from the physical and imaginative territory of his game?

The chocolate makers, however, seem oblivious to the chase occurring around the edge of their factory, apart from Alec watching the girls race around the back (image 20); and a few seconds later (image 26) he is crouched, digging in the sand and watching Kane run after the girls (images 26 and 27). Callum may also be aware of the chase as amidst the commotion he trips over the handle of the trolley (images 26 and 27), having successfully avoided it several times throughout the game as he gathered water from the trough (images 1, 11, 18 and 20). For Kane, expelling the girls from the physical and imaginative territory of the game is a serious exercise. He is serious in his intent and also in playing it out in character from the moment he growls at the girls (image 17) until he chases after them (images 21–28) in his deliberately awkward, stumbling gait and returns (images 29 and 29a) satisfied that his territory is free from invaders. If his chocolate workers had not explicitly acknowledged his leading flows to any great extent, the girls fleeing the territory were doing so – actually in physical terms as they race away from Kane and virtually in terms of supporting Kane's positional ~~leadership~~ in the chocolate factory game; actually fleeing the territory of the sandpit and virtually fleeing the territory of their game. In this mo(ve)ment, Kane's leading has flowed beyond the territory of the chocolate factory through the girls' territory in a rhizo wandering though both games. This changing leading flow presents as the rhizo conjunction of *and...and...and...* opening (to) the multidimensional complexity of ~~leadership~~ through the chocolate factory game. It is then unsurprising that within the game a monster game emerges and Kane, as Willy Wonka, segues into monster.

introducing an (e)merging monster game

With/in and around the physical and imaginative territory of the chocolate factory game, there are intersecting lines of flight as other games emerge from within and merge with the chocolate factory game. A muddy monster game, involving Nic, Josh, Alec and Kane, is one such game. As this snippet opens (images 2 and 3, in Storyboards 3.7–3.10), Nic is working as one of the chocolate makers and Alec is playing alongside with a digger. Kane is prowling around the water trough positioned in the sandpit, chanting and making strange sounds. Josh wanders into the scene a little later. To begin with Kane presents as Willy Wonka, but a(nother) rhizo reading presents him as emerging monster. This monster character segues through various players as the plot evolves, in the process illuminating the children playing out their power-fullness alongside and amongst one another. Whether the monster theme that emerges is an aside, an entertaining deviation or a common part of such plots is incidental. What is interesting is its (e)merging *and* that it works to enhance the chocolate factory game *and* that in the process of playing out the monster theme, the children enact a complex understanding of the Deleuzo-Guattarian conjunctive, *and...and...and...*

Note: The numbering of the images of the *Chocolate factory* (Storyboards 3.1– 3.6) now becomes a marker for all three games happening at the same time during this four-minute play episode, so the following images in the *Monster game* storyboards (Storyboards 3.1–3.10) are numbered to coincide with those in the *Chocolate factory* storyboards. Where an image from the *Chocolate factory* storyboards is also used in the *Monster game* storyboards, the number stays the same, as 2, 3, 4, etc. For example, the *(e)merging Monster game* becomes apparent in the midst of the *Chocolate factory* game so the first *Monster game* storyboard image is marked as number 2. There are also numbers inserted where other images are significant to the activity of the *Monster game*. For example, between images 8 and 9 in the *Chocolate factory* storyboards, significant activity in the *Monster game* is marked as images 8a and 8b.

the monster game ~ 'Whaaah! Bad muddy monster!'[2]

As the children play out their games – performing curricular understandings – unexpected themes emerge, unexpected turns are taken, these themes and turns becoming part of the game or lines of flight to follow. There may be resistance and occasionally a player will abandon both game and playmates, but in various ways these lines of flight are utilized to progress the game. In the monster game, which segues through the chocolate factory, the monster character is played out by a stream of players, through the interactions of Kane, Nic, Josh and Alec. In the process of expressing their power-fullness as monster characters relative to one another, they find ways of involving themselves in others' storylines and ways of involving others in their own storylines. The lines of flight they follow become ways of including other players and (their) ideas, enriching, extending and progressing the game through an understanding of *and...and...and...* The monster is not a fixed, stable character, but flows from one to another – through Kane through Nic through Josh through Alec through Kane. A linear understanding of curriculum is disrupted in that the character/role does not disappear when the player disappears. For example, monster-Josh carries on from where monster-Nic leaves off. Their curricular performativity also destabilizes binary understandings such as monster|victim goodies|baddies insider|outsider as they each segue *seamlessly* through becomings of all these (hence lack of commas) in various space-times becoming-monster becoming-victim becoming-goodie becoming-baddie becoming-insider becoming-outsider.

As the snippet opens, Kane is wandering about apparently in an imaginative world of his own, making strange sounds. Although, at first glance, he seems detached from managing the chocolate factory enterprise, when he moves in to view Callum and Rylie's dispute over the flat trowel, he seems very involved. He immediately returns to making odd noises and he seems to be both Willy Wonka and becoming-monster in a rhizo mo(ve)ment. Another becoming-monster character evolving in this curricular performativity of *and...and...and...* is the role played by Nic (images 3, 4 and 5), who also seems distanced from the chocolate factory even though he is mixing the sand and water with his hands. But, like Kane, Nic is obviously engaged in the chocolate factory plot as well, apparent when Nic responds to Kane's yelling to grab a chocolate – Nic is the only one to grab a handful of sand from Kane's bucket, as requested/invited.

However, Nic has something else in mind to do with his muddied hands as he scoops up handfuls of wet sand – as circled in image 6. Suddenly, he rears up in monster mode with his hands at shoulder height, fingers splayed and slightly curled (image 8a), and confronts Josh (image 8b). In this moment, the presence of a monster, a supposedly negative force, intensifies the play plateau, affirming the game's procession as the unfolding plot, emerging characters and roles are played out. If Kane is shaping up to becoming the leading monster figure, he is now upstaged by this new monster~Nic who confronts Josh, a newcomer to the scene. Nic on the periphery of the chocolate making becomes insider in the monster game and confronts outsider Josh. But, undaunted, Josh stands his ground, which opens a way for him to become insider as well, as they each display and express their singular power-fullness. Similar to Nic usurping Kane's expression of power-fullness by assuming a 'bigger' monster role, Josh is challenging Nic's power-fullness by refusing to back off. Josh has now become a power-full player as well. And, while expressing their singular power-fullness, together they become another force in that this emerging monster game challenges the physical and imaginative territory, which until now has been largely occupied by Kane's chocolate-making enterprise. If Kane has any ambition to be sole controller of the territory and of the chocolate-making enterprise, this is now disrupted through this (e)merging monster line of flight.

But, is Nic as monster assured of ongoing power-fullness? As he moves away from Josh, in search of another victim, Josh is raising his hands in monster mode (images 9 and 10). This is the moment that Callum shouts at him: *Yes! Willy Wonka and chocolate fact'ry's here!* In the chocolate factory interpretation, it is easy to assume that Josh is raising his hands in defence. But, the monster interpretation opens to other possibilities, namely, that Josh is not concerned about Callum's announcement, at close proximity, deafeningly loud, directed at him...*and...*that he is interested in becoming-monster, to either play alongside Nic...*and...*to meet any further challenges from Nic head-on. For now, it looks as if Josh as becoming-monster is preparing to move into monster mode himself.

Alec seems to be engaging with the monster theme as well as he becomes intent on muddying his hands. He has moved from playing with his digger (image 8a) to observing the interaction between Nic and Josh (image 8b) to dunking his hands in the trough (images 9 – partly obscured by Rylie – and 10) to rubbing his hands in the sand at his feet (image 11 – partly obscured by Rylie). Nic tries to attract Alec's attention but, failing to do so, turns back to Josh, seated in the deck (image 11) and rushes him, hands raised.

> Nic: *Muddy monster!*
> Josh stares but doesn't move.

Moments later, Nic leaves the scene, his monster character perhaps thwarted by Alec's and then Josh's passive resistance. By refusing a victim response, both have hindered Nic progressing his monster role, although all could have agreed to play together. So Josh's power-fullness seems to have overruled Nic's. Alternatively, Nic is expressing his power-fullness in another way, by choosing not to continue. Rhizo readings of the activity of *and...and...and...* of this activity generates a multiplicity of possible understandings rather than any one *or* other in particular. Josh and Alec then proceed to further this conjunctive *and...and... and...* understanding. Josh becomes leading monster and moves the game on by chasing after Alec, who, although raising his muddied hands at Josh, turns (image 15a) and runs away (images 15b and 15c). Perhaps this monster chase is a tacitly collaborative interlude with little concern about who is being chased by whom, as long as a chase happens – the activity of the performance, the performativity. Josh seems not to mind who he is chasing and as Alec returns to the trough to muddy his hands, Josh hisses at an outside observer (image 18). His targets expended, he sits on the deck (image 20). But Kane has now adopted a monster mode as he goes after the girls (images 21–25) and, when Josh notices this, he rushes towards Kane-as-monster-chasing-the-girls (image 25c), although Kane remains focused on the girls. Josh-as-monster now fades and Kane resumes as leading monster in the closing moments of the data snippet.

Like a 'stream...that undermines its banks and picks up speed in the middle' (Deleuze & Guattari, 1987: 23), the fluidity of the monster role – of who plays the part and how – not only opens the flow of power-fullness to all, it also opens other spaces for the monster game and opens possibilities for Kane in his becoming-Willy Wonka flow of leading. The characters slip and slide from one game to the other, each intensifying the other. Even when rejected – for example, when players refuse to act as victims – the play processes on: when Nic rejects Josh's refusal to become victim and leaves the game, the play continues regardless. The game is not disrupted, it irrupts elsewhere as Josh, Alec and Kane follow other lines of flight, expressing their power-fullness, singularly and together.

Of interest is Nic, Josh and Alec's peripheral involvement in the chocolate making, which opens possibilities for flowing together with/through (an)other line(s) of flight. A behaviourist reading, and perhaps a sociological one, may say their lack of involvement causes them to create a disturbance to make their own space in the chocolate factory game. However, a generative rhizo reading perceives both Nic and Josh as having the space(s) to imagine and perform other threads of the storyline. Their imaginings flow simultaneously in a line of flight that enables both of them to work as becoming-protagonist *and* becoming-antagonist all at once. When Nic (becoming-protagonist) rears up as a monster (image 8a), Alec skirts around him en route to the trough, and Josh, otherwise unoccupied, is the only one left in Nic's path. Josh does not acquiesce; instead he plays an adversarial role. Even though he steps back, he demands that Nic back off (image 8b), signalling his opposition (as becoming-antagonist) to Nic's monster character. But in doing so, it can also be said that Josh is becoming-protagonist and as Nic then turned away from him, Nic is becoming-antagonist. It is not that there is any actual *opposition* to the monster character; rather monster-Nic and the emerging monster-Josh play *appositionally*[3] with the monster character, illuminating the complexity of the activity unfolding. So, a monster game emerges through Nic, Josh and Alec's intersecting lines of flight – they engage, juxtaposed, playing out their power-fullness, in close proximity, each adopting various becoming-monsters.

Disrupting the claim that behaviourism would make, that children's play follows unidirectional, cause and effect patterns, these children's curricular performativity illuminates a multidimensionality of understandings. In a rhizo reading, Kane, Nic, Josh and Alec segue through the monster character and the monster morphs through their singular and collective renditions of the role of becoming-monster. There is no sense of a dichotomous relationship of either|or-ness, of a monster game and a separate chocolate factory, of goodies *or* baddies. It is about both, that is, *and...and...and...* The monster game emerges to intensify the play plateau – until then dominated by the chocolate factory game – becoming and illuminating other dimensions of the complexity in/of/at (the) play. Intersecting with the chocolate factory game as a complex activity, in which Kane, Callum, Rylie and Nic enact rhizo leading flows, is the monster game, in which Nic, Josh, Alec and Kane express their emerging power-fullness and demonstrate understandings of *and...and...and...* The plots (e)merge as the game processes and (e)merge to process the game.

With/in and around the games, rhizome is working ceaselessly. Turning to the girls' Goldilocks game furthers *and...and...and...* of embodied rhizo-gendered performativity.

introducing Goldilocks[4]

The sandpit is an area reportedly dominated by boys and their games (MacNaughton, 2000) and when girls enter the area they often play cooking-type games on the periphery of boys' activity. My intention here is not to play into the binary of girl|boy or to dichotomize their activity, rather it is to illuminate the complexity of gendered relations (Davies, 2003) played out and perceptible through the girls' Goldilocks game. As the data snippet opens, Libby, Lee and Alice are focused on digging. This soon becomes a cake-making exercise and then segues into a Goldilocks game. In the same way that the boys are playing out *Charlie and the*

Chocolate Factory, Libby, Lee and Alice are playing with the culturally familiar *Goldilocks and the Three Bears* story, which draws them into traditionally gendered roles. The girls play at being traditional girl – passive homemaker – narrating the actual and imagined spaces of their game as they go. Much of the time they acquiesce to this image of girl, but they also break through those traditional boundaries as Alice becomes guardian of their physical space and as they all work in the closing moments of the snippet to move the imaginative space of their game outside the territory of the boys' games and outside the sandpit. On the surface it appears that through this Goldilocks game the girls are playing out a traditionally gendered image of girl as passive, weak and victim, but a generative rhizo reading entangled with/in shadows offers another. I suggest their flight from Kane and the sandpit can be understood as an expression of their power-fullness as 'strong girls', with victim~strong girl becoming an embodied performance.

Note

The numbering of the Goldilocks storyboard images (Storyboards 3.11–3.16) follows the pattern of the monster game storyboards.

the Goldilocks game ~ 'We're playing Goldilocks!'

Having selected their tools by colour and begun digging, Libby, Lee and Alice soon encounter trouble with operating in the space they have chosen. They begin relatively close to the chocolate-making activity (image 2), but as soon as they start to fill the bucket hanging unattended from the pulley, the boys move them on. Apart from Lee's momentarily defiant gesture of grabbing hold of the bucket on the pulley and grinning (image 2a), they acquiesce to the boys' demands by finding another bucket and moving further away. Their digging then turns into a cake-making exercise (image 2b) and the Goldilocks theme emerges. However, the physical territory of their game is still not settled and they relocate to establish their home by the back fence (image 2c). While they seem unconcerned about playing their game in close proximity to the boys, they move further away from the boys' activity. From their new home, they announce their storyline, telling me about their game and confirming details with one another (images 5a, 5b and 5c).

They are now secure enough in their space to engage in conversation about the presence of the boys, which is apparently a concern, although more in relation to the imaginative space of their game than the physical space they are de~territorializing. What Lee envisages hiding from is not clear (image 5b). Maybe she thinks they need to hide from the boys in an attempt to protect the physical and imaginative territory of their Goldilocks game... *and*... maybe they are pretending they are the bears and need to hide so Goldilocks can make her appearance. Given the challenges from the boys to their occupation of the physical space and given their desires to make their game work, it is feasible that they are responding to both: to being girls hiding from the boys – by the back fence they are, for the most part, out of the boys' line of sight; to being bears hiding from Goldilocks – in the imaginative space of the game if they say they are out of sight of Goldilocks, they are. In this always already (im)partial rhizo reading such simultaneity is generative, not contradictory.

Libby seems less concerned about the boys knowing what they are doing as she publicly calls Goldilocks into be(com)ing. Alice is now becoming-guardian as she acknowledges Goldilocks' imminent arrival despite the boys being there and, different from her previous comment, Lee both accepts the boys' presence but denies they will have any affect on their game, saying: *but they're not Goldilocks*. While earlier submitting to the boys moving them on, the girls are now standing strong together (image 5c).

In these opening moments of the snippet, through generating a narrative of their game, the girls define the physical and imaginative spaces they are de~territorializing, and it is apparent that Alice is also becoming-defender of their space, similar to Kane's defending the chocolate factory space. Alice has been standing guard in their home at the back of the sandpit and surveying the scene since Libby announced they were playing Goldilocks. Of the three, Alice seems most aware of the boys who, one way or another, are attempting to commandeer the whole sandpit area. For example: Nic has passed through their territory, clapping his muddied, soon-to-be monster hands (image 5b); Kane is overseeing the chocolate factory activity (image 5c); and, Alec has pushed his digger in a loop in front of the girls' home (image 5d). The extent to which Nic, Kane and Alec are aware of the girls' difficulty in claiming territory in the sandpit and/or mounting a counter-challenge is incidental to Alice's attention to their movements.

As becoming-guardian, Alice has cast traditional passive girl aside to become a proactive becoming-protector of their territory – she suddenly rushes Kane as he makes an announcements (image 5e) and jumps decisively to a halt to watch him (image 5f). Although she does not end up very close to him, her jump is close enough to startle him in his announcement, which stops midstream. She seems to be challenging his verbal invasion of the Goldilocks game space; in her jump she both alerts Kane to her perception of the chocolate-making game being a potential threat to the Goldilocks game... *and*... she presents herself as a threat to Kane. She now claims the space as Goldilocks territory and ensures their safety as they play out the game.

Under Alice's guardianship, Libby and Lee are meanwhile preoccupied with making what was cake but is now porridge (image 7a), with Lee gathering water from the trough alongside the boys (image 7b). Their game is working smoothly. They continue to discuss their Goldilocks storyline, at this moment seeming to be more intent in talking about what they are going to do rather then actually doing it. It is repetitive, but maybe they are confirming their understandings of how they want the game to work (image 16). Apparently more confident in the space, Libby, Lee and Alice have moved from the far edge of the sandpit to a spot quite close to Kane (image 16), who is standing on the edging by the pulley. Although he seems preoccupied with his own activity (image 17), his suddenly loud growling response to Libby's closeness indicates he is very aware of the Goldilocks activity.

Operating as rhizome, following various lines of flight of the children's play, with no cognizance of what the data might illuminate and in particular unaware that the girls' territory was about to be compromised yet again, as Libby starts to speak I pan the camera away, back to the boys at the chocolate-making activity. So exactly where she places the porridge bowl is impossible to ascertain. But, it is obviously too close to Kane for his liking – maybe only a metre away – and the girls apparently accept his view as there is a gasp and a squeal, signalling their hasty exit. As they run off, in the chaos that follows, on the surface it looks like the demise of their game, that the girls have acquiesced yet again to the boys' claim on the territory, ending the Goldilocks game.

But are they fleeing the boys' territory and does their flight mark the end of the game? A generative reading says otherwise, that in this moment of crisis a new line of flight emerges. If Kane has morphed into bear, their flight with Kane chasing them moves the game along albeit before the girls were prepared for it, that is, before they had narrated their version of this surprise encounter in the traditional storyline. While they never explicitly identify their roles, in mixing the porridge they likely imagine themselves as the bears, but in fleeing the sandpit, it seems they have all become Goldilocks. In this altered storyline, they are undoubtedly fleeing Kane's space, but not his chocolate factory space, rather his growly bear space. Had the intent been to escape the chocolate factory space, Libby would have abandoned the bowl of porridge and chosen the shortest and easiest route of escape by jumping over the edging where they were standing and running away from the sandpit. Instead, Libby leading and carrying the bowl of porridge, their actual flight processes *through* the sandpit (image 19) as they race around the back of the sandpit (image 20), momentarily retrace their steps (image 25a), then turn back in the direction they were first going (image 25b). Given that the girls, until now, seem to have acquiesced to the boys' desires to dominate the sandpit with their chocolate factory enterprise and the monster game, at first glance the girls' flight appears to be more of the same.

However, a rhizo reading, (im)partially challenged by Davies' (2003) call to learn to think beyond the male|female binary, is that to intensify the game to their satisfaction, they need to leave the sandpit area – the home of the bears – and race off through the imaginative woods that the playground likely represents. Thus, if they had exited the scene via the shortest, easiest route, they could be perceived to have become *actual* victims of the boys and of their Goldilocks game, but escaping the space in the way that they did, they become *virtual* victims fleeing the *imaginative* territory of their game. But, a Deleuzian reading considers flight as a creative response (Deleuze & Guattari, 1987: 55), so is there any difference to the actuality and virtuality of these supposed victim roles? Yes and no – the actual and the virtual are intertwined and their difference and sameness resides in the liminal space between. That is, the virtual is played out in the actual world, the virtual being an extension of, and feeding into the actual... *and*... the actual lived experience is (re)lived in the virtual or imagined world of the game, the lived experience informing the virtual, imagined space of the game. So, determining where the game is situated in any moment – in the actual or virtual worlds – is confounded by it being all at once in both. Had the game 'ended' in conventional terms, then the girls could be perceived as victims of the boys and of their own game. But the game continued – simultaneously in both actual and virtual worlds, as (a) panicked flight.

The panic seems to be chaotic in terms of the girls being in a state of utter confusion and disorder, with Libby unable to decide which way to go. But considering chaos as resonating with the complexity of the space-time, her state of panic only appears random as she responds to this new situation. In terms of continuing the storyline, the chaos was necessary. When Libby is surprised by Kane's growl, it is not an event she has anticipated (yet) in the narration of the storyline. As she rushes one way, then the other and back again, dropping the porridge bowl is of no concern – after all it should be back in the bears' house; also without it running to escape is easier. They all become Goldilocks, enacting a flight from the bears that no script or actor could better as they tacitly co-opt Kane into a growly bear role. Kane goes after them and his gait is bear-like; he is lumbering, not oddly, but with style (image 26).

In a Deleuzo-Guattarian understanding a territorial assemblage gathers forces, at times precipitating a sudden confrontation or departure that likely brings on a 'movement of absolute deterritorialization: "Goodbye, I'm leaving and I won't be back"' (Deleuze & Guattari, 1987: 327). Thus, their seemingly traditionally gendered performance becomes an expression of their power-fullness as strong girls, not weak, victimized girls. Libby, Lee and Alice appear to be victims in the traditional image of girl; alternatively, they are embodied as strong girls in this supposed victim role to satisfy the traditional Goldilocks storyline and to enhance their game as they engage with/in de~territorializing activity. As the territory of their game connects with the territory of others, a line of flight opens enabling a preservation of their territory, differently. Preserving their territory in this moment means re-situating themselves as characters in their game (they flee), re-siting the physical space of the game (outside the sandpit area), and reciting anew the actual storyline of the game (Goldilocks subsequently morphs into a game of strong girls). This reading affirms the productivity of the children's desire – not as determination but as affect – their flight reflecting neither lack nor negativity. Rather, the children constantly (re)constitute the power-fullness of their subjectivity through de~territorializing their game and themselves. In their flight, they de~territorialize their characterized becomings... and... they de~territorialize the traditional Goldilocks storyline... and... they de~territorialize the play space they are working with/in.

This Deleuzo-Guattarian affective reading sees such flight – physically exiting the sandpit and following a line of flight with/in the storyline – as functional, productive and expressive of the force or power-fullness of desires of their feminine subjectivity. Deleuze and Guattari (1987) draw on ethology to perceive flights within milieu as conquests or creations.

Since [any] milieu always confronts a milieu of exteriority with which the animal is engaged and in which it takes necessary risks, a *line of flight* must be preserved to enable the animal to regain its associated milieu when danger appears. A second kind of line of flight arises when the associated milieu is rocked by blows from the exterior, forcing the animal to abandon it and strike up an association with new portions of exteriority, this time leaning on its interior milieus like fragile crutches...the animal is more a fleer than a fighter, but its flights are also conquests, creations.

(Deleuze & Guattari, 1987: 55, original italics, underline added)

To link this to the Goldilocks girls' flight from the sandpit, I re-site the above quotation, inciting a Deleuzo-Guattarian revolution. 'The question is not: is it true? But: does it work? What new thoughts does it make it possible to think?' (Massumi, 1987a: xv). As invited by Massumi, and taking Deleuze and Guattari at their word, I thus put phrases to work from their original. I consider that the milieu here is constituted by the children, both girls and boys, the physical territory they are playing in (sandpit) and the imaginative territory (storylines of games) that is being played out. Any milieu, such as the players, storyline and territory of the Goldilocks game always confronts a milieu of exteriority with which the children engage. In this moment, the milieu of exteriority is Kane, playing Willy Wonka~monster, the storylines and other players of the boys' games. The girls' engagement is with creating a space to play alongside the boys and with guarding that space. Ensuring their wellbeing within the space – when Alice jumps Kane and ensuring their access to the water – necessitates the girls taking risks. But lines of flight also need to be preserved to ensure the safety of the girls' physical and imaginative territory stayed safe, regardless of the boys' activity. The girls first relocated to the back fence, distancing themselves from the chocolate factory but the necessity to follow another line of flight arises when the milieu of their game is subjected to blows from the exterior. These blows are marked by Kane's growl – his expression of power-fullness as WillyWonka~monster and now, it appears, as bear. The girls opt to abandon the physical space, the sandpit, and strike up an association with new portions of exteriority as they flee into another part of the playground, this time leaning on its interior milieus like fragile crutches. The fragility of their storyline is illuminated as the storyline now segues away from Goldilocks and the sandpit to irrupt in another space later. The girls choose to flee not fight, and in a Deleuzo-Guattarian reading, their flight is both creation and conquest. Some of the milieu, indeed the Goldilocks milieu itself, may be abandoned, but another is territorialized – the activity of de~territorialization.

In this sense, playing victim then becomes an expression of the power-fullness of their gendered understandings of themselves. The girls project the kind of understanding 'in which all sorts of hybrids are engendered in a joyful play of creative mutations' (Braidotti, 1996: 313) as they mutate the storyline by calling the bear into existence and then co-opting Kane (as bear) as their reason to flee. Braidotti might call this expression of their emerging subjectivity a 'line of evasion from the morbid mutual dependence of feminine and masculine' (p. 313) or maybe she would see Libby, Lee and Alice as 'nomadic subject[s] of collectively negotiated trajectories' (p. 314). In response to whether following the traditional Goldilocks storyline exacerbated any images of gendered weakness, I cannot ignore the procession of the game after this data snippet – they went on to become 'strong girls' (their description of themselves), 'saving' (their expression again) Ani from Kane who continued his storyline as bear~monster in the playground beyond the sandpit. Inevitably, segue-ing into strong girls refuses a reading of victim. My reading is thus (no) more or less (im)partial and (im)plausible – victim~strong girl becomes an embodied performance and opens spaces of possibilities for Libby, Lee and Alice's rethinking themselves in curriculum and opens spaces of possibilities for educationists' rethinking the curricular performativity of children's games.

opening into flowing through/with intersecting lines of flight

Deleuze and Guattari (1987: 325) point to the importance of noticing that new assemblages form within territorial assemblages, describing them as innovative openings of passage and relay. Within this book~assemblage, mo(ve)ments of productivity of assemblages emerge as plateaus open in/on/to other plateaus, milieus open to milieus, middles to middles, the multiplicity is never ending, ever-intensifying, like a refrain. Lines of flight, the forces of de~territorialization affecting the territory itself, continually changing and altering it, and the assemblage of the territory always already moves into other assemblages, generating (a) milieu of space-time co-existence. So while the chocolate factory, monster and Goldilocks games are singular assemblages they also combine, mutually and reciprocally (re)constituting themselves as a fragmented whole. (Re)turning to the four-minute snippet of data of these three games is like a refrain, pausing to gather force both inside and from outside the territory. The refrain of the intersecting lines of flight among/through these games finds its force-fullness inside...*and*...with/in/through these forces proceeds outside into other territories. Working with intersecting lines of flight, several maps (of the three games) are combined (Map 3.1) to generate a collective mapping of them all, a map that opens to the complex ways that children make their curricular understandings work.

intersecting lines of flight ~ chocolate factory~monster~Goldilocks

On the surface, at times the activity in the sandpit was bedlam, but through processing rhizoanalytically through the complexity of the chaos, it becomes chaoplexy in/at/of play, that is, complexly chaotic interconnections among players...*and*... storylines of several games, each (e)merging with the others as lines of flight intersect...*and*...flights negotiating a multiplicity of curricular performativity...Plots emerge in the playing...*and*...games merge as players commingle...*and*...games

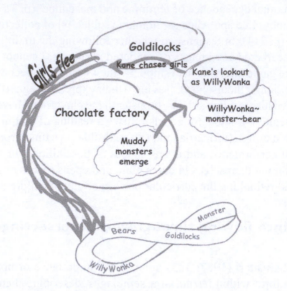

Map 3.1 Intersecting lines of flight: shifting plateaus of play(ing) segueing through Willy Wonka~monster~bear~Goldilocks

intensify in the boundless spaces...*and*...Goldilocks, the chocolate factory and the monster games de~territorialize the others...*and*...they (e)merge in other spaces, following lines of flight. In the liminal spaces in-between of *and...and...and...*as storylines and roles segue and characters morph, linkages (e)merge and the non-linear procession of the games becomes apparent.

In narrating the storyline, there are moments when various children incite others into their own performativity, calling other characters into becoming. For example, Lee calls as she's running: *He's got a really big growl!* (Goldilocks image 27), which seems as much statement of what has happened, as reminder to Kane to keep growling. In response Kane shouts *Mi-ine!* (image 28). But, most markedly, in the seeming panic of the closing moments of this snippet, the timings demonstrate the children's disruption of a linearly ordered, progressive game. The timings show that things actually happened after it was claimed they were happening. For example, as the timings from the video footage indicate, Lee claims Kane is following them (42.24) before he moves off the edging eight seconds later (42.32) and Kane announces he had a good idea (to chase the girls away) (42.28), eight seconds after they run off (in anticipation of being chased) (42.20).

42.18   Libby: ...*put Goldilocks poison porridge <u>he-re</u>.*
42.19   Kane: *Grrrrraaaagggghhhh!!*
42.20   One of the girls gasps then squeals as they run off.
42.24   Lee, as they are running: *Aaahhh! He's following us! C'mon!*
42.25   The girls are now running across the back of the sandpit.

42.28   Kane, still standing on the edging: *Huh! I have an idea!*
42.28   At the same moment, Libby halts their escape and they stop running.
42.31   Kane then jumps down off edging.
42.32   Kane: *Grraaaaghhh!* and now runs after the girls.

The tacit understanding of processing through their games is seen in their interactivity. The moment Kane says he has an idea, Libby stops her flight and turns to run back towards him, perhaps to make it a more credible chase. The girls have decided that Kane is following them and begin their flight before he has indicated, at least explicitly, that he is about to do so. It is only as they pause to look back at him that he jumps down and stumbles after them. The interactivity among the children, as players in their games, is a complex linkage, a multiplicity of lines of flight, which assembles as a rhizo plateau, but only for a moment as in the same instant everything de~territorializes. Change(s) continue(s).

Play is like (a) plateau(s) of clouds sculpting skyscapes,[5] flowing as one, singularly and severally, constantly changing. No mark between growl, gasp and squeal, only a liminal merging of one into a(nother) line of flight, with mere glimpses, insights and moments of light. No positivist clarity here. The most clearly it can be stated is that emergence of 'matters of expression' characterize the territory (Deleuze & Guattari, 1987: 315). The territory – the multiplicity of the children and the singular but merging Goldilocks~chocolate factory~monster games – is marked by/with territorializing conditions and expressions, the territory rapidly constituting all at once through play-fully productive mo(ve)ments. Many moments in the snippet illustrate flashes of such rapidity, such as the rapidity with which the Goldilocks game and chocolate factory~monster game de~territorialize one another – Libby puts the porridge bowl down~Kane growls~the girls flee~Kane goes after them. The de~territorializing happens in a flash, the activity all at once (re)creating the territory.

Foregrounding the intersecting lines of these games makes visible the complex environments the children generate and their sophistication in performing (with/in) such complexity. Each storyline grows through tangled systems involving the players of the game and children playing in nearby games with supposedly different, yet intersecting storylines. As well, it seems that in the play(ing), each game takes on aspects of the adjacent games and simultaneously affects the storylines of the others. Willy Wonka~monster~bear makes perceptible the commingling and perhaps interdependency of all three games, storylines, players and the physical space they territorialize in the sandpit. Throughout, the children are performing their understandings of curriculum. They make perceptible their doing (of) curriculum – how they process through/with curriculum, how they go about 'curriculum-ing', how they perform curriculum, how they make curriculum work for their learning – all expressions of living curriculum.

A condition characterizing the territory is their social(izing) activity, as they play with their close friends – those participating in the same game – and as they engage with players nearby and with adjacent games. In this performativity they are not only experimenting with their understandings of ~~leadership~~ and gendered-ness, but they are demonstrating that each of the games is more than itself, that it becomes something of the others and that each of the players become something of the other players, both players within their own games and players within other games. In contrast to conventional perspectives of curriculum that operate in terms of specific subjects and skills, the children in this data snippet demonstrate that learning emerges through a curricular milieu that is non-linear in form and expression; they show an understanding of rhizo processes at work, that any particular curricular focus is inseparable from others, as the *Te Whāriki* definition of curriculum intimates (Ministry of Education, 1996: 10). The intra-activity of their dramatic performance and oral expressions intermingle within expressions of social communications and with various media representations of children's literature – through film (*Charlie and the Chocolate Factory*), books (Goldilocks and the three bears) and TV (monsters/superheroes) – and with their imaginings of these.

Children thrive within the complexity of their spontaneous play(ing) and linear processes are not necessary to the fruitful play(ing) of generative learning~living experiences of curriculum. They are adept at responding to opportunities as they present, whenever...*and*...however...*and*...whatever...*and*...with understandings that linear processes obstruct generativity. When children flow freely through their ideas, their innovative, creativity imaginings are illuminated. For example, we see a conventional approach to gendered performance interrupted through their victim~strong girls embodied performance, which does not require the boys to agree to certain ways of operating. Rather, the girls' expressions of power-fullness open (to) a generative line of flight, one that de-territorializes the games, their subjectivities and adult understandings of (non-)gendered activity. As the children flow freely, so any ~~leadership~~ subject positions or leading flows of subjectivity are similarly fluid, collaborative and co-operative in varying ways. Thus attempting to formalize such curricular opportunities for the children to be 'taught' social(izing) performance is challenging if not impossible. However, curricular opportunities open (to) possibilities for working with children's own expressions of generating their own understandings of their own learning and in these intersecting, de~territorializing lines of flight we catch glimpses of the children engaged in conditions and expressions of what matters for them in the social worlds around them.

Notes

1   See the Chocolate Factory Storyboards: Storyboards 3.1–3.6 (colour plate section).
2   See the Monster Game Storyboards: Storyboards 3.7–3.10 (colour plate section).
3   Opposition from L. *opponere*, 'set against' signals either/or relations. Apposition, 'the positioning of things next to each other' (*COD*), signals '*and...and...and...*'.
4   See the Goldilocks Storyboards: Storyboards 3.11–3.16 (colour plate section).
5. For a performance of cloud sculpting within curriculum inquiry see: W. Sellers & N. Gough (2008) Currere and cloud-sculpting. *In* J.G. Knowles, S, Promislow & A.L. Cole (eds) *Creating scholastistry: Imagining the arts-informed thesis or dissertation.* Halifax: Backalong Books, 223–23.

Children and childhood

opening the children~childhood plateau

In this plateau, I work with poststructuralist feminist understandings of children and childhood; commingling, are (my) westernized understandings, reflected in my subjectivity as white woman~wife~mother~grandmother~early childhood teacher~teacher educator~always already learner. Introducing singularities and monad to disrupt the adult|child binary, I work through contemporary discourses of children and childhood that situate children as having rights, as rich and agentic, for example, towards an understanding of becoming-child(ren), a dynamic perception of children operating both singularly and severally, as one and many, always already processing through conditions of change, in matters of becoming something different. Connections to *Te Whāriki* (Ministry of Education, 1996) are woven through the conversation.

poststructuralist understandings of children and childhood

Understandings of children and childhood are inextricably intertwined in that childhood is a period in which children live their lives and also a part of society. As well, while childhood is a temporary period for children, it is an ongoing social structure. However, the modernist notion of the scientifically universal child progressing naturally through specific age-related stages of development of childhood promotes an individualized, homogenous child with isolated childhood experiences. Whereas the concept of childhood, in poststructuralist thinking, is represented, as socially constructed, historically contingent, culturally situated and contextually bound (Cannella & Viruru, 2004), in these understandings it is impossible to define what childhood might be or how it should proceed. Rather, a conceptual multiplicity abounds, entangling notions of children and childhood within historical and contemporary understandings. Dahlberg, Moss and Pence say:

> ...there is no such thing as 'the child' or 'childhood', an essential being and state waiting to be discovered, defined, realized, so that we can say to

ourselves and others 'that is how children are, that is what childhood is'. Instead, there are many children and many childhoods, each constructed by our 'understandings of childhood and what children are and should be'.

(Dahlberg, Moss & Pence, 1999: 43)

Thus, as a cultural (re)production, childhood is complex, fluid and contextualized, and is shaped and understood differently by singular children and the worlds they operate with/in. What then becomes apparent is 'the power of discursive and interactive practices to create and sustain individual subjectivities and social structures' (Davies, 1994: 20). In poststructuralist thinking the universally individualized child is decentred and children are viewed complexly in a-centred arrangements – singularly, severally, always already in particular cultural/institutional contexts.

singularities~monad

Deleuze's (1993) understanding of singularities is useful here. Unlike the individual subject, which is perceived to be structurally embedded in life, singularities are complexly embodied in processes of living as indiscrete inside~outside systems that are constantly changing to the extent that 'a singularity cannot achieve total self-consciousness, since if it did know itself, the self that it knew would not be the same as the self that did the knowing' (Readings, 1996: 116). Conley (2005) further explains: a 'singularity shifts and bears different inflections in different contexts but is always related to perception, subjectivity, affectivity and creation' (p. 253); and Braidotti (2001) says that a singularized body is 'collectively defined, interrelational and external; it is impersonal but highly singular...not an atomized individual but a moment in a chain of being that passes...nomadically...[through] multiple becomings' (p. 407). Such inside~outside flow between a singular body and its environs disrupts the conception of an individualized, stable child.

The Deleuzian 'monad' also works with embodied inside~outside worlds – 'the world is included in each one in the form of perceptions...the monad does not exist outside of other monads' (Deleuze, 1993: 86). With/in the (im)perceptible finiteness of its own inside becomings, the infinity of becomings of the outside world is expressed, and vice versa – monad is always already (in)finite and infinitesimal. Monad expresses oneness that enfolds a multiplicity and a multiplicity that unfolds the oneness, each folding continually moving through/with/in the other; singularities and monad together re-cite/site 'the' modernist 'child'. As such, singularities negotiate territories of other singularities and children and childhood are inextricably intertwined. Children are no longer individuals but assemblages of singularities embodied in particular territories; childhood is similarly disrupted as an individualized, isolated experience. Children and their childhoods become perceptible as a slip-sliding inside~outside~monadic~nomadic flow. Oscillating, ebbing and flowing, resisting the imposition of a progressive, linear continuum – although a continuum engages with variable extension in the overlapping of adjacent elements it also assumes an uninterrupted, ordered, traceable sequence. In contrast, flow is perceptible as 'matter in movement, in flux, in variation, matter as conveyor of singularities and traits of expression…matter-flow can only be *followed*' (Deleuze & Guattari, 1987: 409, original italics). Thus matter-flow cannot be determined as a tracing, only mapped in open space-times.

subjectivity and monadic~nomadic flow

Linked to notions of the individualized child and monadic children are understandings of subject and subjectivity. 'The subject' represents a modernist assumption of a logocentric, generic individual, whereas 'subjectivity' assembles as inside~outside flows of social worlds (re)constituting subjects. Subjectivity perceived as a shifting, fragmented, multifaceted, contradictory condition (Davies, 1994) expresses the diversity of lived experience; always already dynamic, changing and multidimensional with/in particular discourses and practices; always already constituted by/through these as subject-in-process, in a multiplicity of worlds. The ex-subject, now monad, is produced in the discursive practices of social worlds, becoming a multiplicity of contradictory subjectivities dispersed through a plurality of spaces. This multiplicity further disrupts any lingering assumptions of a unitary, pre-given psychological subject who is socialized only from the outside. Braidotti (2001) explains the movement around subjectivity as a 'social imaginary, [as] a network of forces and interconnections that constitute subjects in multiple, complex, and multilayered ways. Subjects are…simultaneously constructed and destabilized by interpellations that hit them at all levels [all at once]' (p. 385). This is complexly multidimensional, a Deleuzo-Guattarian nomadic subjectivity of nomadic~monadic flow. The unitary subject is disrupted with subjectivity characterized as constituted and constitutive, embodied and situated as a desiring-machine (Deleuze & Guattari, 1987), fragmented, re-cited/sited with/in/through various mo(ve)ments of monadic~nomadic flow.

In opening (to) possibilities for understanding children and childhood as a monad~nomad multiplicity within poststructuralist thinking, I turn to the modernist adult|child binary, rejecting its dichotomous categorizing of children as not-yet-adults that homogenizes children, relegates them as inferior and obscures the diversity of their childhoods.

adult|child binary

Disrupting the modernist adult|child binary is significant to the project of (re)conceiving children and their childhood(s). Within dichotomous thinking, society divides its members into childhood and adulthood, with transition into adulthood the ultimate goal and adulthood claiming distinctive rights and privileges, but also having obligations. However, even as monad children mature into adulthood, the inferior status of children as a group remains. For example, (middle class) adult platitudes present childhood as a golden age in which children are to be untroubled by adult concerns, such as work and social responsibility. Although this expresses concern for children's physical and emotional wellbeing, it subordinates children in the family, school and the wider community and is imbued with disdaining ageist values and attitudes towards children. Intersections among child and adult, and childhood and adulthood are complex and fraught with contradictions as past and present meet, for example, adult experience as children living childhoods in an earlier time are different from children's experiences of childhood now (Mayall, 2002). When children are confronted with historic adult knowledge, temporal differences ascribed to childhood and adulthood become apparent, although exploring the space of difference opens (to) possibilities for generating both unique and common understandings. Moss (2002) urges that we think more broadly about early childhood across life's course to avoid the marginalization of young children.

In the process of subordinating children within protected social roles, generational boundaries between childhood and adulthood become more distinct. However, Suransky (1982) argues that the predominating adult agenda shaped by technological and institutional imperatives is eroding childhood; similarly, Postman (1994: 98) believes that the division between childhood and adulthood is disappearing, with children perceived as 'adult-child' or 'kidult' (Bird, 2003: 45). Through popular entertainment, news and advertising, adult information and values become accessible to children, so that 'behavior, language, attitudes, and desires – even the physical appearance – of adults and children are becoming increasingly indistinguishable' (Postman, 1994: 4). Yet, within this kidult culture, Postman notes that children's understandings of themselves are that they are children, the adult responsibility here being to embrace their agentic definition.

In deconstructing early childhood education, Cannella (1997) disrupts the modernist binarial assumption that children are unable to be perceived as competent, knowledgeable and empowered until they reach the privileged position of adult. She promotes children as younger human beings and although *younger* risks implying there is an older, more desirable position, her critique is influential. The child is decentred as children are viewed complexly as young people of monadic singularity; childhood is similarly disrupted, no longer specific but distributed through shifting sites of emergence. Butler (1990) affirms that abandoning the terms 'children' and 'childhood' is unnecessary, as to be constituted is not to be determined. Considering possibilities for re(con)ceiving children and childhood invites/incites also a response to the multiple voices of feminism, calling to question dominating ideologies, knowledges and educational practices. The hierarchical concept of the adult|child binary, which absents children, distorts their social positioning and compromises their contribution, thus comes to the attention of feminist scholarship, which implicitly sustains children as young people, rather than not-yet-adult.

Casting aside the adult|child binary I conceive children and childhood as an assemblage, as a heterogeneous multiplicity of desire and productivity involving lived experiences and associated social forces similar to those which adults experience. This thinking perceives children as young human beings of monadic singularity living childhoods that are more than a mere pathway to adulthood. Childhood is a celebratory performance of living, not a problem in life to be resolved or worked through, and in this, children are due unqualified respect. As a living~learning experience that all human beings negotiate, childhood involves space-times where by children experience life in all its complexity and ambiguity. Children are thus conceived as power-full players in their childhoods and in society, capable of communicating a knowledgeable, sophisticated desire for their childhoods and for what they would be(come).

(e)merging images and subject positionings of children in childhood(s)

Psycho/sociological discourses perceive children and their childhood(s) in various ways. Historically, three sets of themes dominate images of childhood: the child as weak, innocent and needy, requiring rescue and protection; the child as evil, monster or threat, from whom society needs protection if order and progress are to be maintained; and the child as miniature or embryonic adult, perceived as a redemptive agent ensuring futurity (e.g. Woodrow & Brennan, 2001; Moss & Petrie, 2002). More recently, within poststructuralist thinking, emerging subject positionings explain children as adult commodity; agentic, younger human beings (e.g. Cannella, 1997; Sorin, 2003); with rights (e.g. Moss & Petrie, 2002; Bird, 2003); as social problem (Corsaro, 1997); and as 'produsers' (Bruns, 2007: 3), who both use and produce information and knowledge. These understandings of children and childhood weave through different eras, with different ones dominating in different times, influenced, for example, by changing conceptions of the roles of nature and culture.

The notion that childhood is a socially constructed concept and not an independent reality informs understandings of how images and subject positionings work, including how they are shaped by philosophies, attitudes and practices of dominating cultures. Rogoff (2003) disrupts the western discourse of child development, foregrounding how westernized images and subject positionings of children and childhood are commonly perceived as natural, so that questioning them creates discomfort, and is likely to elicit accusations of political bias (Woodrow & Brennan, 2001). Images that present children as passive and childhood as a site of control, while simultaneously embracing aspects of nurture and protection, limit understandings of children and childhood (Woodrow, 1999). In contrast, poststructuralist positionings of subjectivity, always already shifting, fragmented, multidimensional and contradictory, are organized in relation to various discourses and open possibilities for interacting with the world (Davies, 1994).

These modernist images of children as weak, monstrous and embryonic adult pervade current educational practice, as adults act on behalf of children, effectively denying them agency, as children are regarded as objects of study towards improving behaviour, and as children are pushed towards adult-imposed achievement standards and educational maturity. Children are sustained as essentially passive, with the dominating male adult majority deciding what constitutes learning and development, in regard to what children need to know and why, and how they ought to go about it. However, while modernist understandings see these actions as having positive affects for children, their learning and their progress through childhood, a poststructuralist transgressive approach resists positioning children as subjects inferior to adults, immature, naïve, less able, dependent and incompetent. Instead, conceptions of agentic, rich, younger human beings with rights and possibilities open for (re)conceiving children and their childhoods.

However, it is important to note that movement towards the agentic, rich child with rights has not occurred in an orderly, sequential fashion. Rather there has been an ebbing and flowing of merging images and subject positionings of children through childhood(s); a complexity of discourses slip-slides through various space-times. (E)merging subject positionings become a multidimensional complexity of areas of connectivity where particular images of children are (im)perceptible from within a historical tangle of authority, regulation and possibilities for the future as present practices continually dissolve, opening (to) future ones. Much has been written about historically changing images of children; I work only with recent notions of agentic, rich children with rights towards unfolding contemporarily productive understandings of becoming-children, never fixed but always already susceptible to ongoing change.

the agentic child

The constituting of an agentic child positions children as active and influential participants within a variety of social contexts (Cannella & Viruru, 2004). Agentic children are perceived as capably participating in their worlds, appropriating and reproducing aspects of their culture through social interactions, often creating learning experiences beyond that which their teachers may have conceived or thought possible. This understanding considers children as collective producers of culture, as co-constructors of childhood, as co-producers of knowledge, as a social group, as useful, as autonomous social actors (e.g. Prout, 2005). From a westernized educational perspective, viewing children as co-producers (with teachers and other adults) of knowledge foregrounds them as power-full in negotiating their childhoods. However, Lee (1998) argues that considering children as agentic and actively contributing to the social worlds they operate within fails to recognize the notions of dependency and immaturity inherent in agentic action. He claims that this sociological concept of agency privileges competency and completeness and, as an essentialist view, excludes those outside the mainstream, so while this view of children's agency is commonly promoted in early childhood education, the concept is culturally bound. Similarly, Davies (1990) emphasizes that the traditional sociological view, which constitutes individuals as having choice and as being able to act on those choices, is a misplaced assumption that lacks cognizance of complex and contradictory belief systems, such as those around individual rights and the productivity of the collective and around notions of gendered-ness.

While attempting to ensure that children as a societal group have voice and are visible, how agency translates into practice is inherently problematic as it functions within the parameters of childhood having minority status. Although disrupting the adult|child binary may produce anxiety about an erosion or disappearance of childhood as we know it, it opens possibilities for both adults and children in that arbitrary, generational boundaries, for example, dissolve and become less constraining. But such sociological perspectives remain problematic. When agency is considered dependent on having a 'voice', encouraging children's participation risks silencing groups of children who operate within tenuous social worlds of diverse lived experiences, socially and culturally. For example, participation is an acceptable notion for children living in families where a culture of negotiation exists – negotiation between parents of the family and between parents and children. Such negotiation and self-expression are western, middle-class cultural constructions, not common to all cultures, although such attributes are implicit in *Te Whāriki* and are promoted in Aotearoa New Zealand early childhood settings. As Davies (1990) says, 'all available discursive practices are not something any individual can automatically take up' (p. 342). So this, now westernized, and most likely middle class, agentic child works to privilege an already privileged group of children even though agency is likely to be produced in different ways in different social and cultural contexts. With negotiation skills perceived as a civilizing process and preparation for adult life in a westernized democracy, anomalies arise in that promoting the agentic child also works to tame the monster child and to affirm the status of childhood as a preparatory process for life in which the child is futuristic adult and redemptive agent. The agentic child, culturally bound, continues to be susceptible to adverse affects and effects of dichotomizing adult|child.

From a poststructuralist perspective, agency is contingent within contradictory and shifting positionings, accepting and resisting social beliefs about individuals and groups, and accepting and resisting operations around associated social lore. Davies foregrounds the following questions as significant to becoming agentic, as children (and adults) continually learn to fit in and also become agents of change:

> How is an individual's subjectivity, their idea of who they are, their particular way of making sense of themselves and of the social world, developed? How is it that we find the words, the concepts, the ideas, with which to say who we are? How do we become one who takes up or resists various discursive practices who modifies one practice in relation to another – who chooses between various positions and practices made available?
>
> (Davies, 1990: 345)

What becomes apparent is that theorizing *any* image of children and childhood risks homogenization, and if teachers and adults fail to generate opportunities for divergent ways of children seeing and making sense of the world, we risk reverting to universal conceptions despite diverse lived experiences. Although subject positionings of children and childhood admit to being unstable, non-unitary and contestable, even the weaving of subject positionings that work to (re)conceive children as active and contingent members of society and of childhood can limit children's world-views, as any (adult-construed) discourse ultimately affects how children see themselves. Agency is (a) supposedly shared and participatory (enterprise), but there is a sense that an agentic child emerges only through adult authorization, providing necessary discursive and social resources and when a personal sense of agency is endowed (Davies, 1990). Ongoing critique and transgressive thinking is thus significant to avoiding limiting children through a use of conceptualizations that un/intentionally sustain adult control and children's acquiescence.

a child with rights

At first glance the child with rights has agency, but a second glance reveals it is also permeated with passivity. Recently, in early childhood education, discourses of the needy child have moved towards a child with rights – to freedom, self-determination, equality and citizenship – but this value-laden, problematic image maintains the minority status of childhood, with children becoming subjects of an emancipatory project (Moss & Petrie, 2002). Children's needs are reinscribed to a human rights discourse that makes issues visible and more readily contestable, but, although this entitles children, as young human beings, to be active agents with personal desires for enacting personal goals, children remain under the jurisdiction of adults and are not entirely autonomous. There is scope for independent thought and action and some capability for children to act on their own behalf, but rights tend to be granted by adults. Also, the child with rights still needs protection against oppression (Dahlberg & Moss, 2005), such protection assuming expert-adult knowledge of children's needs and desires. Not denying that protection from abuse is often necessary, there is an underlying assumption of a conceptual vulnerability that exacerbates inequitable, inferior positioning in both family and society.

Furthering the problematic, the notion of the free-thinking child with rights assumes cultural homogeneity in regard to the place and limits of autonomous actions, and tension arises between understandings of individual rights and collective interdependence within diverse culturally located families/whānau/communities.[1] Cannella and Viruru's understanding is that the adult|child hierarchy works through all discourses to colonize children:

> Our Enlightened, modern, and even postmodern discourses have conspired to create a group of the invisibly colonized – those who are so dominated that they are disqualified (without adult awareness) as human beings...*While we would not hesitate to stress that children themselves do not necessarily accept or function within this colonization*, we would stress the ideas that within the adult mind and constitution, the colonization of children is complete and without question.
>
> (Cannella & Viruru, 2004: 118, italics added)

That children reject adults colonizing their childhoods is demonstrated by children's expressions of power-fullness – for example, in Marcy resisting adult demands on her activity (*Letter to Marcy* in *Preceding echoes*) and in Tim's confronting my colonizing of his space (*Becoming-child(ren) becoming-power-full* plateau). However, for the moment, a rights discourse seems useful for including children in wider societal understandings of entitlements and responsibility as it disrupts the 'expert needs discourse' (Bird, 2003: 43) and opens (to) possibilities for children's active participation in decision making about their childhoods and their learning. Both children and adults are entitled to be heard, to have their concerns taken into account; simultaneously, children and adults are obliged to listen to, and take into account others' concerns. Individual and collective rights of children and adults are co-implicated – children become social participants, with adults conceived as 'protecting *children's rights*, rather than protecting *children*' (Moss & Petrie, 2002: 106, original italics). (E)merging from/with/in the agentic young human being with rights is the rich child.

the rich child

The rich child (Moss & Petrie, 2002), commonly associated with the early childhood education in Reggio Emilia (Rinaldi, 2006), operates in a perceptibly agentic setting. This child is rich in potential, strong, powerful, competent, social and an interdependent agent, understood as a member of the social group of childhood, which is important in its own right and is a significant phase of life that leaves traces on adulthood. The concern is with who the child is now, with the adult world bearing responsibility for children having opportunities within the present, rather than regarding children as redemptive agents of their own future. Children's extensive relations among parents, other adults, children, their communities and wider society are of great importance within the rich child image. Such extended relations decentre the nuclear family with a totalitarian responsibility for children's welfare; instead, both parents and children are now conceived as contributing members of communities, which reciprocate by providing support. These relationships acknowledge that childhood is played out in many settings. Children's friendships represent ways for more active involvement in the wider community, as together children generate their own cultural expressions to enhance their 'sphere of social agency' (Moss & Petrie, 2002: 104). The rich child is a subjective person with citizenship rights, not an object of adult demands; collectively, children as citizens are a social group in their own right with rights and strengths. This interdependent approach works to ensure that children's optimal involvement contributes to an accrual of collective benefits to the adult world (Moss & Penn, 1996; Lero, 2000).

However, in that the development of children's human capital is an investment in the social capital of the adult world, this rich child again becomes a potential object of exploitation, a resource for future investment. When children are considered fully operational, productive young human beings, space-times open (to) possibilities for genuine interdependence among children and adults and their social worlds. Such spaces are rife with ambiguity and contradiction; as rich children express their own flows of power-fullness, their richness becomes a resource for the adult world. Also, when supposedly expert adult conceptions are used to classify children and childhood through subject positionings that they – the adults – deem either desirable or problematic, the complex understandings of the rich child are denied.

the rich child and *Te Whāriki*

The rich child is readily accepted as a desirable image for early childhood practice in Aotearoa New Zealand, which aims to provide agentic environments that foster children as active participants in their own learning. Much of *Te Whāriki* can be read as supporting this rich child image, given the underpinning philosophical aspiration for children 'to grow up as competent and confident learners and communicators, healthy in mind, body, and spirit, secure in their sense of belonging and in the knowledge that they make a valued contribution to society' (Ministry of Education, 1996: 9). It highlights children's family and community as places of 'socially and culturally meditated learning' and the critical role of 'reciprocal and responsive relationships' among these (p. 9). Positive aspects of the rich child's agency and rights are alluded to, as children are afforded opportunities to 'reflect on alternative ways for doing things; make connections across time and place; establish different kinds of relationships; and encounter different points of view' (p. 9). However, subject positionings are both affirmed and problematized in the principles and strands of *Te Whāriki*, as conceptual understandings of children as agentic, rich and with rights are entangled in western assumptions of children as essentially weak, needy and embryonic adult, these latter assumptions enmeshed in the general provision of early childhood services. Let me illustrate some of these entanglements and their ensuing contradictions.

Te Whāriki principles of empowerment, holistic development, family and community, and relationships are suggestive of agency, but not without difficulties. Although a common understanding of empowerment is that 'children will have the opportunity to create and act on their own ideas' (Ministry of Education, 1996: 40), a problematic with empowerment is that there is an implicit understanding that a superior body from the outside will endow children with dispositions for operating more effectively, in adult world terms. Also, while holistic development weaves together intricate patterns of experience and meaning rather than emphasizing the acquisition of discrete skills, there is an expectation that early childhood practitioners will have 'an understanding of Māori views on child development' (p. 41), despite the underpinning developmental perspectives of *Te Whāriki* being informed by western psychology. The principles of family and community and relationships seem to cross cultures more readily, but in an essentially westernized educational environment actually honouring ideas that 'different cultures have different child-rearing patterns' and fostering 'culturally appropriate ways of communicating' (p. 42) is not straightforward. In relation to child rearing patterns, for example, *Te Whāriki* assumes independence as the ideal, but whānau embodies *inter*dependence. As for fostering communication, not all cultures deem it appropriate for children to express their opinions and desires, particularly to older adults.

The strands are similarly complicated in their linkages to images of children and childhood. Although the intent of the strands promotes a rich child, like the principles, this is culturally bound. The strand of well-being~mana atua states: 'The health and well-being of the child are protected and nurtured' (Ministry of Education, 1996: 15). Keeping young human beings safe, physically and emotionally, is to be lauded but this strand does operate from within the weak~innocent~needy image, perpetuating the adult|child binary and valorizing the powerful, competent adult. What is deemed 'safe', and why, thus requires serious critique. Communication~mana reo reflects the image of a child with rights, stating: 'The languages and symbols of their own and other cultures are promoted and protected' (p. 16) but a genuine realization of the inherent intent demands a de-colonizing of education. Exploration~mana aotūroa, in which 'the child learns through active exploration of the environment' (p. 16), promotes an agentic child who is expected to develop reasoning strategies, but reasoning is a modernist attribute embedded in structuralist thought, which conflicts with ambiguously and contradictorily complex ways of the world. In belonging~mana whenua, 'children and their families feel a sense of belonging' (p. 15). This links to the promotion of extensive relations of the rich child image, however families of traditional Māori or Pacific Peoples, for example, may find that 'limits and boundaries of acceptable behaviour' (p. 15) differ from those promoted in westernized settings. Contribution~mana tangata expects that: 'Opportunities for learning are equitable, and each child's contribution is valued' (p. 16). A simplified translation of mana tangata is 'human rights, integrity, status' (Ryan, 1997: 143), including honouring cultural rights.[2] Social and spiritual connotations are embodied in Māori understandings in that mana tangata is about not standing alone but being at one with one's people. This conflicts with the individualized child with rights suggested in *Te Whāriki*, whereby 'children are affirmed as individuals' (Ministry of Education, 1996: 16).

These linkages between well-being~mana atua, communication~mana reo, exploration~mana aotūroa, belonging~mana whenua and contribution~mana tangata are a chaotically complex system, lacking structuralist coherence although being presented as a set of orderly continuums. However, in a transgressive critique, as soon as a link is made it is disrupted in a de~territorializing movement that renders it impossible to establish any sort of orderly pattern of categorizing images of children and childhood as traditional discourses demand. This lack of consistency both disturbs and is disturbing to developmentally based thinking; it also opens (to) possibilities for thinking through subject positionings otherwise, in other ways.

Conceivably, a rich child application of *Te Whāriki* opens possibilities for productive linkages in valuing whānau relations that are extensive, collective and interdependent. But a cursory check of the goals for children's development attached to the strands again highlights the inherent westernized thinking, and not only in terms of 'development'. For example: 'an expectation that [children] take responsibility for their own learning' (Ministry of Education, 1996: 84) implies an individualistic approach, not necessarily one of interdependence; and, developing 'working theories about Planet Earth and beyond' (p. 90) implies use of western, modernist scientific reasoning, which marginalizes mythological explanations of Māori and Pacific People's cultures. Also, the expectation for children to develop 'a growing recognition and enjoyment of "nonsense" explanations' (p. 90) is intriguing. This use of the term 'nonsense' signals the adult|child binary, whereby (westernized) adult understandings trivialize children's interpretations about how the world works.

Yet, still more challenges emerge. The images of children and childhood discussed above disrupt notions of the child as incomplete, immature and passive, and childhood as universal, normalizable and normalizing. However, involving the notion of a metaphorical image, which tends towards the representation of something – albeit a concept created in the mind – suggests that certain qualities will be exhibited. In contrast, a philosophical 'subject positioning' is more slippery, furthering the disruption in attempting to cast aside any remnants of potentially structuralist classification...*and*...the Deleuzo-Guattarian imaginary of becoming-child(ren) – introduced in *Preceding echoes* – opens (to) possibilities for complex and mobile understandings of subject positionings that may (e)merge from/with/in the images above but resist being fixed with/in any specifics.

...a becoming-intermezzo...

Before elaborating a Deleuzo-Guattarian (1987) understanding of becoming, it is important to note that this is significantly different from psycho/sociological perspectives. In psychological and sociological terms 'being' and 'becoming' work to reduce the child to always being in states of incomplete development, albeit destined to become something more, such as mature adult. However, the Deleuzo-Guattarian imaginary of becoming offers possibilities for working a conception of children as embodied be(com)ings. This imaginary moves outside fixed *images* of children and childhood and opens (to) possibilities for subject *positionings*. In its use as a metaphorical figure of speech, 'image' evokes a sense of likeness, reflecting the outside and judged as being extremely typical, thus promoting a unitary and non-contradictory self, embedded in a stabilizing identity. In contrast, an 'imaginary' is dynamic, a 'symbolic glue' flow operating in spaces of transitions and transactions; it is 'sticky...it catches on as it goes' (Braidotti, 2001: 384) lacking transparency and purity. It is an oscillating, (im)pure characterizing affect, a force affect working with the activity of thinking not just the thought itself.[3]

This *becoming* imaginary considers children and childhood as subjective systems, characterized by ceaseless change and alteration. Children and childhood are no longer (in)complete bodies, but perceivable as differing epistemologies in which dynamic processes are ongoing, being both subject and object of per-petual change through de~territorializing processes – the systems always already in flux, recursively changing. Becoming, in this sense, works as an antidote to *being* and *identity* – these presume a stable, rational individual – conceiving of bodies as constantly changing assemblages of forces. The notion of becoming – as in becoming-child – is a way to 'get outside the dualisms...to be-between, to pass between, [to act and be with/in] the intermezzo' or the milieu (Deleuze & Guat-tari, 1987: 277). Working in rhizo ways with becoming-child opens possibilities for different linkages and intersections that collapse present practices in search of different ways of thinking around (re)conceptualizing children and childhood; also, for exploring the situated productivity of subjectivities of children in ways that decentre hierarchical arrangements that specify and regulate 'normality'. Becoming-children and becoming-adult are thus distributed through common ter-ritory; and, re(con)ceiving childhood is a(n) (e)merging hybrid amidst an array of troubled ageist discourses.

becoming-

Within the web-like interactions of rhizo thinking, of interconnectedness and intersections, becoming is not about becoming anything specific – 'becoming is the very dynamism of change, situated between heterogeneous terms and tend-ing towards no particular goal or end-state' (Stagoll, 2005: 21). Becoming is about happenings of the in-between always in flow of becoming-*something*, such as becoming-child. In this flowing, becomings give birth to (e)merging subject positionings – in liminal mo(ve)ments, at intersections of in-between-ness, within the *inter* of connectedness – so as to produce 'nothing other than itself'; it is the becoming itself that matters, 'not the supposedly fixed terms through which that which becomes passes' (Deleuze & Guattari, 1987: 238).

> A line of becoming is not defined by points that it connects or by points that compose it; on the contrary, it passes *between* points, it comes up through the middle...a line of becoming has neither beginning or end, departure nor arrival, origin or destination...A line of becoming has only a middle. The middle is not an average; it is fast motion, it is the absolute speed of move-ment. A becoming is always in the middle; one can only get to it by the mid-dle. A becoming is neither one nor two, nor the relation of the two; it is the in-between, the border or line of flight...
>
> (Deleuze & Guattari, 1987: 293, original italics)

In-between bodies are thus a 'flux of successive becomings' (Braidotti, 2001: 391). In a complex array the embodied subjectivity is perceptible as 'a play of forces, a transformer and relay of energy, a surface of intensities' (p. 391). Consid-ering the subjective positioning of singular children, 'the child [does] not become, it is *becoming* itself that is a child' (Deleuze & Guattari, 1987: 277, italics added).

Amidst the liminality of intersecting forces and spatiotemporal connections, life~work~play space-times are a milieu of inseparable becomings, an endlessly becoming-multiplicity, constantly negotiable and de~territorializing.

becoming-child(ren)

Becoming for Deleuze and Guattari (1987) is incommensurable with the static, sociological notion of being as becoming something more in subsequent states of being. Understandings of becoming-child and becoming-adult are 'not a correspondence between relations' (p. 237); it is not about child becoming adult. Deleuzo-Guattarian becoming does not involve a series of progression and/or regression culminating in specific ends; it dispels notions of incompleteness, such as incompetent child developing into rational adult. This becoming works within liminal spaces that (e)merge around borderlines and boundaries, at intersections where transgressive thought~thinking~doing~acting occur. Spaces for incipiently different ways of thinking (e)merge from/with/in conditions of the in-between, middle or milieu.

In contrast to any linearly ordered structure associated with psychological and sociological perspectives that require subjects to achieve completeness, Deleuze and Guattari (1987) work with 'zones of proximity and undecidability' (p. 507), in which there is 'no preformed logical order' (p. 251). In such conditions, 'becoming is a verb with a consistency all its own; it does not reduce to, or lead back to, "appearing," "being," "equalling," or "producing"' (p. 239). What matters for Deleuze and Guattari concerns not so much *what it is*, but *how it is qualified*. For example, it is not about identifying with something as in child becoming adult, it is about qualifying being as in becoming-child, in such a way that 'a becoming lacks a subject distinct from itself' (p. 238), each becoming the other; the *act* of becoming is all it ever is. As with all becomings, becoming-child(ren) is always already becoming-something different.

It should be noted, however, that these Deleuzo-Guattarian zones of proximity and undecidability, which slip-slide in mo(ve)ments of continual change, differ from Vygotsky's zones of proximal development in which children are scaffolded through plateaus of learning – these plateaus being spaces where little or no change is occurring – to progress to what is perceived as more advanced positions of development. The points of scaffolding that mark this hierarchical progression are stepped in a developmental sequence and signify an advancement of competency. For Deleuze and Guattari, proximity expresses only an inexact or undecidable nearness and plateaus are a-centred, horizontal planes open to continual (re)negotiation. They are planes of immanence that are not transcended, not discarded in favour of something bigger or better. Rather passages are constantly (re)turned to, the plane de~territorialized, knowing that space-times (re)negotiated are always already different in every way as the body of the territory and the bodies in passage have become-something different. Living~learning on these planes is never repeatable or the same. On planes of immanence becomings are expressed in dynamic conditions of becoming-children becoming-adult becoming-adulthood becoming-childhood and so on...

In this way becoming-something different perturbs the structuralist thought that favours reductionist and historic relations of subjects|objects. Becoming-something different is not defined by specific characteristics but by populations of bodies, variable both between and within milieus (Deleuze & Guattari, 1987: 239). So, becoming-child is a condition of populations of children in diverse milieus, thus my preference for expressions of becoming-child(ren), this embodying both one and several. Becoming-child(ren) is thus an expression of a population of bodies of singular child and a severalty of children becoming; and children's play(ing) is a condition of that becoming. Becoming-child(ren) is not evolutionary or filial, it is not progressive or serial; it is involutionary, it *in*volves creative symbiosis such as enactive~intra-active play(ing). Lenz Taguchi (2010) introduces notions of intra-activity into early childhood pedagogy for moving outside a purely inter-personal approach, instead embodying intra-active relations that work with/through the in-between activity of all living and material bodies.

Mechanical play is the usually imperceptible allowance for movement in a machine to enable it to run; similarly, becoming is (im)perceptible activity that children operate with/in/through their growing and learning, their living~learning. Just as mechanical play is perceptible only when a machine is running, so becoming is (im)perceptible only in the activity of living~learning, when both living~learning and becoming are simultaneously in play. It is thus not a matter of knowing what becoming is, it is about understanding how it works. Becoming happens between/through/among/with/in coursings of bodies operating with/in de~territorializing spaces, with/in un/in/defin/ed/able territories, whereby various criteria come into play in the course of events unfolding. Despite this (im)perceptibility of becoming, we can 'see' becoming at play – perceived as flows of becomings – like we see a stream by perceiving the flow of water. It is the experience of presence, of being entangled in various space-times that opens (to) perception. Such intra-active presence of/with/in experience is perceptible in the following tale.

Semetsky (2006) tells the Russian story of a four-year-old kindergarten child who, through her familiarity with some stories, pretended she could read until she was presented with, or presenced by a book she had not seen or heard before. Mortified by her impending exposure to the group of children listening, what emerged (im)perceptibly through her panic was becoming-child becoming-reader. As she opened her mouth to confess that she could not really read, her eyes fell on the page and she heard herself quietly and rhythmically saying the words:

> One half of me was reading, and the other was listening in sublime horror...I was reading page after page as if in a dream...simultaneously I was seeing the text all at once and letters very black and pictures very bright and myself too surrounded by the kids.
>
> (Semetsky, 2006: 109)

The book ended, the children disbanded, the child was alone with her new knowledge; she could read, without understanding how. Later she feared she had forgotten and took a book from her mother's shelf. To her amazement, she recognized words even though the text made no sense to her. In this story, 'the concept becomes the narrative, and the subject becomes subject of expression' (Deleuze, 1993: 127), with/in a dynamic process of becoming-reader, a condition of the becoming-child. Without explicit instruction she had learned to read; she engaged with the book and the setting – the fear, the teacher, the group of children – and actualized a virtual thought experiment. As Semetsky points out, her becoming-child could not have happened in this moment without these immanent connections – 'conditions enabling the possibility of accessing the otherwise inaccessible may indeed be created and realized in experience…Something that was virtual… became actualized in a singular experience in the material world' (Deleuze, 1993: 120). Becoming-child becoming-imperceptibility becoming-reader becoming-multiplicity linking child~learning~playing~reading~understanding~curriculum ~currere~curriculum-ing…

Although Guss (2005) does not work directly with Deleuzian philosophy, she similarly illuminates becoming-child(ren) as she troubles the identity of children's dramatic play(ing). She shows children embodied with/in fantasy play(ing) in 'a state of continual becoming' (p. 240). A game of 'house' morphs into a performance of fantasy actions that is 'generative and expressive of personality and culture [becoming] a process of discovery of the here and now, rather than a rehearsal of (male-dominated, adult-dominated) models for functioning in later life' (p. 241). In a play of becoming-child, Tessa and Hilde in the data of her research segue through a game about a wolf. Tessa singularly and simultaneously is becoming-mother~wolf catcher~props person~sound producer~wolf~narrator~ young goat~pig~dramatist, momentarily becoming-each several times over. Hilde's roles are less extensive but no less intensive as becoming-narrator~dramatist-narrator~wolf-catcher. In Guss's analysis, Tessa is engaged in processes of constant change of: fairytale narratives, actions and meanings about the wolf; dramatic monologue that her teacher used in telling wolf stories to the children; and herself. In a Deleuzo-Guattarian reading, Tessa is playing out her singular but multiplicitous becoming. As she segues through the characters, she reveals herself as becoming-child playing out her understandings of various characters. While the Russian story (Semetsky, 2006) explicates the immanence of becoming-child, Tessa and Hilde (Guss, 2005) make perceptible more of the complexity of becoming-child(ren). This involves enactive~intractive play(ing) of each singular becoming-child in a creative symbiosis, severally becoming child(ren), resonating with Deleuze and Guattari (1987): 'Since each of us was several, there was already quite a crowd' (p. 3).

In another mo(ve)ment Olsson (2009) unfolds the workings of becoming-child, using Deleuze and Guattari's (1987) imaginary of territorializing activity to trouble the notion of identity of the learning of the young child. By superimposing a photograph of a surfer on photographs of a toddler's novice steps she creates a palimpsest of a child learning to walk with the movements of a surfer on a surf-board. Olsson says:

> I saw my little niece Nona's attempts to start walking. She was lying on her stomach, arms and hands level with her armpits, a sudden jump up to a squat position, the slight raising of the legs, the arms balancing horizontal to the body...[similar to the surfer]...lying on the board with the hands level with the armpits, the fast jump up into a squat position with the feet close to the hands, the slight raising of the legs, the arms balancing horizontally to the body...
>
> (Olsson, 2009: 1–2)

This linkage is not so much redefining how children learn to walk, rather it opens another way of appreciating one child's manner of learning to walk as an 'apprenticeship of walking' (Borgnon, 2007: 265), (re)conceiving 'the child' as becoming-child. Stella Nona is a 'hybridized' child who defies definition. 'She is no longer the child with the attributes of naturalness and development; she is a mixture of all that *and* the skilled, closer-to-his-twenties, wild-at-heart guy' (Borgnon, 2007: 264–5, original italics). Becoming-child as beginning-walker is expressed as movements of de~territorialization – Stella Nona disrupts the adult|child binary, as does Borgnon/Olsson – both toddler and surfer negotiating the divide to be understood as the other. Adult and child are no longer separate identities; rather, each is already always the other. Transgressing this (im)perceptible generational divide, Stella Nona is the 'becoming-child of the adult as well as of the child' (Deleuze & Guattari, 1987: 277), this dissolving the conceptual separation of age. This morphing of toddler~surfer illuminates becoming-child(ren) as rhizo bodies, disturbing and decentring any hierarchical developmental or socially reproductive agenda.

> The girl and the child do not become, it is becoming itself that is a child or a girl. The child does not become an adult any more than the girl becomes a woman; the girl is the becoming-woman of each sex, just as the child is the becoming-young of every age...It is Age itself that is a becoming-child...
>
> (Deleuze & Guattari, 1987: 277)

In dispensing with sequential, age-related developmental stages, body and mind are linked as operational in a 'new flux of self' (Braidotti, 2003: 46). Understanding Stella Nona as becoming-child~beginning-walker moves outside conventional territory and reforms (as) another territory. But it does not 'stop' 'there', 'within' 'a' 'new' territory of space-time. Its movement resists such latent over-coding and disrupts an organizing tendency. What happens is that we become involved in constant change and alteration through movements of de~territorialization. As we and the territories within which we operate are always already changing, so an assemblage of forces expressed through encounters with one another moves to negotiate the territory, through space-time connectivity. Braidotti (2001) explains such an assemblage of forces that activate becoming thus: 'A pattern of de-territorialization takes place [between us and Stella Nona], which runs parallel to and in-and-out of respective and mutual existences, but certainly does not stop there' (p. 405). The becoming-child of Stella Nona learning to walk as becoming-walker intersects with the becoming-child within adult understandings; in flux, dynamically (re)constituting in connections with in/animate others, constantly moving, always already becoming. So that in this shifting mo(ve)ment, 'the condition of childhood comes gradually to be seen no longer as an unformed adult subjectivity, but as a form of subjectivity in itself' (Kennedy, 2002: 157), not valorizing but foreshadowing possible worlds to be encountered.

So becoming is not only about slip-sliding moments of change, it is perceptible as a continuously (re)constituting *movement*, which embodies dynamics of change *and* dynamic changes, which having achieved a condition of alterity simultaneously dissolves into movements of recursively changing processes. Becoming embodies mobility, as expressions of motion and rest, speed and slowness, and flows of intensities. Grosz (1994a) says that becomings are 'always a multiplicity, the movement of (trans)formation from one "thing" to another that in no way resembles it' (p. 204). So, becoming-child is not about *who* the child might be now or become as a specific identity – not as a child now, not as an adult-constructed ideal child, not as a future-adult. The imaginary, becoming-child(ren) involves a milieu of never-ending processes of becoming. Explicating Deleuze (1994), Lenz Taguchi (2010) says it is about 'becoming different in itself – rather than being different in relation to another' (p. 15). The becoming-child co-exists with/in itself as a condition of becoming, within transgressive spaces, different from before, becoming something beyond before. In asymmetrical zigzag movements, becoming is a doubled (ad)venture – 'that which one becomes becomes no less than the one that becomes' (Grosz, 1994b: 305). So, becoming-child becomes no less, yet neither does s/he become more; becoming-child intensifies the singularity while the singularity expands through conditions of continual alteration. Becoming-child always already changes and (re)constitutes her/him/self, (in)discernibly, (im)perceptibly without culmination, becoming-something different, beyond before...thus dispelling any structuralist ideas that becoming is a correspondence of relationships, a resemblance, an imitation or even a series of progressions/regressions.

Becoming as intra-activity of the in-between works with/in/through a middle comprising mo(ve)ments of de~territorializing lines of flight. Becoming-child is thus a work of passage, always in the middle. For example, in playing games, as in the data worked with here, each/any/every becoming-child embodies and is embodied within a milieu of becomings. In processes of becoming, linkages are formed among various characters and roles. As they flow with/in the spoken or unspoken producing of the game, becoming-children morph, unexpectedly, seamlessly, into various characters – becoming-mother becoming-pilot becoming-doctor becoming-baby becoming-co-pilot becoming-nurse becoming-sick baby – each always already played out singularly and severally (see the *Play(ing)* plateau). Each player draws, and is drawn by others into zones of undecidability, a flow of energy and movement as one becomes the other(s), becoming-child(ren) constantly in flux, so that all that is real is the becoming itself.

three becoming(s)-child(ren)

In the following juxtaposition of (the) becomings of three young people, I open possible readings of what matters to (a) young child(ren) within childhood(s) in some ways far apart – as one, three and five year olds, living in suburban London, Sydney and Auckland – and in other ways sharing a severalty of intra-active becomings. Through these poetic inscriptions, I work towards (re)inscribing the worlds of these children, to perturb the authoritative tendency of academic text and disturb developmental pretexts. Welcoming glimpses of their becomings interrupts any potential authority claimed by behaviourist and developmental interpretations by leaving the children's activity to do the talking, without intervention of researcher analysis and doing away with interpretive and/or de/constructive literature. Although the poems were generated through adult wor(l)ds, I have endeavoured to transgress an adult(erated) authorial voice, inasmuch as that is ever possible, to (re)story a few moments of becoming-child(ren) becoming-intense becoming-imperceptible becoming-power-full becoming-curriculum.

becoming-Taylah…one year old
greets the day and everyone in it   joyfully   with enthusiasm
toddles around lounge through kitchen down hallway
each trip closer to a run   running is tripping without falling over
tidies bathroom drawer made safe for explorations
re-allocating stuff to bath and floor
treasures for the senses   softpinkpowder puff
shared with Granni   against her cheek and mine
tells Daddy stories on the phone   excited   animated   babbling   laughing
indecipherable (to adult ear)   it is a very funny story
brings gumboots and Mummy's shoes to go exploring outside
but it's too cold out there
squats low   head lowered   squeals discontent
it makes no sense   adult non-sense
earlier in the watery warmth of winter sun I played with the dribbling hose
you turned it on for me   it was wet   I was wet   the water cold
I was cold   it was OK   what's different?
tired   off to bed   in Mummy's arms   waves nite-nite to Daddy and Poppa and me
as delighted with sleeping as exploring the day
livingworld   loving   oving Taylah   knowing~loving   experiencing~living
sunny rays of expressions
becoming-Taylah becoming-child(ren)

becoming-Leo…three (or thirty three?)
becoming-Leo in London   too far away   greets each day at full volume
withenthusiasm   now!
skype-talks to Pa Wazz   announcing *Today I am going to sing…*
hands clasped at his chest   a carol   weaving intricacies of words and melody
some other day some other opera house?
enterSpiderman   stage left   suitablysuited in 'jamas   cape flowing
body extended   leaps   bounds   dives   entices Daddy to play along
cushions reallocated to other (landing) spaces
(whose?) living room disrupt(ur)ed
puffing   panting   talking superhero into action
Daddy (ex-arch-superhero) fades into audience with Pa
(an)other imaginary(?) world(s)
plays at his kitchen alongside actual kitchen   cooks   eats   talks
shares chicken soup   a concoction of pretend food   plastic and imaginary
in photo album Leo cavorts under sprinkler with Mummy in Italy
tastes sand and sea at Ti Papa Point and Greek Island
rides on horse and mower at 'home' (home?)
Aotearoa New Zealand
wrapped in wool   swings between Daddy and Uncle Bo in Berlin
in hat coat mitt braves his Barnes playground
no!   Daddy *braves* the playground and the cold
becoming-Leo embraces coldness~less~hot
a dynamo of   in   with   play(ing)

becoming-Caelan…nearly five years young
starts earlier than the grown-ups   returns to where he left off last night
more or less   never still except when sleeping
bodyracing   keeping pace with thoughts and with thinking
there are darts to be (re)created   launched in unpredictable lines of flight
some fly better than others   but all are successful   somehow
smoothpathways   sudden spirals   spectacular crashes
crayons to be used   pages to be filled
expressions of becoming-Caelan foreshadowing his becoming-world
there is the trampoline
jump bounce boing turn twist jump bump
balls to kick bat bowl chuck wham whack
whoppersnickered   wah-pa-changed   ski-dooshed   blonkered
newwords   with Daddy   every day
when his path is crossed he responds with his four year old sensibilities
draws (on) power-full responses   working to ensure his desires are understood
working to understand others' desires   for him
negotiating social lores and landscapes with/in grown-up worlds
different flows   flowing differently

through space-times of his worlds and space-times of worlds of others
becoming-Caelan   knows already it is we who have to learn
becoming-Nanni~Mummy~Daddy~Poppa

These becoming(s)-child(ren) open (to) possibilities for thinking otherwise, other ways, towards (re)imagining a heterogeneity of children's matters of experiencing learning~living. They offer opportunities for appreciating (e)merging hybridity with/in a flux of ongoing becoming(s). What is at least momentarily perceptible is the dynamism of change of becoming that characterizes these (and likely other) becoming-children.

leaving the plateau

Transgressing the images of children and associated discourses that characterize childhood, I have opened (to) incipiently different space-times embodied with/in an imaginary of becoming-child(ren). As adults attempting generative understandings we can participate in these space-times, rather than as adults characterizing children and their childhoods in prescriptive, presumptive terms. Functioning as becoming-adults in relations of becoming-children, becoming-children are no longer inferior beings maturing into a superior condition of adulthood. Becoming-children are young human beings embodied in becoming-childhoods. Through various becomings they are expressing their understandings of living~learning. What they will be(come) is (im)perceptible only within their immanent becoming; the condition of children and childhood becomes conditional. Possibilities also open for young children to (re)imagine their understandings of themselves and their learning as becoming-learners; and for opening adult understandings to the play(ing) of their learning that produces curricular understandings – theirs and ours – and what these might become.

Childhood is constituted of/by ongoing phenomena; for becoming-children~becoming-adults it is a never-ending experience. While it is a part of life that warrants attention for what it is in the present (its presencing), as the future becomes the present, 'past' memories of our childhoods (as becoming-child~becoming adult) are unsettled and unsettling in conditions of continual (re)imagin(ary)ing. Like Silin (2003), I wonder whether adulthood is merely a time in which we have *expanded*, not necessarily *improved* ways for understanding our experience. So that becoming-children~becoming-adults together live interstitially amidst past~present~future, with childhood conceivably a dynamic presence in our adult lives as well as a time already lived. Always already becoming-child~becoming-adult   always   already   becoming-child~becoming-adult always already becoming-something different beyond before...

Notes

1 Whānau is the extended family, which includes not only blood relatives but also others closely connected within everyday living experiences of parents and children.

2 See also the Mataatua Declaration on Cultural and Intellectual Property Rights of Indigenous Peoples First International Conference on the Cultural and Intellectual Property Rights of Indigenous Peoples, Whakatane, 12–18 June 1983, Aotearoa New Zealand. Online at:www.fphlcc.ca/downloads/mana-tangata.pdf (accessed 27.05.12).

3 There is an interesting conversation yet to (e)merge around the sticky glue of the philosophical imaginary and the cosmic glue of the Higgs boson subatomic particle, recently discovered in physics (announced 4 July 2012); both 'glues' elusive and (im)perceptible.

Rhizo~mapping

Maps are of-the-moment, brought into being through practices (embodied, social, technical), always *remade every time they are engaged with; mapping is a process of constant reterritorialization. As such, maps are transitory and fleeting, being contingent, relational and context-dependent. Maps are practices – they are always* mappings, *spatial practices enacted to solve relational problems...*

(Kitchin & Dodge, 2007: 335, emphasis in original)

Map making features in some games of the research data. In these, each player drawing a map is integral to the game starting up and being played out. Maps are made at various times through the games, some before embarking on the game. Others are made and re-made as the game unfolds, so that, while expressing intentions and expectations for the game, these are not always proposed in advance. These maps are an open '*plan(e)*, not a phantasy' (Deleuze & Guattari, 1987: 260, original italics) in terms of how the children express the imagery and how they use them for playing the game; they are neither a prescription for the game nor an authoritative statement about how it will process. Rather, they are pictorial expressions of (e)merging ideas about the game – the storyline, characters and their roles and areas in the playground through which the game and its players might pass. The maps picture imaginative and physical plan(e)s, that is, territorial planes of conditions the games might operate with/in *and* a plan of how the children envisage this happening. They are assemblages – passages, relays, lines of flight – that the children can negotiate to (dis)solve problems, these problems perceived as opportunities for reinventing the storyline. The game emerges self/un/consciously in the playing, as do the maps. Although the maps are literal constructions, they are played with generatively, becoming the game itself.

(re)thinking mapping

Using understandings of play, Perkins (2009) rethinks ideas of mapping. Similarly, I use geographical understandings of maps as practices to rethink children's map making and their play with maps – their map(ping) play(ing). Kitchin, Perkins and Dodge (2009) explore philosophical issues of space, representation and praxis of mapping in geographical terms, noting the significance of map making and map-reading to thinking processes: 'Mapping is epistemological but also deeply ontological – it is both a way of thinking about the world, offering a framework for knowledge, and a set of assertions about the world itself' (p. 1). This elides with Deleuze's (1994) '"thinking" in thought' (p. 147) and to the mapping children use when playing their games. In the data of the research, children engage with maps and mapping as they make maps of their games and play out their mapping in an embodied performance of map(ping) play(ing), of map play and mapping their playing. It involves recursive and multiple processes of map making and mapreading, with the children becoming mappers and with many possible mappings being made, as they read their own map alongside maps drawn by other players in the game. Mapping is thus processual, embodied and dynamic; and maps are inscriptions that are complexly multivocal and contestable, not simply static representations of stable constructions.

In map(ping) play(ing) children picture experiences of their movements through playground spaces and imaginative spaces of their games; they de~territorialize changing space-times of material and social relations among bodies, the playground, programme and artefacts. Mapping is about mobility through/with/in singularly situated contexts, not about being confined to any specific location or fixed to any descriptive moment of its creation. The maps as entities and the associated processual mapping are only ever becoming-mappings with becoming-children. Mapping changes continually with/in encounters of the game linked to the actual map, each (re)reading producing different matters and possibilities of engagement. Co-constitutively, the mapping shapes the games... *and*... the games affect how the map is read as the games become expressions of the children's desires... *and*... the children affect and effectuate the mapping of their games. In this, the tracing of the game plan(e) is continually put back on the map to (re)produce and (re)announce the territory. Maps always already operate through/with/in a milieu of unfolding expressions, conditions and practices.

Children's mapping is performative, as they enact their (im)partial visual inscriptions of their imaginative picturing, conveying the leading flows of shifting authority, confirming subjectivity of play(ers) and announcing various character's mobility. At times they talk about map making; at other times they seem to work with tacit understandings of the map and the game being mapped. In performative understandings of mapping and what maps do – rather than what they represent and mean – maps are conceived as being 'always in a state of becoming; as always mapping; as simultaneously being produced *and* consumed, authored *and* read, designed *and* used, serving as a representation *and* practice; as mutually constituting map/space in a dyadic relationship' (Kitchin *et al.*, 2009: 17, original italics). In this mutually constitutive space, territory does not precede the map, rather maps and territories (e)merge simultaneously: 'Space is constituted through mapping practices, among many others, so that maps are not a reflection of the world, but a re-creation of it; mapping activates territory' (p. 18). This notion of becoming-map~becoming-territory commingles with notions of curriculum as a milieu of becoming, as milieu(s) of becoming-children's curricular performativity.

As with geographical mapmakers, when creating maps the children negotiate 'what to include, how the map will look, and what the map is seeking to communicate' (Kitchin *et al.*, 2009: 9). Affected by singular and collaborative subjectivities, the children's maps are imbued with their various values and judgements; the maps become both products and producers of power-fullness through contested, (im)partial mappings of various children. Maps as inscriptions are thus unstable and complex texts, neither created nor readable in simple ways; rather they are open to, and require, processes of ongoing (re)contextualization in that the map (re)produces and (re)announces territory. Not simply describing territory, maps are 'part of [an] assemblage of people, discursive processes and material things' (p. 16). This opens (to) possibilities for (re)thinking spaces for children to (re)constitute themselves and their games – children working to produce maps of their games... *and*... children working their maps to produce their games.

Kitchin *et al.* (2009) conceive maps as 'unfolding potential; as conduits of possibilities; as the sites of imagination and action in the world (p. 18). Through processes of de~territorializing, mapping continuously remakes territory, each re-make (re)producing differing consequences. This doubled mapping de~territorializing activity that passes through re-territorialization produces a variety of affects of reciprocal flow – it is always already 'open and connectable in all of its dimensions; it is detachable, reversible, susceptible to constant modification. It can be torn, reversed...reworked by an individual, group, or social formation' (Deleuze & Guattari, 1987: 12). Mapping is thus always already open curricular performativity, opening (to) milieus of (im)perceptible or (un)imagined possibilities of activity.

map(ping) play(ing)

Rhizo~mapping involves a complex interplay of following lines of flight and nomadically flowing through various territories, such as physical or imaginative spaces, storylines of games and player relations. As any part of a rhizome is always already connected to any other (Deleuze & Guattari, 1987: 7), an assemblage of ceaseless and ongoing connections amasses as an a-centred milieu of perpetual and dynamic change. In rhizo~mapping, there are no points or positions, no specific end or entry points, no beginnings and endings; there are only lines or relays of passage. Working with these de~territorializing lines of flight opens possibilities for connections between what otherwise may be regarded as disparate thoughts, ideas or actions, generating a mass of interconnectivity – an amassing of middles amidst an array of multidimensional movement among open systems. Generating rhizo~mapping thus disturbs arborescent, linear progression, which can only be retraced through the same series of points of structuration and 'always comes back "to the same"' (p. 12). In contrast, a rhizo map always already opens (to) possibilities for mo(ve)ments of connectivity.

The children's use of maps – map(ping) play(ing) – in the data shows rhizo~mapping at work as they make maps, using them as a play resource and to think through processing (through) their games. In map(ping) play(ing), maps and mapping, and play and playing (e)merge through/with/in creative and imaginary performative plan(e)s of the games. The games like the maps never fully material-ize but are perpetually (e)merging as the plan de~territorializes the plane and the plane (re)distributes the plan. How children make maps within the contexts of their games, and how they make their maps work within those de~territorializing (re)distributing space-times offer glimpses into their curricular understandings. There are various snippets in the data that illuminate different aspects of map making (map play) and playing out of their maps (mapping playing), with which the children engage.

Tim and Piri opening map making

Tim and Piri prepare for their bad guys hunt and make perceptible the significance of a map for calling their imaginary game and its characters into be(com)ing, the maps being part of their hunting gear. Having a map before the game gets under-way matters. The maps confirm participation, and become a way of discussing the storyline and communicating their expectations for the game. Piri's map features a grid-like pattern (Figure 5.1a); Tim draws people on his as well, namely, the bad guys to be hunted as well as Piri and himself as the hunters (Figure 5.1b). Tim's map also doubles as a weapon.

> Piri rolls his map and Tim talks as he draws: *We go spider hunting every day…and we're on a hunting trip…and we're doing a bad people hunt today. Yeah.* (He rolls up his drawing) *And this is my light sabre map.*
> Piri stuffs his map into the top of his waistband: *Treasure map.*
> Tim: *The treasure map. There's my circle to turn it on.* (He shows me the light

Figure 5.1a Piri's map of the bad guys hunt

Figure 5.1b Tim's map depicts the bad guys as well as the hunting game

sabre 'switch', then sings) *We're hunting, we're hunting.* (He unrolls his map) *And we need something special on it, how to know it.*

Piri: *I don't.*

Tim: *We need to draw our, some bad guys.*

Piri: *Let's go hunting.*

Tim: *Not yet, Piri. First I need to draw the bad guys. They got so many bad guys. There they are, all the bad guys are there and now we need to roll them up.*

Within this mapping conversation, Tim and Piri negotiate what the map will include, how it will look and what it is to communicate. For Tim it is a bad guys hunt and although Piri does not dispute this, he brings a treasure component into the game and Tim embraces this. Their maps do not picture any particular route to be travelled, they are about mobility through the game plan(e)s rather than particular positions and locations.

Kane, Nadia and Bella mapping their pathway(s)

In the middle of their game an inter/ir/ruption occurs as Kane, Nadia and Bella pause to make maps of/for their game and un/intentionally, in this mapping mo(ve)ment, their (e)merging lines of flight momentarily meld the constantly fracturing group. For some time Kane has been trying to co-opt Nadia, Bella, Adam, Alec and Callum into playing out his ideas for a chocolate factory game.[1] Kane has not gained their full attention although the group is following him around the playground, albeit with deviations as they pause to play on various equipment – 'a social field is always animated by all kinds of movements of decoding and deterritorialization affecting "masses" and operating at different speeds' (Deleuze & Guattari, 1987: 220). They each talk about their own ideas for the game but Kane persists with his overcoding venture of trying to control the flow of the play. Eventually they make their way to an art area, where he, Nadia and Bella make maps (Figures 5.2a & b).

Figure 5.2a Watch what the map's gonna tell you

Figure 5.2b This is the map where we get lost

Kane tells Nadia that his map is about *where we know where to go*. Nadia listens but says her map is *the map where we get lost*.

Kane: *So we have to go past the chocolate waterfall, back past me, and then we go up the river, and then we go... 'Scuse me, watch what the map's gonna tell you. You go past the chocolate waterfall. Hey everybody look at the map! We go past the chocolate waterfall through the reeds, then at the river and then, ah, we head to our space rocket and then we're at [...]. So we have to all go the right way, we have to go past the waterfall. So we have to go a really slo-ow way. That's going to take a long, long, long, long, long, long time.*

Nadia rolls up her map: *This is the map where we get lost, OK?*

Kane, rolling his map: *Well this is the map.*

Nadia, adding more to her map: *Yeah, but this is the map where we get lost.*

Kane: *Mmmm and this is the map where we know where to go.*

Nadia hands her map to Kane and leads the way outside.

Kane appreciates the value of the maps for communicating (his) intentions for the game plan(e) and for ensuring they all go the right way or his way and that they understand that his is the map to be followed. But Nadia brings a critical, diffractive reading to their use of maps. She seems to appreciate the diverse ways in which maps are produced and used and that there is no one right way to do either. It seems that her map is to ensure they do or do not get lost and to help them find their way if/when they do. With a continual refrain of attempting to draw the group into his ideas for the game, Kane manages through the map making to 'distribute game roles and functions within the territorial assemblage' (Deleuze & Guattari, 1987: 327), an assemblage of game~players~maps. The maps become a space of negotiation among players, a space where Kane and his overcoding rigid lines of thought or 'rigid segmentarity' of intentions for the game can come together with Nadia's 'relatively supple line of interlaced codes and territorialities' and with their lines of flight as singularly and severally they flow as nomad~rhizome, 'ventur[ing] a fluid and active escape, sow[ing] deterritorialization everywhere' (p. 222). Despite thinking he was in charge, it is Nadia who continues to promote the smooth space of the game and leads the way to the playground outside.

Tim and Zak's mapping machinic

In their dinosaur spider hunt, Tim and Zak open a milieu of mapping as their maps both legitimize and contest their participation in the game, this generating conflict and a passage through. In these doubled mo(ve)ments their mapping becomes a machinic of power-fullness, a desiring machine of the unconscious – when complications arise around their actual mapping of the game, it is the maps themselves that open a way for the players to negotiate the complexities and intensify the milieu of the game. Firstly, their maps are significant to their game starting up. When I ask what they need to play the game, Zak says: *We need a map and....*

Tim adds: *And the horseys.* So, they require other gear but making maps comes first; and later re-making them as the game processes inscribes their singular and several desires for the game. The maps make perceptible that having a game-plan(e) matters as well as being an actual picturing of the game-plan(e) itself. Although the maps announce their entry into the game, they are fluid, contestable and constantly (re)negotiable – 'a map that is always detachable, connectable, reversible, modifiable, and has multiple entryways and exits and its own lines of flight' (Deleuze & Guattari, 1987: 21).

However, in the moment that it becomes apparent they need to modify their maps, a problem arises around their convoluted understandings of the hunt. They are sitting in their trolley using a toy cash register seeking a reading of whether it is time to hunt dinosaurs, despite Tim's earlier announcement that they were on a spider hunt.

> Tim: *Let's see if it's dinosaur time. No dinosaur time today.*
> Zak: *Let's see it. Oh you're right it's no dinosaur time today.*
> Tim: *'Cos it's Saturday, no dinosaur time on Saturdays, are there?*

Although they already have maps, having established that it is not dinosaur time, they decide that they need to make new maps. Tim runs off to make his while Zak guards the trolley and when Tim returns with his new map, without seeing what Tim has drawn, Zak runs inside to the drawing table. Tim now guards the trolley and he shows me his map with a spider on it, then, abandoning the trolley, he goes after Zak who is drawing a dinosaur map. When Tim realizes this their (mis)understandings about the game unfold.

> Zak: *Um I'm gonna make a better map for a dinosaur hunt. I made a spider map but I don't want a spider map...I'm going to make another dinosaur map...*
> Tim: *We're not going on a dinosaur hunt. We're going on a spider hunt.*
> Zak: *Uummm...um, I thought you said we're going on a, on a dinosaur hunt.*
> Tim: *No dinosaur hunt. Spider hunt! Do a spider one!*
> Zak: *No-o because it's almost finished...*
> Tim: *Huuh! Ok I'm going to have to do a spider hunt by myself.*
> Zak: *Well we we I wanna um...I thought you said you wanted to go on a dinosaur hunt.*
> Tim: *No dinosaur hunt! Spider hunt!*
> Zak: *Why do you want to go on a spider hunt?*
> Tim: *'Cos I wanna I need to go on it.*
> Zak has another idea about his drawing: *Oh what alright it's it's it's a dinosaur spider instead!*
> The tension between them melts as Tim squeals and jumps from one foot to the other: *It's a dinosaur spider hunt! Let's go!*
> Zak beams as they run off together.
> Tim: *We got to go on a dinosaur spider hunt.*

thinking about children's curricular performativity

As well as being a site of conflict, Tim and Zak's maps become a site of resolution. A developmental, behaviourist reading would likely see this as extremely well executed conflict resolution and in these terms, Zak's expertise is undeniable. But a Deleuzo-Guattarian reading complexifies the (mis)understanding of the milieu as legitimizing and contestable, presenting both Tim and Zak as powerfull negotiators of challenging territory, productively re/dis/solving the problem. In this moment of putting the tracing back into the(ir) map – 'Plug the tracings back into the map, connect the roots or trees back up with a rhizome' (Deleuze & Guattari, 1987: 14) – each negotiates the site of the other's engagement with the game as they pause to (re)make their hunting maps. Momentarily, the tracing of their singular intended storyline limits the game. It seems they have different maps generated through not so much conflicting as convoluted understandings from the outset, but it is not until Tim approaches Zak at the drawing table that these differences become apparent and an opportunity to re/dis/solve their differing expectations opens. The tracing – the (fixed) understanding that each has – is impeding the game's processing and the (open) mapping enterprise. The tracing obstructs the game; an a signifying rupture appears; a new line of flight emerges – 'Once a rhizome has been obstructed, arborified, it's all over, no desire stirs; for it's always by rhizome that desire moves and produces' (p. 14). While (re)making the maps stymied the game momentarily, in negotiating a newly (e)merging line of flight, an opening occurs for continuing by bringing the tracing of the hunt together with two maps of possibilities for playing out the hunting maps.

> There are knots of arborescence in rhizomes, and rhizomatic offshoots in roots…The important point is that the root-tree and canal-rhizome are not two opposed models: the first operates as a transcendent model and tracing, even if it engenders its own escapes; the second operates as an immanent process that overturns the model and outlines a map, even if it constitutes its own hierarchies…It is not a question of…this or that category of thought. It is a question of a model that is perpetually in construction or collapsing, and of a process that is perpetually prolonging itself, breaking off and starting up again.
>
> (Deleuze & Guattari, 1987: 20)

In breaking off and starting again, Tim and Zak play out their (mis)understanding. Tim's tracing engenders its own, arguably despotic, escape as he states that he wants and needs to go on a spider hunt; Zak's idea for a dinosaur-spider hunt opens out an immanent process that becomes a new mapping for the game. Zak's way through is not despotic, even though the new combined reading of their maps – for a dinosaur-spider hunt – force-fully overtakes the old map's tracing. But, as the tracing is plugged into the map, the tracing melds with the map, generating something of a palimpsest that furthers the game and assures their negotiation through/with/in it. Mapping the game both is and is not disrupted; a commingled Tim~Zak becomes a knot of arborescence, singularly blocking the other's desire as rhizo offshoot. In behaviourist terms, this interruption disrupts the smooth flow of the game, but negotiating Deleuzo-Guattarian smooth spaces involves eruption, irruption and disruption for negotiating unexpected passages for the game.

However, the de~territorializing refrain – 'expressive qualities that constitute territorial motifs' (Deleuze & Guattari, 1987: 317) – of (mis)understandings between Tim and Zak (un)surprisingly breaks the game. They now disagree over Piri joining the game; Tim invites him to participate but Zak argues that he can't because he doesn't have a map. This time their disagreement breaks the game and no way to start it up again is apparent to either. The map reverts to tracing, which is to be protected. As Tim walks off, he waves his map at Zak, saying: *I'm gonna put this in my locker and you can never find it!* The tracing of the maps is intact but its passage through the mapping is broken yet even this seemingly stagnating space-time is merely part of the oscillating refrain of rhizome as flows of desire connect with overcoded rigidity but in an a-hierarchical way so that each is always already (e)merging with/from the other. 'Childhood scenes, children's games: the starting point is a childlike refrain, but the child has wings already...Opening the assemblage onto a cosmic force...one was already present in the other' (Deleuze & Guattari, 1987: 350)...*and...*the game~players~map assemblage continues in a different expression on another day as Tim and Piri take up hunting together after Zak turns five and goes to school.[2] Tim and Zak's dinosaur spider hunt map making occurred on a Thursday; Zak left for school the next day; and on the following Monday, Tim and Piri made maps for their bad guys hunt. The maps were continually becoming the never-ending hunting game, the map(ping)s calling both the games and the players into conditions of be(com)ing in an ever intensifying milieu of map(ping) play(ing).

mapping (a) milieu(s) of curricular performativity

The children's approach to map(ping) play(ing) makes perceptible their curricular performativity within the context of conventional curriculum conceptions that the adult world imposes on young children. The children's curricular performativity around map making and playing out their maps becomes a milieu of learning. The maps communicate desire for the games, characters to be played and players' subjectivities, this desire constantly changing as the children process through singular and several expectations for the game. The maps open (to) possibilities for the social and material spaces to (e)merge with/in the imaginative territory of the game. Their maps continually illuminate and dissolve problems as the children flow through various lines of flight, in the process (dis)agreeing to continue playing together or to con/di/verge in this game-plan(e) or another. Through their map(ping) play(ing) we are afforded glimpses into their ways of approaching curriculum, which seems to be more about thinking differently than any particularized understandings. Through/with/in imaginary games, the children work with tacit learning of the self/un/conscious, working with their desires alongside (those of) others, imparting understandings of an embodied unconscious with/in the multiplicity of social and material bodies. This disrupts cognition as a prime function of human bodies, disturbing the foothold of pervasive structuralist approaches to learning and understandings of curriculum. Linear processes are irrelevant to children operating productively in play, in informal, spontaneous learning situations and experiences. As they flow freely with/in/through their ideas they (re)create generative learning experiences for themselves and those around them. Attempting to think differently about the ways children generate learning opportunities problematizes structural, developmental and behaviourist perspectives, as well as opening (to) glimpses of how this might happen otherwise.

Maps picture ebbs and flows of the rhizo movement of games and children commingling in (a) curricular milieu(s). There is one and there are many or several – child/ren, game(s) and milieu(s). Mapping matters of rhizo conditions and expressions avoids pathologizing children and opens (to) insights about curricular performativity. Maps as fragmented wholes, offer a picture of an extensive~intensive milieu of space-times, in which both space and time are irreducible to a linear conception. They picture mobility and expressions of activity, with de~territorializing lines of flight flowing through/with/in the milieu(s) mapped. An assemblage of map(ping) play(ing) – maps of play (the games) and mapping of playing the games – makes perceptible workings of children's curricular understandings as (a) milieu(s) of becoming, in which a horizontal plane of becoming-children becoming-curricular performativity is illuminated.

Notes

1   On a different day from the chocolate factory game discussed in the *Children performing curriculum complexly* plateau and with a different group of children.
2   In Aotearoa New Zealand children most often start school on their fifth birthday, so group dynamics in early childhood settings constantly change as children leave for school and new children come in to fill vacancies in the register.

Play(ing)

opening the plateau

Theory of children's play and actual activity of their playing is the work of this plateau about play(ing). What unfolds within this conversation is a play-full engagement with 'Play which is more than play' (Trueit, 2006) through a rhizopoietic juxtaposition. From this emerges a tripled juxtaposition of my intra-activity with two transcriptions – one of a data snippet of children playing a game in the family corner, another of the same children (re)playing their play(ing) as they watched the video of themselves playing. These juxtapositions are intra-active pieces of embodied onto-epistemological (Barad, 2007) activity through/within which theories of being (ontology) and knowing (epistemology) explicated in each text work(s) with the other(s).

conceptions of play

Much has been written about play from diverse disciplinary fields, such as biology, ethology, folklore, literary criticism, leisure science, education, psychology, sociology, anthropology, history and communications. But it is psychological and sociological perspectives that dominate in early childhood education, with play considered a natural condition of childhood and the 'natural media of children' (Rhedding-Jones, 2003: 244). The pedagogy of play is basic to early childhood studies but it is often given minimal attention in texts used in preservice early childhood teacher education. In the literature, play is presented as progress, power, fantasy and self, adaptation, existential optimism, hegemony, social context, transformation, performance, and world upside down (Sutton-Smith, 1995, 1997) and, although some take a discursive approach involving characteristics of play and lingering historical discourses, the theory addressed remains primarily with the developmental. However, any conversation about play(ing) cannot deny the complexity involved, exemplified in Sutton-Smith's (1997) indexed references for play.

A critical view considers the concept of play as elusive, as defying definition, and those who attempt definitions often do so without concern that it is a contested issue, not only pedagogically but also culturally. Even in the claimed sociocultural approach of recent curriculum documents, perspectives of the dominant white, middle-class majority as well as a developmental pedagogical approach pervade; that play is important to learning in the early years is arguably a taken-for-granted concept but not always well understood. Although I would argue that play constitutes significant learning experiences, it should be signalled that this is a westernized understanding. Play-based learning is defined in *The Early Years Learning Framework for Australia* (EYLF) as 'a context for learning through which children organize and make sense of their social worlds, as they engage actively with people, objects and representations' (Department of Education Employment and Workplace Relations & Council of Australian Governments, 2009: 6). While this is open to different cultural understandings, what follows embodies western ideals, explicated as enabling: personal expression; curiosity and creativity; connections to prior learning; interpersonal relations; and, a sense of well-being (p. 9). This is not dissimilar to what is implied in *Te Whāriki* (Ministry of Education, 1996).

Although the Aotearoa New Zealand early childhood curriculum statement does not directly address play, the value of play is inherent to its reading. Notions of play are woven throughout, somewhat buried in statements such as the importance of early childhood settings having a library of information for parents about 'the value of play in learning and development' (Ministry of Education, 1996: 83). Play is promoted in *Te Whāriki* as 'open-ended exploration' (p. 41), with open resources, using materials that children can 'change and interact with' (p. 43), in open situations where play activities 'invite rather than compel participation' (p. 40), in open relations where children learn through 'trying out their ideas with adults and other children (p. 43). In contrast, the Australian EYLF explicitly identifies play-based learning as key, in terms of social engagement and enhancing children's thinking. However, the more implicit assumption in *Te Whāriki* of play as learning is unsurprising given the philosophical history of early childhood education in Aotearoa New Zealand. The kindergarten movement, established in 1906, was influenced by Froebelian notions of the setting as a child's garden and play as children's work (Liebschner, 1992). Also, the contiguous playcentre movement, established in 1941, works through the philosophical principle of child-initiated play. Moreover, in the mid-1950s, Clarence Beeby as Minister of Education introduced the 'playway' into new entrants classes[1] in schools, endorsing a free play space of an hour each morning called 'developmental' that provided opportunities for creative expression within the formal syllabus. By the 1980s this free play space was often called 'choosing time' and generally happened during the afternoon; in some schools this no longer exists, in others it is still part of the daily programme. Unsurprisingly, the notion of free play and how it is prioritized ranges through a variety of interpretations, manifesting in different ways according to school policies and teachers' personal philosophies. For example, free play within the classroom may be a time when children choose to work at a selection of work stations, such as art, blocks or computers for a designated time; free play may not happen every day; free play may be relegated to times before school and

Plate 3.1 Chocolate factory game

1 Nic, Rylie and Callum are making chocolate in Willy Wonka's chocolate factory.
Rylie (singing): *We're making chocolatey yes yes yes yes yes...*
Callum (singing): *Yes yes yes yes...*
Nic (singing): *Yes yes yes yes...*

2 Kane is parading as Willy Wonka, overseeing the chocolate-making enterprise, he is chanting: *uddoduddabbeedaa... ubbadda...*
Callum: *We're making it sweeter. Yummy tastes good eh? Yummy, tastes chocolater eh?*

Callum, Rylie and Nic work with a sandy-watery mixture in the buckets and tray. Kane prowls around making odd noises: *uddoduddabbeedaaubbadda.* He picks up handfuls of sand and throws them down.

Callum and Rylie argue over a trowel. Kane walks in from behind to satisfy himself that the chocolate-making is progressing: *C'mon, let's see about that chocolate...*

Plate 3.2 Chocolate factory game

Kane jiggles his bucket attached to the pulley, yelling to the chocolate-makers: *Charlie and the chocolate...C'mon grab a chocolate and put it in the container to make some chocolate!* Nic grabs a handful of sand from Kane's bucket while Callum and Rylie continue with their mixing.

Alec has joined in with mixing the chocolate. Josh has entered the scene and is watching. Kane, in charge of the pulley, which is jammed, continues to jiggle his bucket.

Callum suddenly yells at Josh: *Yes! Willy Wonka and chocolate fact'ry's here!* Josh holds his hands up, as if in defence.

Plate 3.3 Chocolate factory game

Rylie and Callum continue to collect water from the trough and mix their chocolate.

Kane grabs handfuls of sand to replenish his bucket of chocolate.

He steps up onto the edging and calls: *Anybody want chocolate?*

Callum yells back without looking up: *No! Not that chap in the chocolate factory that makes it!*
Kane continues: *C'mo-on! Chocola-ate! Chocolate!*

Plate 3.4 Chocolate factory game

Kane surveys the chocolate-making. The girls in the background are discussing their separate storyline about Goldilocks.

Kane drops his handfuls of sand into his bucket. Moments later, the girls move closer to Kane and he growls: *Grrraaaggghhh!!!* The girls race off.

The boys continue, oblivious to Kane's growl and the girls' flight. Callum carries a trowel of water to the bucket, Rylie works with the mixture in the tray and Alec mixes the chocolate in the trough with his hands as the girls run past.

The girls suddenly stop and turn to look back towards Kane.

Kane jumps awkwardly off the edging, saying: *Huh! I have an idea… versutshuvannagh…grrraaaggghhh!*

Plate 3.5 Chocolate factory game

...and in an odd stumbling gait lurches after the girls, chuckling: *Huhhah*

Kane chases the girls from the scene. Callum en route to the sandy-water trough, trips over trolley handle and swears.

Plate 3.6 Chocolate factory game

Kane growls*: Mi-ine!* As he protects the chocolate factory domain.

Kane goes back to the pulley*: Aarrrgh! Ha ha ha!*

Plate 3.7 Monster game

Kane is wandering around making odd noises. He presents as both Willy Wonka and monster.

Kane is grabbing handfuls of sand and throwing them down: *…uddoduddabbeedaaubbadda…* Nic, sleeves rolled up, is working the sand and water mix with his hands.

Nic, intent on mixing the sand with his hands, is oblivious to Callum and Rylie tussling over a trowel.

After checking that Callum and Rylie are on task with the chocolate-making, Kane continues with his odd noises…*akkagagga…*

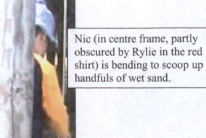

Nic (in centre frame, partly obscured by Rylie in the red shirt) is bending to scoop up handfuls of wet sand.

Plate 3.8 Monster game

8a Nic rears up and shouts: *Whaaah! Bad muddy monster*…He raises his sandy hands, fingers splayed and slightly curled.

8b Alec

Nic confronts Josh, who steps back a pace. Josh: *Leave me alone.* Josh stares at Nic and doesn't move. Nic: *Muddy monster*…Alec observes the interchange.

9 Nic moves away from Josh and heads towards the trough, where Alec (partly obscured by Rylie) is now wetting his hands.

10 Josh holds up his hands in monster mode as Callum shouts at him: …*Willy Wonka and the chocolate fact'ry's here!*

11 Alec (obscured by Rylie) is crouched by the trough, muddying his hands. Nic approaches Josh as he sits on the deck.

15a Nic, having 'washed' his hands in the trough, pulls his sleeves down. For a moment Josh and Alec faced each other, hands raised, but as Josh steps towards Alec, Alec turns and runs off.

Plate 3.9 Monster game

Hissing and stomping his feet as he goes, Josh strides after Alec.

Alec runs back in, chased by Josh. Nic has left the scene

The chase short-lived, Alec returns to the trough to muddy his hands. Josh (far left) hisses at an outsider.

Alec continues to muddy his hands.

Josh sits on the deck. Alec watches the girls run across the back of the sandpit.

Plate 3.10 Monster game

Kane jumps awkwardly off the edging: *Huh! I have an idea…versutshuvannagh …grraaaggghh!* In an odd stumbling gait he lurches after the girls, chuckling: *Huhhah.*

Josh (far right), hands raised in monster mode, leaves the deck and runs towards Kane.

Kane stumbles in after the girls. Alec crouched by the trough turns to observe Kane's approach/Josh's exit.

Kane growls: *Mi-ine!* as he continues after the girls.

Plate 3.11 Goldilocks game

Libby, Lee and Alice have selected their tools by colour and are close to the boys' activity. Libby: *We're playing digging.*

In response to being told they cannot play with the bucket on the pulley, Lee grabs the rope and grins defiantly. Rylie concedes: *You can get some water though.*

The digging soon turns into cake-making.

They gather their tools, Libby carrying the cake, and relocate to the back fence to establish their home.

Plate 3.12 Goldilocks game

⑤a Libby: *Do you know what we're playing? We're playing Goldilocks!*

⑤b Nic walks through clapping his sandy hands. Libby, pointing to the back fence: *We pretended the cake and it's over there and there's our home.* Lee: *And we better hide cos Goldilocks is at the fence, eh?*

⑤c Libby and Lee join Alice by the fence at the back of the sandpit. Libby announces: *Goldilocks comes!* Alice: *And when those boys are there too, eh?* Kane is standing nearby.

⑤d Lee brings a trowel of water for the cake mixture: *We gotta have heaps of water to make it stick.* Libby attends to the 'cake', now porridge, in the bushes: *I make the porridge now.* Alec makes a track with his digger that loops around in front of the girls. Alice surveys the scene.

Plate 3.13 Goldilocks game

Libby puts more sand into the porridge. Alice rushes past, towards Kane, who is announcing: *Charlie and the chocolate...*

Lee collects more water from the trough. Alice watches Kane as he shouts: *Anybody else want to make chocolate?*

Alice maintains the watch.

Lee gathers water from the trough alongside Nic and Rylie (obscured by Nic).

Plate 3.14 Goldilocks game

The girls discuss their storyline. Lee: *Yeah we should do it it in the other...where the bears where the, where they go in after...* Alice: *When they see her and go back, eh?* Libby: *And and and Goldilocks...*Libby, holding a bowl of sand: *Hey um ah um I know, this can be Goldilocks' porridge and we can make the peasey pudding porridge...It's a good one. We'll get the peasey porridge as well and put Goldilocks' poison porridge he-re.* She places it on the sandpit edgeing close to Kane.
Kane: *Grrraaaggghhh!!* Lee squeals.

They rush off, across the back of the sandpit, Libby in the lead, holding the bowl of porridge. Lee: *Aaahhh! He's following us! C'mo-on!*

Libby stops suddenly and turns to look back in the direction of Kane. Lee crashes into her. Libby loses balance momentarily but doesn't fall. Alice walks up behind.

Plate 3.15 Goldilocks game

Kane jumps awkwardly off the edging: *Huh! I have an idea...versutshuvannagh ...grraaaggghh!* He lumbers after the girls, chuckling: *Huhhah.*

Libby, followed by Alice then Lee, retraces her steps back towards their home.

As Libby sees Kane lumbering towards them, she quickly turns again to run back behind the trough, pushing between Lee and Alice.

Libby crashes between Lee and Alice and the bowl falls from her hands, but she doesn't hesitate. Lee and Alice pause to look where it's fallen.
Libby, as she runs: *Oooohhhh!*

Plate 3.16 Goldilocks game

Kane appears, stumbling randomly after the girls.
Lee: *Eeeee!*
Libby races around the edge of the sandpit, gasping: *He doesn't go round...ooooh...*Lee and Alice are close behind.

Libby leads their flight out of the sandpit as Kane waddles after them.
Lee: *He's got a really big growl...*

The girls have gone. Kane growls after them: *Mi-ine!*

Kane: *Aarrrgh! Ha ha ha!*

during breaks; or it may be part of a democratic, participatory approach in which children organize their daily activities.[2] Thus, in varying ways, notions of play are a characteristic of early years education in Aotearoa New Zealand. Contemporarily, Wood (2004) articulates a pedagogy of play, in which play is conceived as providing planned and purposeful opportunities for teaching and learning within variable sociocultural contexts; and Hill (2006) takes a social justice approach in considering play as a response to life.

While *Te Whāriki* works with bicultural philosophical principles – incorporating traditional Māori and western approaches – it is westernized understandings of play that underpin its workings. *Te Whāriki* takes a non-prescriptive approach and makes no attempt to define play but it implies that play is a natural condition of early childhood activity and that all children play. It refers to the 'value of play in learning and development' (Ministry of Education, 1996: 83), with play seen as exploration of natural, physical and material worlds, and as social interactions that constitute a sense of belonging in the setting. Although there is no limiting definition, there is little attempt to rescue play from 'natural' social and psychological understandings, and the text contains remnants of Parten's (1933, cited in Hyun, 1998) outdated typology of solitary, parallel and co-operative play. However, I continue with caution, as the cultural critique of play that follows inevitably works with (my) westernized understandings, but in working with rhizome the philosophical links to current perspectives of pedagogy of play ostensibly open (to) possibilities for wider readings.

Rationalizing discourses of play describe play as being natural, spontaneous, pleasurable, developmentally appropriate, dramatic, free, pretend, exploratory, representational, creative, to name a few. In discussions about what constitutes so-called 'normal' play, developmental stages of play and types of play dominate, producing matrices of regulation useful to developmentally appropriate practice [DAP], all this legitimizing the adult gaze for monitoring progress (Fleer, 1995). Establishing such specific sets of thought and knowledge about play has become effective in governing early childhood education through predominating views of what is rational, technical and practical. This is significant to both producing and silencing children, curriculum and teachers, the corollary being observation of play for management of children. Play as a cultural artefact and the naturally playing child as a social construct are seldom questioned let alone critiqued (Cannella, 1997; Rhedding-Jones, 2003). The centrality afforded play within conventional discourses and the effects of such positioning in early childhood education is culturally significant; how play is understood varies among cultures, problematizing play as an artefact of a white, middle-class culture (Cannella & Viruru, 2004).

Westernized sociocultural understandings present play as a community of practice, reflecting the spaces and relationships of children's sociocultural worlds but these tend to be dominated by developmental theories. Together developmental and sociocultural perspectives work to normalize and regulate children's behaviour by classifying play as, for example, appropriate/inappropriate, individual/social or advanced/delayed. These discourses then become technologies for governing young children and early childhood education (Cannella, 1997). Power relations enmeshed in play-as-work are thus problematized as a technique of social control. In espousing play as the work of young children, adults influence, construct and manage play environments that reflect culturally created agenda for controlling children (Cannella & Viruru, 2004). Further, from a technicist perspective, the player-as-worker is shaped and managed according to principles of work, with the playing child promoted as producing a 'self-managing subject' (Gibbons, 2007: 303). However, children as singularities with their own desires for play(ing) and learning operating on horizontal, fluid planes of rhizo connections with others – other children and other planes – invite ruptures of complexity rather than predictable, traceable networks that both DAP and traditional sociocultural interpretations attempt.

Play(ing) is complex; it is ambiguously related to games in that 'games can be seen as a subset of play…[and] play is a characteristic of games' (Perkins, 2009: 171). Unsurprisingly, it is theorized in different ways. In a seminal analysis, Sutton-Smith and Magee (1989) assert that play perceived as fun trivializes it as a structure within curriculum, while psychological and cognitive readings of children's play attempts an order and rationality that satisfies adult perspectives and desires to control play and refine children's behaviour. From an ideologically similar understanding, Ranz-Smith (2007) suggests that fostering a sense of play in the learning process might threaten adult perceptions of what learning ought to be. Alongside this, Ailwood (2003) reveals the culturally mediated, adult-imposed relations of power and control that are concealed within the taken-for-granted concept of play. Also, in Cannella and Viruru's (2004) analysis, play is a cultural artefact and is central also to the (re)production of western culture. For De Castell and Jenson (2003), play and learning are mutually constitutive and their conjunction is transformative to both. Ultimately, Harker (2005) calls for understandings that any theorizing of playing must engage with a blurring of boundaries among children and adults, childhood and adulthood, towards destabilizing unequal power relations and promoting irreducibly shared spaces. Avoiding the stasis and limitation of definition or representation, Harker opens understandings of play(ing) as fluid, polymorphous, bending, looping, twisting through continually changing space-times of 'the being of becoming' (p. 52) whereby the play of games is created and the playing happens. He presents play(ing) as a dynamically embodied performance of affects flowing through non/human, non/material, and semiotic, social and incorporeal bodies situated with/in various space-times. Heartened that his geographical discourse casts aside traditional psychologically and sociologically developmental perspectives outlined above, in a similarly modest attempt to avoid the colonizing of the becoming of play(ing), I negotiate more of its horizontal plane of immanence, 'always in it but not of it' (Massumi, 2002: 33), opening (to) the multiplicity…

play-fully (re)conceiving play

Guss (2005) creatively reconceptualizes play as a critically reflective, cultural activity. Destabilizing the notion that playing all too often sustains existing power relations, she devises a cultural-aesthetic methodology, which promotes children as power-full players within their 'play-culture', disrupting cultural hegemony to consider play as critical transformation, as a process not dissimilar to Deleuzo-Guattarian 'becoming'. She shows how, 'in the privacy of the children's play-culture, they have the cultural occasion, space, and liberty to take control' (p. 233), to question, speak for and transform themselves; as with the feminist challenge to male-dominated operations in everyday life, children experiment with and trouble standpoints, turning cultural hegemony on its head. She demonstrates how 'the aesthetic dimension contributes to the children's ability to interpret and communicate meaning, as well as [how] the aesthetic mode and production contributes to a strengthened child-cultural sphere' (p. 235). However, it is Donna Trueit's (2006) 'Play which is more than play' and other contributions in the same journal that inspire anew ways of thinking play(ing), resisting colonizing, concretizing or theorizing. It is a gesture towards (re)thinking play(ing) – play-fully!

Trueit invites a different way of thinking about play. She works with 'binocular vision (double description) for enhanced depth of perception' (Bateson, 1979, cited in Trueit, 2006: 97); and, reflecting *poiesis* (that is, copying for creating, the work of her doctoral dissertation – Trueit, 2005), she speculates on different understandings about play through a conversation linked to mythopoetic discursive practices of archaic times. Her mythopoetic understandings of 'the play' – as performance and as playing by the players – open (to) possibilities for (re)thinking play differently in early childhood curriculum although not through a conventional interpretation of her writing. In a connecting contribution, Doll (2006) discusses 'a new sense of method' (p. 87). He notes the importance of 'inter (or *trans*) action' between reader, writer and text as a reflective, creative, flexible, open, complex conversation that disrupts the rigidity of conventional, multiple step approaches to method. To achieve this, readers~writers need to be supported in developing singularly autobiographical approaches. As with the Deleuzo-Guattarian project, Doll suggests a recursive process whereby a text 'is looked at not only in terms of itself, but also in terms of its relationship with…[the philosophy or other texts] from which it emerged, and in terms of that which has *yet-to-emerge*' (p. 88, italics added) to explore a multiplicity of creative connections. This affirms an emerging desire to find my own way of (re)reading Trueit's text. But, there is more.

In another contribution, 'Playing with our understandings', Smitherman Pratt (2006) presents Aoki's considerations of what it means to understand, namely that understanding 'is never static, fixed, or rigid; rather understanding is always changing, in flux, continually being renewed' (p. 93). Reflecting on Smitherman Pratt's reading of Aoki alongside Doll and Trueit prompts reading~writing as a generative space of possibilities as I open (to) spaces of both 'and/not-and…a space of conjoining and disrupting…a generative space of possibilities, a space wherein in tensioned ambiguity newness emerges' (Aoki, 1996/2005: 318, cited in Smitherman Pratt, 2006: 93). Also, Gough's (2006b) 'Rhizosemiotic play' demonstrates 'the generativity of intertextual readings' (p. 119) and further prompts a desire to play with Trueit's text to find out what might happen by writing around it.

He refers to Deleuze and Guattari's (1987) urge to experiment with rhizome and, like Richardson (2001), I am urged to 'write because I want to find something out…to learn something that I did not know before I wrote it' (p. 35), to uncover what I maybe already know but need to see written down, to drift with illuminations of the shadows. So, with ideas of how I might move towards generating a multiplicity of understanding play, I (re)read Trueit's text and Hand (1988) explicates the approach I will take.

In discussing the philosophical difference between Deleuze and Foucault, Hand (1988) notes that 'both Deleuze and Foucault recognize that the relationship between their work resembles the *partial and fragmentary relationships* between theory and practice that can no longer be understood in terms of totalization' (p. xlii, italics added). He presents a series of 'de-individualizing principles' that Foucault identifies in Deleuze's work, one of these being: 'Develop action, *thought, and desires by proliferation, juxtaposition, and disjunction, and not by subdivision and pyramidal hierarchization*' (p. xlii, italics added). Reading more of Trueit (2002), I sense a relationship, (im)partial and fragmentary, between our philosophies of curriculum, ways of thinking, style of writing and communication of ideas. Within conventional realms of academe, she is undoubtedly my superior, and although we have neither met nor spoken, a few email communications assure me she is not party to pyramidal hierarchies. There is also a sense that to (re)view her article, 'Play which is more than play', in the usual (linear) way will not satisfy my desire for proliferation as I work to intensify the rhizoanalysis that constitutes this rhizo book~assemblage.

So, to avoid analysing or isolating fragments of her lyrical text, resonating with the spirit of her writing, I transpose the words that speak to me into a *poietic* format, juxtaposing my commentary alongside. It is a play-full negotiation of her work, a way of opening (her) ideas to a rhizo understanding of children's play.[3] Mostly the punctuation is as in Trueit's text but occasionally I cut a sentence short; mostly the sentence structure is the same but in a few instances I trim words from the beginning of a sentence; I omit her citations to optimize the lyricism and minimize disruptions to the flow;[4] and centring the text disturbs a linearly focused reading. By virtue of what I have included and what I have left out, the *poiesis* inevitably reflects my subjective, (im)partial understanding of her text – 'Are we not subject to our own limited "understandings" as we impose our interpretations on others?' (Smitherman Pratt, 2006: 91). Another (re)reading on another day and I might change what is/not included – 'understanding is always changing, in flux, continually being renewed' (p. 93). This (re)reading/writing is processual; I have no idea before doing it what might be uncovered, what understandings might emerge. To the fore is the urge to step aside from the dreary writing of ordinary academic prose, to *po(i)etically* enact 'a threshold occasion: a moment of ecstasis when something moves away from its standing as one thing to become another'.[5] Bringing Trueit's and my texts alongside one another phrase by phrase, I work to illuminate complex relations of these texts, and others, by playing with the idea of playing with Trueit's text, attentive to spaces of possibilities in-between. It is a play-full and I hope thought-provoking (ad)venture with writing as a method of inquiry (Richardson & St. Pierre, 2005), towards understandings incipiently different, about something I/we all assume to know – 'We all know "play," don't we?' (Trueit, 2006: 97) – because of my/our own childhood experiences.

To open a previously unseen reading, what follows is a *poiesis* of Trueit's text on the left with my commentary on the right. As I (re)orient my thinking, away from linearity, a stuttering of (re)thinking~(re)reading~(re)writing coalesces as a multiplicity. The following 'rhizo-imaginary' (Sellers, 2008) becomes a way of negotiating (through) the multiplicity, negotiating (with) Donna,[6] as nomad(s). What follows is a *rhizopoiesis* commingling Donna's and my ideas, working with/ as nomad and rhizome, generating a flowing affect of bodies in-between – a body of texts, a body of ideas, a virtual social body of Donna and me – towards disrupting conventional ideas about play. This reading~writing~thinking conversation is perceptible, abstractly and with/in the actual, as a 'vertical dimension of intensities' (Foucault, 1977, cited in Hand, 1988: xliv).[7]

Mythopoesis of play Play-fully engaging with Donna Trueit's (2006) writing about 'Play which is more than play', in which *I* is Donna	A rhizo-poiesis: Children's play(ing) of games
Much has been written about play from various disciplinary perspectives, about the value of play, its relationship to child development and to learning.	The preceding overview of understandings of play illuminates various work(ing)s of the concept of play. In these, developmental approaches are mediated by sociocultural critiques, but modernist thinking pervades.
We all know 'play' don't we?	The assumption that everyone knows about play is foregrounded here by Trueit's facetious question, to which I respond in kind: Of course we all do/n't know about play. Trueit's question points to the tendency to trivialize 'play'. Play goes hand-in-hand with western conceptions of childhood and all adults have passed through (graduated from?) childhood. What more is there to know or be said about it? We played. Play happened. So what?

Why search for new meanings?

Subjectively affected by *my* childhood experiences of play, I bring my scholarly understandings in to the play of play-fully responding to this question. In working (with/through) this mythopoesis, I am alert for re-newed ways of re-thinking play.

I [Donna] hope not only to open up
modernist habits of thought,
but also to suggest that
play might be the organizing principle
of a discursive practice.

Like Trueit, I want to disrupt the modernist agenda that pervades and suggest how we might (re)think play, so I again transpose her ideas, this time from poem into scholarly discourse. In the poem slip-sliding alongside, I map Trueit's ideas; now, in this juxtaposition, I plug the tracing back into the map in a (re)shaping of my thinking; in (re)thinking the poetical (re)reading of her text.

Note: Discursive practices shape, and
are shaped by thought.

As the organizing principle of
mythopoetic (primarily oral) discursive
practices,

I consult the *OED* for a definition of mythopoetic and find it used in reference to Māori: *1. = MYTHOPOEIC adj. 1914 Jrnl. Royal Anthropol. Inst. 44 139. It is clear that the ancestors of the Maori* [sic]*, in common with other races, strove to fathom the unfathomable...The above is part of the result, ideas evolved by a mythopoetic people* (*OED*, Online).[8]
Striving to fathom the unfathomable – not least in Māori navigating to Aotearoa New Zealand and back again many times over,
talking ideas into be(com)ing through storytelling or becoming-myth. What I am attempting here in a mythopoetic gesture?

play signifies recursive relations,
dynamics, and liminality
characteristic of an open system of
representation,

I engage with Trueit's projected flow of movement through play – read play ambiguously here, as performance and as constantly changing movement – with recursivity, intra-active systems,

one that has far greater complexity
than the modernist practices of
representation
that continue to hold us captive.

speed and flow, thresholds in-between, openings.
Complex, and hard to shake off modernist trappings of representation – language, discourses and the notion of representation itself. Biesta and Osberg (2007) outline complexity's challenge to representation: a static, passive, or representational view of knowledge relies on a binary understanding, 'which holds that the world is simply present in and of itself and that we can acquire knowledge of it…[a] binary logic of representational epistemology…that there is a real world that knowledge somehow reflects' (p. 24); 'that knowledge is an accurate representation of something that is separate from knowledge itself' (Osberg, Biesta, & Cilliers, 2008: 213). Rather, knowledge and reality 'are part of the same emerging complex system which is never fully "present" in any (discrete) moment in time' (p. 213). These authors call this 'emergence'. Emergence explicates active and adaptive understandings 'towards questions about engagement and response' (p. 213), releasing us from modernist captivity, opening (to) sites of emergence.

In modernist discursive practices one
observes play,
objectifies play as a 'thing' or an
'event',
and represents 'play' definitely.
However,
modernist discursive practices are
(1) very different than the dominant
discursive practices that preceded
them; and
(2) these prior practices probably
cannot be fully appreciated

In the preceding review about play, pervasive modernist practices linger. 'Play' is under scrutiny as Ailwood's (2003) analysis disrupts long held relatively simplistic and naïve understandings, bringing other agenda out of the shadows.
But, play is still objectified as something that happens, as an experiential event and an eventful experience, albeit with poststructuralist leanings. Alternatively, Trueit's engagement

from our now too distant stance.
[But,]
we can *speculate* – and it is necessary
for us to do so,
because in regard to 'methods of representation and the recasting of meaning'
there have been
'universes of thought evolving into
other universes of thought'.

with cosmological ideas that precede
modernism, although distant and
speculative, opens an oscillation
through past~present~future space-
times or universes of thought. A
change from always thinking forward
in relation to the not-so-distant past; a
change towards thinking differently?
Beyond representation; thinking emergence? Beyond before?

Due to the recasting of meaning,
I am led to consider the implications of
another meaning
of play as 'the play',
as in theatrical performance,
as an acted re-presentation of a story.
I speculate that the play is not the thing
itself,
but rather,
the play is a site of far greater
complexity,
a *nexus*, or perhaps, a *temenos*,
in Ancient Greek thought 'a sacred
space within which special rules apply
and in which extraordinary events are
free to occur'.

Epistemology addressed, play(ing) with
play(ing) becomes the conversation and
a linkage appears to children playing
their imaginary games (of playing) and
the games they play (the play), particularly those informed by children's literature, the media and popular culture.
So the game is not perceived as the
thing itself but as a site of emergence,
a milieu of various becomings, spaces
of convergence and (con)fusion. As
children and games converge, adults
may see only confusion among/within
children's games (in early childhood
settings). Yet, the *temenos* or space-
times of early childhood requires educationists' respect for the children and
their understandings played out in their
games. Along with the children, we
must expect the unexpected and accept
the surprise of its occurrence within this
play-site of complexity.

The play is not just the play: it is much
more.
And it is the 'more-ness' in this sacred
space of play
I wish to bring forward:
the staging of cultural education
(*paedeia*)
leading to creativity and
transformation.

So…the play is not just the play; the
play is not just the game; the game is
not just the play; the game is not just
the game. More-ness or *and…and…
and* is foregrounded within the
paedeia of the setting.

The *OED* (Online)[9] elaborates *paedeia*
thus: *1904 S. H. BUTCHER Harvard*

In this place, in this ancient time,
the play was not just entertainment it
was education;
recreation was for re-creation.

*Lect. on Greek Subj. ii. 124 The Greek
Paideia (ΠΑΙΔΕΙΑ) in its full sense
involves the union of intellectual and
moral qualities. It is on the one hand
mental illumination, an enlarged
outlook on life; but it also implies a
refinement and delicacy of feeling, a
deepening of the sympathetic emotions, a scorn of what is self-seeking,
ignoble, dishonourable – a scorn bred
of loving familiarity with poets and
philosophers, with all that is fortifying
in thought or elevating in imagination.*

The creativity and alterity characteristic of milieu(s) of children's games
emerge through/with such understandings of the culture of the setting in
all its complexity. Becoming-something different is perceptible in the
(re)creation that happens through the
game and its play(ing). Entertainment
and education; play and learning are
mutually constitutive and their conjunction alters both (De Castell & Jenson, 2003).

In this sacred space of play
extraordinary events occur.
Energy flows through all things,
bringing contiguity.
The free play of forces brings in to
relations:
players [the children];
time
[of past, present and future relationships and games (to be) played];
senses: speaking, hearing, seeing,
feeling;
and inter-subjectivities
[fairytale and popular culture heroes
and heroines].

Yet, is this extraordinary, considering the complexity of this play-site?
And, considering the chaos of energy,
forces, players, time, senses, intra-
active relations of subjectivity?
Toscano (2005) explains chaos in
Deleuzian understandings as infinite
speed of forms and entities emerging and disappearing simultaneously
leaving no points of reference. So,
as energy ebbs and flows through
both children and their games,
(im)perceptible borders/~~borders~~ are
crossed over and crossed out and the
free play of forces –the play or movement of what happens between forces
– becomes an(other) affect. Children

as players within games merge within human and material relations: as they relate to one another and brush alongside others' relations with others; remembering past relations and present affects, experiencing relations of the now, envisaging relations as they may be in the future... *and*... into the chaos of in-between spaces come memories of games already played... *and*... energy of present games and expectations of what these games may/will become. The children bring their senses into play as they negotiate relationships and the storyline of their game, drawing characters in and drawing from the characters as they are played out.

There is a flowing together
that forms an unbroken sequence in time
and uninterrupted expanse in space.
There is a dynamic system of patterns and transformation
that 'makes it possible to deal with unresolvable differences and contradictions'
in a relational manner.
Recognizing patterns and rhythms.
Recognition by 'patterns of resemblances'
means that of *bundles* of relations must be seen
rather than one set of relations,
or isolated events.
While all situations are contextual, one is,
in a mythopoetic culture,
looking at *an* event as a bundle of relations over time.

Children within games flow together, sometimes together and sometimes multidirectionally. The storyline may not emerge as expected by any/all of the players and in that sense it is disrupted. In another sense, as long as the game continues it is unbroken. But, even if/when time intervenes (e.g. tidy-up time or home time), the games most often only pause, to be taken up the next day or soon after... *and*... when the play-space is interrupted, the game is likely to erupt in another play-space, similar or altered. Patterns and rhythms of play within games and of games seem tacitly understood by the players. With practice, through generating the data and working with it, these become perceptible. Play can be seen as a heterogeneous bundle of relations, ideas and understandings that have 'merged and collided over time' (Ailwood, 2003: 295), constantly oscillating.

This backwards and forward looking
marks the threshold of play,
for in this culture, the play,
as a sacred *temenos*
where extraordinary events are free to
occur,
insists on the flow of dynamical
interactions.

In the oscillation, the constant moving
backwards and forwards through the
storyline of the game now and through
reflections of storylines already
played, thresholds are glimpsed in
stop~start moments as games and
players turn ebbs into flows. Perhaps
it is more of a fibrillation, a quivering
of uncoordinated movement(s)? In
liminal spaces of the games and their
playing, intra-active flows (e)merge.

The dynamic flow of play is
complicated,
but the energy might be thought of
deriving from the use of language
(which is why I suggest play is the
organizing principle
of mythopoetic discursive practices).

Play and its playing are complex
and its energy is illuminated in the
children's talking their way through
storylines. Play, I suggest, is also
a methodology, a way of children
expressing complex understandings
and a way of opening those understandings to adults. But, immediately
I think of cultural lore: inasmuch as
anthropology may want to understand
the lore of ~~other~~ cultures, why does it
assume that other/ed cultures might
want to share their understandings?
Just because adults want to know,
doesn't necessarily mean children
want to tell. But, we can be(come)
with them in their curricular spaces.
Perhaps we need to (re)learn to play,
in adult space-times and with children.
If we want children to work in shared
spaces towards shared understandings,
why not share their play(ing), engaging in their play-full activity? Why not
(re)learn play(ing)?

The audience members are drawn out
of themselves,
their energy flowing outward,
towards the events enacted on stage,
reacting to the performance;
and energy from the performer is
absorbed,

So, adult-outsiders become part of
the audience but must be willing to
be drawn into the play and the game,
towards the players, responding to
the playing. We see other parts of the
audience playing their part, players of
bordering games becoming part of the

drawn into,
as the viewer receives this version of
the tale.

This active engagement and
participation,
giving and receiving,
attention and reflection,
is part of *paideia*,
being drawn into oneself,
drawn continuously forward.
Each performer and participating
viewer
allows him or herself to be drawn in to
the movement
and find the play,
the slip, in a situation,
to be in the movement,
and to work with the movement,
to find – to *create* – variations.

But there are multiple sites of play in
the play,
and the flow of reflexivity and
reflection
infuses all,
permeating individuals with cultural
values of creating,
perhaps even creating as an ethical
responsibility
– creating *self*.

Self in this sense is not an object,
but rather seems almost another site of
play,
of reflexivity, reflection and
connection,
with the other and with tradition.

energy as the games brush alongside one another, merge and collide, in response to the performativity of players of other games. The energy melds; energy of the game and its players and energy of outsiders and the exteriority of the milieu. Each understands the game in her/his own way.

Players interact with the exteriority, aspiring singularly and severally to the multiplicity of the *paedeia*, players oscillating through inside and outside, so the inside becomes the outside, insider becomes outsider, inside(r)~outside(r). Drawn into the movement or the machinic play of the play, into the liminality of play's constant motion.

Play(ing) with/in the slip. Here the storyline (e)merges, in response to what has already happened, responding to creations of the players, to players' creativity. And, I am glimpsing an emerging storyline around 'play'.

In the multiplicity of the milieu, of playing in the games, of the games in play, the children collectively and collaboratively negotiate their storyline(s), in an ethics of processing through their own becoming, and merging and colliding with others in their becoming. Becoming-child/ren (e)merging.

Not being a particular some*one*. Be(com)ing something different. Becoming-child, singularly and severally. Becoming-children, different, yet understandable within the lore of the *paedeia*.

Gadamer (1998: 103–9) associates play with performance and the dynamism of play with creating self.
He says:

The movement of playing has no goal that brings it to an end;
rather, it renews itself in constant repetition.
The movement backward
and forward
is obviously so central to play that it makes no difference
who or what performs this movement.

The player is subsumed by the play, playing without purpose or effort, absorbed into the structure of play, and relaxed by it.
First and foremost play is self-representation. All presentation is potentially a representation for someone.
Play before an audience becomes
the play
and
openness toward the spectator is part of the closedness of the play.
The audience only completes what the play as such is:
a process that takes place 'in between'.

Play does not have its being in the player's consciousness or attitude, but on the contrary play draws her/him into its dominion and fills her/him with its spirit.

Moving through, moving with, moving in games~playing~becoming-child/ren.

The games are never-ending. They pause only as children tire of negotiating storylines or when the programme says it's time for something else. Like rhizome, they shoot in (an)other moment(s), later, tomorrow, next week. Games keep going, newly different in different moments. For the game to continue, characters and roles shift within moments of movement, within movement of moments. What matters is the game continues.

The game takes over, draws the players in, with no ~~end~~ other than the processual condition. Process *is*. Means and ~~end~~.

Play is about becoming-something differently qualified, in whatever way matters. The gaming (presentation) is about always already becoming-…
Within space-times of the setting and programme, insider~outsider becomes the storyline.
Openness and closed-ness in never ending de~territorializing movement, de~territorializing play (verb/noun), de~territorializing play (adjective/noun), interrelations among insider~outsider players contesting the game and the storyline processing in the in-between. Play – what children do and machinic movement.

The players *become* the game, both develop into and are accepted as the game and enhance the game.

The player experiences
the game as a reality that surpasses
her/him
all the more the case where the
game is itself 'intended' as such a
reality –
for instance,
the play which appears as presentation
for an audience.

The game and its storyline become more than the collective contributions of the players.
It becomes a milieu, an 'interior milieu of impulses and exterior milieu of circumstances' (Deleuze & Guattari, 1987: 317).

Each performative occasion is an opportunity to create,
to reinterpret and to grow through the experience.
The extraordinary occurrence of play, the 'more-ness'.
derives from the powerful dynamism of relations and interactions,
the circumstances for the emergence of the new
and for transformation.

Becoming-(something different), becoming-(…)

There is no playing down the complexity of play, of play as movement. Elusive, indefinable, dynamically changing, (e)merging.

This semantic play does not provide a neologism for *play*,
a word – like 'spirit' – that defies defining.
It presents only a speculative re-description
of play as dynamic flow
through which systems – cosmological, mythological, human, and natural –
are transgressed,
transcended,
and transformed.

However, these semantics have not overwritten or over-played play with any newly coined expression. Play and play(ing) escape concretizing. But, a way of thinking play differently – finding a way beyond thinking of play as thing or event and thinking of play verbally, as dynamism and movement, as a milieu of becoming. 'Becoming is the pure movement evident in changes *between* particular events…[It is] a characteristic of the very production of events. It is not that the time of change exists between one event and another, but that every event is but a unique instant of production in a continual flow of changes evident in the cosmos. The only thing "shared" by events is their having become different in the course of their production' (Stagoll, 2005: 21–2, original italics).

Play, as the organizing principle of
discursive practices
or re-presentation (re-enactment) in
Ancient Greece,
blows open
the tight
and constraining
discursive practices of representation
in modernity.

But then, we all know about 'play',
don't we?

Following Trueit's playing mythopo-
etically with play, I would approach
discourses of play play-fully. I would
blow open the modernist representation of the centrality of play to supposed developmentalist advantage. I
would work to disrupt thinking that
considers play as governmentality, and
more. I would present a *rhizopoietic*
offering of play as a machinic assemblage, a milieu of becoming... *and*... I
would not pretend to know anything
about play as children understand
it until I (re)learn to be a player as
children are in their childhoods, until
I (re)learn to play as children do. Sutton-Smith (1997) says: 'We all play
occasionally, and we all know what
playing feels like' (p. 1). But, do we?
It is like drawing and painting; when
we stop doing it, we forget, we stop
learning how to do it. When we stop
playing, we stop learning how to do it;
we stop learning what play(ing) is; we
stop understanding play(ing).

Rhizopoiesis

This *rhizopoiesis* is a play-full (ad)venture of juxtaposing Donna's~my understandings to perturb the linearity of conventional academic writing and the page.
Continuing the play (as performativity, game and constantly changing movement),
I recursively and speculatively (re)turn to (re)negotiate the (re)reading. Processing
as nomad through a generative space of possibilities with/in the doubled rhizopoietic mapping, the juxtaposing of my commentary alongside a play-fully poetic
version of Trueit's article becomes a virtual collaboration of an actual palimpsest
in a commingling of artistic material, to open through poetry another iteration of
play(ing). Feminine écriture, in this moment exemplified by the works of Trueit
(2006) and Richardson (1992), opens to other *poietic* readings. Coetzee (2007)
writes that the 'masters [sic] of information have forgotten about poetry, where
words may have a meaning quite different from what the lexicon says, where
the metaphoric spark is always one jump ahead of the decoding function, where
another, unforeseen reading is always possible' (p. 23). In this doubled, if not multiple reading~writing~reading, my preference for difference, flows and mobile

arrangements is illuminated, in the process transgressing uniformity, unities and systems. Also, with/in this gesture of 'disjunctive affirmation' (Hand, 1988: xliv), non-sedentary, nomadic productivity is made perceptible.

In play-fully engaging *rhizopoietically* with play which is more than play, the (ad)venture is with disrupting the idealization of children's play that pervades much of play theorization and with interrupting order and rationality towards a Deleuzo-Guattarian affective reading that defies ownership, colonization and specific positionality. In this affective register, while play(ing) is not thought-less (Harker, 2005), neither does it prioritize non-cognitive, physical, emotional processes; instead, it opens (to) possibilities for a-rational, a-ordered processing to (e)merge. This averts a modernist, civilizing tendency 'to take away play's muddy complexity and reduce it to some kind of pure fun, pure intrinsic moti-vation, pure flow, rid of all encumbrances' (Sutton-Smith & Magee, 1989: 54) and also turns away from ways of controlling it – both children's play(ing) and theorizing about it. Continuing with the complexity, aware that I risk concretizing anew children's play(ing), in the closing words of this plateau, I present play as intensities of becoming.

(re)conceiving play as intensities of becoming

What comes to the fore in the play of ideas above is that play is not so much thing or event but movement, with/in/through which change occurs, continually. Gadamer (1982) considers play as 'the to-and-fro movement which is not tied to any goal which would bring it to an end' (p. 93) such as in 'the play of light, the play of waves, the play of the components in a bearing case, the inner play of limbs, the play of forces, the play of gnats, even a play on words' (p. 93). This sense of play as light and constantly changing movements generates an openness as the movement of the play becomes somewhat indescribable, indefinable – an elusive mo(ve)ment. This may go some way towards explaining difficulties in defining the play that children do. Hodgkin (1985) suggests that in human play '[o]penness is incorporated within a larger system so that the whole system may function without breakdown under the probable range of stresses to which it may be subject' (pp. 27–8). Through this openness of potential space, of a 'time-space field – a field which is open to the future' (p. 28), play continues. In Deleuzo-Guat-tarian understandings, children's play(ing) happens in this kind of potential space as a machinic assemblage. In such potential, liminal spaces an intensity of forces operates, these forces being 'the *relation between* forces' (Boundas, 2005: 131, italics added). In all these understandings, it is the play in-between that generates movement – if there is insufficient play, things seize, nothing happens.

In a machine, it is ball bearings moving that create the play, the balls moving every which way against one another, generating a play of forces in-between. This movement of forces at play is like the machinic assemblage of children's play – unavoidably elusive, constantly in motion, moving multidirectionally, never-endingly multidimensional, always already becoming-intensities of liminality.

The sketch of play becoming spandrel pictures (Figure 6.1), a way of imag(in)ing this between-ness or liminality. Here the play of movement of machinic forces opens to spaces that spandrels create. Play and spandrel simultaneously move with/in/to opportune space-time moments between.

A spandrel is the area between the curves of adjoining arches and the horizontal between the tops of each arch, or ceiling; it exists *with* arch *and* ceiling; on its own it is nothing. Play as spandrel is a multiplicity of the operations of children, games, context, and artefacts. Like spandrel, play cannot exist in isolation as a particular thing. Neither is play an event or a happening even; it is a 'hap', a 'watershed moment', a 'happenstance', which attends to the 'unexpected consequence…[of] sudden insight…The hap may be anticipated…but will more likely be a matter of happenstance' (Davis, 1996: 257). Play as hap and happenstance of mo(ve)ments is constantly changing in spaces among children, their intra-activity, the imaginative and physical territories that they operate within, characters of games and artefacts at hand – all existing only in relation to (an)other(s), nothing without others; like spandrel and mechanical play.

It now appears that turning back in on itself – a process of eversion – the elusiveness of mo(ve)ments of mechanical play and spandrel spaces makes perceptible the machinic movement and space-times of children's play, thus interrupting any defining frustration about what play is not. A mathematical artwork – a sculpture of eversion – (Figure 6.2) provides imagery that resonates with the machinic assemblage of children's play(ing) as 'inside out' and 'outside in' mo(ve)ments through storylines, characters, roles, themes, physical territories and relationships of their games. The sculpture shown here demonstrates how drawing out an inside reshapes as an outside of the same form; an inside out and outside in turning back on/into itself. As with de~territorializating mo(ve)ments of play(ing), inside and outside simultaneously become the other.

Eversion, then, invites a generative reading of Sutton-Smith and Magee's (1989) notion of play as reversibility, which they conceive as a world turned upsidedown.

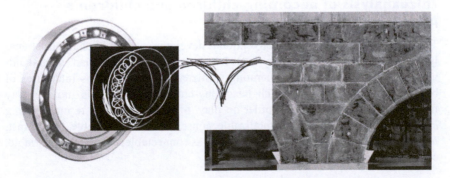

Figure 6.1 Play (movement in-between) becomes spandrel (spaces in-between) (image by Warren Sellers)

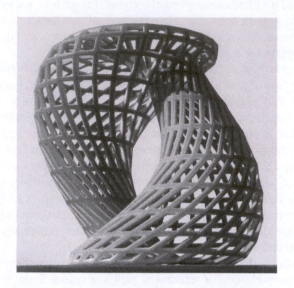

Figure 6.2 Picturing eversion~turning inside out (sculpture and image by Professor Carlo H. Séquin, University of California, Berkeley, see http://www.cs.berkeley.edu/~sequin/ART/AMS_MathImagery/Torus-Eversion_Halfway-Point.jpg)

In its complexity, 'the world of play…is…both up and upside down at the same time' (p. 60); with/in chaos, order and disorder combine. If children's play(ing) could be imaged, it might look like this image of eversion, like a constantly changing bubble un/re/folding, in/re/e/verting, continually de~territorializing, a multiplicity of multidimensionality at play, always already elusive and intensifying. I imag(in)e play as intensities of becoming, and as becoming-intensities of play.

rhizoanalysis of becoming-children and children's play(ing)

Transgressing and disrupting conventional developmental and behaviourist analysing of children and their play(ing), I turn to Deleuzo-Guattarian understandings of intensities, towards generating a rhizoanalysis of play as intensities of becoming in/through/with which becoming-children work. This moves away from imposing an arborescent order on play, of identifying it in terms of being *extensive* – divisible, unifiable, totalizable, conscious and organizable. In contrast, *intensive* multiplicities are made perceptible as connectable, changeable, variable, communicable, constituted through

> particles that do not divide without changing in nature, and distances that do not vary without entering another multiplicity and that constantly construct

and dismantle themselves in the course of their communications, as they cross over into each other at, beyond, or before a certain threshold.

(Deleuze & Guattari, 1987: 33)

Intensities grow inwards and outwards all at once amassing as conglomerations that both spread and become more dense, entangling in an 'asymmetrical block of becoming, an instantaneous zigzag' (p. 278), such as becoming-child(ren) becoming-intense becoming-(im)perceptible. But, how to perceive what is imperceptible? Deleuze and Guattari say that we perceive the imperceptible through movements of difference, not in relations between points but in the middle between: 'Look only at the movements' (p. 282). By not focusing on the objects of our gaze things can be more perceptible. For example, not looking directly at but focusing one's gaze alongside the constellation Mātāriki (Pleiades) in the night sky makes it easier to see with the naked eye. Not focusing on developmental, behaviourist perspectives of children's play(ing) that try to pin play down, opens possibilities for perceiving something incipiently different within the shadows.

The transcription used here of the video-recorded snippet of Maria, Fleur and Lucy playing together, makes perceptible the intensity of their play(ing). From my outsider view the speed of the flow leaves an impression of total disorder as they drift through a scenario that makes little sense, other than it seems that Maria has an agenda of control and in various ways the others are willing to play along. But this is a pervasive developmental analysis and, as I open to the complexity at play, a more generative reading emerges. This generativity continues through the rhizoanalysis as I work towards furthering possibilities of (im)perceptibility of the happenings – a hap of becoming-imperceptible becoming-child(ren) becoming-intense. The game seems to take on a life of its own and I have difficulty in keeping up with the play, but as I engage with the chaotic flow, it becomes an a-ordered intensity with a complex storyline albeit beyond the total comprehension of a non-player. Through the next 17 minutes, the game flows rapidly, the game overtaking and taking over the players. To avoid being inadvertently caught in positivist assumptions of interpreting meaning through a theoretical analysis (Lather, 1992), I opt for a play-full, spontaneous response. Resisting a seriously fractured behavioural analysis that focuses on cognitive, social and emotional development, I transgress notions of individualized children and illuminate them as simultaneously singular and several. In mo(ve)ments of severalty singular children become perceptible through relations of movement and rest and through their capacity to affect and be affected by the others (Deleuze, 1988). This avoids isolating each child and categorizing their activity. Similarly, disrupting a conventional analysis of pulling things apart in an attempt to see things differently, I work with putting things together in slip-sliding arrangements. Through a differently fracturing move I take a *rhizopoietic* approach to transcribing the data, working with the children's conversation making a complex map of the play(ing), not just a simplified tracing.

A threefold juxtaposition of bringing my commentary alongside the children's conversations from two occasions – Maria, Fleur and Lucy playing a game and later the children watching the video-recorded recording of their game – opens possibilities for the rhizoanalysis to flow as the game does, in slip-sliding ebbs and flows of movement and speed – 'a movement may be very fast, but that does not give it speed; a speed may be very slow, or even immobile, yet it is still speed. Movement is extensive; speed is intensive' (Deleuze & Guattari, 1987: 381). Not breaking the transcription into bits/bytes, but leaving it together with its moments of incoherence that become differently cohesive, not interrupting the movement and speed of this snippet of children's play(ing) becomes an improvisational performance, a happenstance of mis/dis/connections. The juxtaposition opens a provisional~improvisational reading with possibilities for moving through the (im)perceptible liminality of the transcriptions – (a) rhizo-imaginary (Sellers, 2008) – like a painting or poem, where the artist~author presents a creative work for viewers~readers to take from it what they will.

Mo(ve)ments of game, children and juxtaposition are fluid, inconsistent, unpredictable. The extensive~intensive threefold juxtaposition speeds through the wording of the texts in mo(ve)ments of rhizo performativity, unfolding a rhizo storying of data, opening (to) rhizo-reading opportunities of changing reading~writing performativity. As the children's play(ing) of their game plan(e) changes as it passes from one player to another so the juxtaposed reading changes for each reader~reading of the play(ing). The centre column opens a rhizoanalysis of the transcription of the game in the left column with the right column displaying more of the data, namely of Maria and Fleur watching the video of themselves playing. Sited/cited thus, the children's conversations both open and close the reading, the data here used differently, performatively, not to support the analysis (Lather, 1992). While each of the transcriptions constitutes some of the rhizoanalysis, they are singular, each telling some of the severalty of the story. Together they make perceptible the intensity of the game, simultaneously working to intensify adult understandings of the play(ing).

Much of Maria and Fleur's conversation is in dramatized, sing-song voices, used to express the various characters they are playing; when in this mode, their conversation is transcribed in *Arial font*. When they are confirming the processing of the storyline, they speak in ordinary voices (marked by Times New Roman). I provide minimal details of their movements to explain the physical flow of the game, leaving their conversations to tell a story of their play(ing). I note that in transcribing the (re)playing of their game, I am aware of the dominance of my comments and questions, inappropriately driven by a pervasive, adult(erated) desire to make meaning despite being aware at the time that the children were intent on watching, not conversing. (See the discussion of researcher~participant power-fullness in the *Becoming-child(ren) becoming-power-full* plateau.)

Maria and Lucy are in their home in the family corner. Fleur is in the adjacent kitchen/shop. Adam is playing by himself in the kitchen. In the play(ing) Fleur and Maria slip-slide through character roles, narrator and clarifying the storyline, indicated by voice changes. In the review session, the (re)playing, the storyline of the game is elusive as it moves rapidly through various themes; a plan(e) marked and constituted by changing characters.

The game	Rhizo interaction	(Re)playing the game
Maria: *Um, bubba, would you like to come to the shop with me? I'll just pretend we're going to get some things.*	First impressions are that Maria is intent on controlling the game and the players; that it is a game designed for the expression of her power-fullness. The game seems a confusion of storylines that Maria is orchestrating and that Fleur and Lucy are happy to play along. Fleur occasionally looks despondent but these moments soon dissolve as she narrates her intentions for the game. Lucy doesn't mind being shut in the wardrobe – she can easily push it open – and seems happy in her explicitly passive role. It is Maria who is often agitated, mostly expressing annoyance at Fleur's participation in the game. But this is reading like a behaviourist analysis…	MS: *Now you're in the family corner. Maria's telling you what to do.*
Fleur: *And I'll do, I'll be the shop.*		Fleur: *Bossing me around.* (grins). *I wanna go back to the thing where it was funny because that was the best part.*
Maria phones Fleur: *Ring ring. Ring ring. Are you shutting yet?*		MS: *We'll watch the funny bit later. Let's carry on from here…OK we'll watch it once more.*
Fleur: *No, I'm I'm I'm I'm the, ring ring, um I am the I'm the office and I'm not I'm the shop I'm not I I'm I'm the shop.*		They all do puzzles while 'watching' the video.
Maria: *OK, bye, thanks. We'll be there soon as we can, OK? Bye.*		MS: *…now we're in the shop. Lucy's being the baby? What are you calling her (to Maria), Bubba or something?*
Maria and Lucy go to the kitchen/shop.		Maria (looks up): *Yeah. Oh, she'll like Bubba.*
Maria: *Oh hello, nice to see…do you have any beef or yoghurt or anything to buy?*		MS: *Aahh. And here's Maria ringing up the shop lady. 'Ring ring,' you said. What are you trying to find out? I think you were trying to find out whether they were still open.*
Fleur: *No we don't. We've got these things in here. You need this for your bubba?*		
Maria: *No no no.*	In a generative reading, the game and the players are an assemblage, distinguished not by form or function but by 'movement and rest, slowness and speed'. These ebbs and flows of movement and speed subordinate 'forms of structures' and 'types of development' (Deleuze & Guattari, 1987: 254–5), such as structures of conventional,	Maria: *Yeah.*
Maria puts toy food items in her bag.		MS: *And Fleur said that she was…the office?*
Fleur: *Can you just sing and don't talk. Yup. And then tell me that crazy thing and then I'll ring up something more.*		Fleur: *Yeah.*
Maria hands money to Fleur: *Here you*		MS (to Fleur): *What does that mean?*

go. (voice change) And you give me that back.

Fleur: No just say this is another money thing.

Maria, back at home: Bubba? Get in. This is your bed. Maria shuts Lucy in the wardrobe. And you can, Bubby, come out, jump out. Now. Today I need to go get some mushrooms…I'm going to take this. Maria selects a bag.

Maria, in shop: I'm having guests…um I need…

Fleur: No my time is shut.

Maria: No go to the next-door neighbours'.

Fleur: Oh yeah.

Maria: Um hello next-door neighbours um we have to go to the [...] and we didn't bring enough food so can we, so can we have food?

Fleur: No-o, the shop's closing down.

Maria: No! No! Fleur! You're not the shop person, you're a next door neighbour, OK. Fleur: Um give me, um you're supposed to give me some money. Maria, going back to her home: I'll just get my money. (back in shop) Now here you go. (voice change) I'll pay you back.

behaviourist views of children's play and psycho/social developmental views of children. The oscillating rapidity and slowness with which Maria negotiates the storyline constitutes her as a multiplicity, connecting the infiniteness of her becoming-child to the complexity constituted by relations with the others, all simultaneously involved in becomings-child(ren). When disjunctions occur in their connecting, these are more like jumps in/of moments that 'do not arrive on time, or arrive after everything is over' (p. 255), these mis-takes or ruptures becoming part of the game plan(e). Maria is often frustrated by the mis/dis/connecting. Fleur works (with) it.

Lucy's involvement is a doubled performance. She is included in the play(ing) but the subject positioning that she adopts silence her – as baby, she cannot talk and has decisions made for her. Yet, as becoming-Lucy, she is active in her complicity. Deleuze and Guattari (1987) say:

Fleur: No I was shopping…

Lucy is watching the TV, Maria and Fleur are doing puzzles. What were you using for money?

Maria: Ah, food. It was fake money.

MS: Now you're back home…where's Lucy…So that was Lucy's bed in the cupboard? Ooooh…(Lucy looks up.) What was it like in the cupboard?

Lucy says nothing and goes back to the puzzle.

MS: Is it scary?

Zoe: It is scary in the beginning.

Maria: No-o.

Zoe: It is scary in the cupboard.

MS to Lucy: Did you mind being shut in? Lucy grins at Maria.

Zoe: That's scary.

MS to Zoe: Do you get shut in the cupboard sometimes? Zoe doesn't reply.

Maria replies: No.

MS: Why not?

Maria: I'm the mother.

MS: When you're playing in the family corner does Lucy shut you in the cupboard sometimes?

Maria shakes head: No no. I don't like

I'll pay you first, OK?
Fleur: I'll just give you some...this...
Maria: No don't like bread today. I'll have this.

Fleur: Want this?
Maria: No thank you.
Fleur: Brrngbrrnng. Brrngbrrnng.
Maria, in home: Oh no! Cos we haven't got any food and Bubba ated all the things. OK then.

Adam, with tray of food: Bubby?
Maria: Bubba's over there.
Fleur enters the home space and grabs the tray: No no no no no. I'll give it to her. (then to Maria) That's Bubba's food.
Maria: Oh thank you. Bubba, that's for you. (hands tray to Lucy, seated in wardrobe – voice change) Just pretend you don't like that pepper bread. (voice change) You like that? Um sorry Bubba didn't like the pepper bread. So she won't have that.
Maria (to Lucy): Aah, just pretend you are sick. Um, now... (gets doctor's bag off shelf)
Fleur comes back with tray: Baby girl, there's some parsnip.

To every relation of movement and rest, speed and slowness grouping together an infinity of parts, there corresponds a degree of power. To the relations composing, decomposing, or modifying an individual there correspond intensities that affect it, augmenting or diminishing its power to act; these intensities come from external parts or from the individual's own parts. Affects are becomings. (p. 256)

In her silence, Lucy affects a power-fullness of her own as becoming-child becoming-Lucy becoming-intense becoming-imperceptible.

When Fleur refuses Maria's overbearing tendencies, the game plan(e) does not totally fail, it merely falters, 'for there is a way in which the failure of the plan(e) is part of the plan(e) itself' (p. 259). The game, with a life of its own, takes over – the game plan(e) is infinite:

being in the cupboard.
MS: Lucy doesn't mind being in the cupboard, does she?

MS: What are you doing there, Fleur?
Fleur looks up: Cheese on toast.
Maria: And there's Adam.
MS: What was Adam? You were the mum and Lucy was the baby. And who was Fleur?
Maria: Ahh, the big sister.
MS: And what about Adam? Who was he?
Maria: The papa.
MS: So you had food in your bed. But then you handed it back? Did it taste any good? What was it? (to Lucy) Was it some toast? Oh...

Maria goes back and says the baby doesn't like it? (to Maria) Why didn't she like it?
Maria: Because it had pepper on it. Pepper's too hot for babies.
They are still doing puzzles, not watching the video, talking amongst themselves.
MS: What's Fleur saying?

Maria: *No no. Bubba doesn't like anything. Thanks for that. You already gave her that slice. OK. Bye. I'm, I'm hurrying. I'm going to take Bubba to the doctor. And I'm really late for the plane. So goodbye.* Fleur: *Do you have to bring Bubba to the doctor'? Hey, just say this is the doctor's place.* Maria: *No, that's not... (voice change) Let's go. Oh, I'm going to be late for my appointment.* Fleur: *Did you say I was the doctor?* Maria pushes Fleur: *No! Go! I am the doctor. It'll be an emergency, at the emergency doctor. (voice change) Bubba we're leaving. Here's your bag. You pack all your stuff in that, OK?* Lucy comes out of wardrobe: *I'll do mine.* Maria: *Oh, Bubba, you'll have to hurry up cos we'll miss the plane.* Adam: *Hello there.* Maria: *I'm just late for the plane.* Adam: *What are you doing?* Maria: *I'm just packing all of my stuff cos I'm going home...to...um my place...um...*	...you can start it in a thousand different ways; you will always find something that comes too late or too early, forcing you to recompose all of your relations of speed and slowness, all of your affects, and to rearrange the overall assemblage. (p. 259) With/in moments of dis/mis/connecting, there is a (re)starting, often signalled by 'No!' from Maria or Fleur. As rhizome, the game plan(e) shatters and (re)starts with/on an old line of flight or a new one, processing with de~territorialization. However, despite the apparent conflict between Maria and Fleur now understood as differing timings of the play(ing) or different lines of flight, it is still tempting to perceive Maria as always being 'ahead' of the play and 'ahead' of Fleur, in particular. On the surface, Maria is the leader, but this arborescent, developmental reading of dominance denies that they are several. In rhizo ways, their movements pick up speed in the middle, perhaps making Maria's activity more apparent. Momen-	Maria: *We're being late for the baggage.* MS:....*that's right you went off in a plane.* Fleur: *After we look at this can we go back to the bit where I say 'stupid old goblin'?* MS: *Here's Maria stuffing her bags. She's ready to go. You were going on the plane (to Maria) Where was the plane going to take you?* Fleur: *To the doctors.* Maria: *Yeah.* MS: *Who was sick? Who was the doctor?* Fleur/Maria (simultaneously): *Maria/I was.* MS. To Maria: *You were the doctor? But who was sick, was anyone sick?* Maria: *Lucy.* MS: *Lucy was sick?*

Adam: *Can I look after your house?* Maria: *Yes, yes, thank you.* Maria, *to Fleur and Adam:* Um goodbye. *Well say goodbye, say goodbye to Nana.* (then to Lucy) *Please, Bubba, hurry or we'll be late…* Maria sits on a chair, Lucy follows; Fleur moves to sit on a third chair. Maria: *No no, Fleur. This is the plane.* Fleur: *Well we need a plane ticket and I need to get one.* Adam: *I have to go now.* Maria, gesturing to Adam to sit on the third chair: *No, here's the plane.* Adam: *Where?* Maria: *Here's the plane.* Adam: *Look after my house very well.* Maria: *No no. Get on the plane, on the plane.* Fleur comes back: *Let's say I'm the driver?* Maria: *No, I'm the driver. Brrmmmm.* (then to Lucy) *And you are playing that you are having the other one.* (Maria knows about co-pilots) *Mmmmmm…mmmmmm…*	tarily, she is under the spotlight but not centre stage as a stable, fixed 'I'. She reflects a desiring unconscious of 'we', a multiplicity she (partially) constitutes and is constituted by, with (n)either subject (n)or object constantly dis/connecting. The becomings of all three (plus Adam) interlink in symbiotic, recursive intensities, growing multi-dimensionally in an (e)mergence of incipiently different relations among themselves. As the characters and their subject positionings shift, becoming-Maria~Fleur~Lucy~Adam segue as nomad~monad. There is neither imitation nor resemblance, only an exploding of heterogeneity, of the game plan(e)and becomings-child(ren). The children's play(ing) of their game plan(e) also changes as it passes from one player to another, and possibly the reading for each reader-reading of the play. Mo(ve)ments of game and children are fluid, inconsistent, unpredictable. Maria, Fleur, Lucy and Adam perform	Maria: *No Lucy was ill.* Fleur: *[…] stupid old Goblin. Will you go back to that part?* MS: *So why wasn't Fleur allowed on the plane?* Maria: *It was a doctor plane. Babies and doctors.* MS: *And did you want Adam to be on the plane?* Maria: *Yeah.* MS: *But he didn't want to be the pilot, did he?* Maria: *And I had to be the pilot.* MS: *Fleur wanted to be the pilot.* Maria: *I got to be the pilot.* MS: *The doctor and the pilot. There you go, flying the plane. Oh Lucy's flying it as well.* Maria: *Yeah, co-pilots too. My dad flies planes.* MS: *You got off the plane, where were you?* Maria: *Stuck at the airport.* Fleur: *I want to go back to the stupid*

as rhizome, stretching and intensifying smooth (undefined, undefinable) spaces of game plan(e) and becoming-children, (re)distributing themselves through these spaces. In becoming alert to their morphing (through) characters and segue-ing (through the) storyline, their becoming-imperceptible moves for a moment from the shadows; how it works becomes perceptible, albeit momentarily. This play-full, generative reading enables an out-of-focus, shifting perception of their becomings-child(ren) as several – since each of them is several there is already quite a crowd (Deleuze & Guattari, 1987) – becoming multiplicitous with/in/through nomadic mo(ve)ments. Becoming-child(ren) becoming-child-hoods, intensities of becoming; becoming-child(ren) becoming-imperceptible becoming-intense through their play(ing) and the (re)play(ing).

old goblin. Maria, we're going back to stupid old goblin part.
Maria: Ok.
Fleur: *You better sit here or you won't see the stupid.*
Maria: *Yes I can see from here.*
MS: *So what were you doing here?*
So you were being the doctor now (to Maria). *Was Maria being the doctor, were you playing doctors now?*
Fleur: *I want to see the stupid old goblin part.*
I rewind the tape.
MS: *Can you remember more about the story?*
Fleur: *I thought that the story was about Fairy Topia.* (then grinning) *I know what it was about, it was about Fairy Opia.*
Maria: *No no Fairy Opia, Fairy Topia.*
MS: *What's Fairy Topia? Is that another game you play?*
Maria: *Yeah. Look, there's the silly old goblin part.*
Fleur: *The silly old goblin part. Yeah.*

Fleur moves to sit on third chair.
Maria guards chair: *No...*(voice change) *Mmmmmm...Right then Bubba, get your bag.*
Lucy: *Yep.*
Maria: *Let's go to the train.*
They return to their home.
Fleur: *Why don't, why don't I be the...*
Maria: *No-o-o! I'm the doctor.*
Fleur: *Hey, I'll sit in the bed and we'll see how she goes.* (voice change) *She's very sick and she can't easily get on.*
Maria: *I know.*
Fleur: *She'll have to have a [...].*
Maria (to Fleur): *Um, can you please get off the bed please.* (to Lucy) *Now Bubba, come and lie on this bed. Bubba, come and lie on this bed.* (she then orders) *You're not the doctor! Go!* (voice change) *Now can you go see all the other sick people?*

Following a line of flight the game segues into one of doctors and nurses – becoming-doctors, becoming-nurses, becoming-sick baby...

leaving these play-full intensities to speak for themselves

In this plateau my (ad)venture has been with play-fully generating a rhizome that tells a story of the extensive intensities of children's play(ing) as a multi-dimensional, complex and slippery ludic out-of-the-ordinary happenstance. It is a 'chorus of many voices…a creative pastiche, a *rhizopoiesis*, a "valid" piece of academic writing allowing for the whether of data stories that refuse and exceed containment, confinement, and codification' (O'Riley, 2003: 53), so that the (re)play(ing), transcribing, juxtaposing, (re)reading become 'both data and analysis without succumbing to interpretation' (p. 53). The tripled juxtaposition opens (to) a rhizo reading, as multidimensional happenstances with/in/through the middle extend and intensify the play and its playing, forcing the play plateau to grow outwards (movement is extensive) and simultaneously pushing on further inwards (speed is intensive). In this multiplicitous milieu of becomings glimpses (e)merge of play(ing) as extensive intensities of becoming-child(ren) becoming-intense becoming-(im)perceptible.

Lucy, Fleur and Maria's activity is a generative play(ing) of/with/through constantly changing characters and subject positionings that promote their own expectations for the storyline(s) and respond to one another's. Maria articulately expresses her power-fullness amidst the others; silent Lucy not necessarily acqui-escing, but playing out her understanding of bubba without instruction or resis-tance; Fleur fibrillating through ideas, listening, dis/agreeing, questioning, playing with/amidst rejection. But, it is Fleur's stuttering moment that eloquently tells of the complexity of/at/with/in play(ing). As she searches for words when answering the phone, to say she is not the shopkeeper but the office person, she performs play and playing as fluid, contextual and unresolvable: *No, I'm I'm I'm I'm the Ring ring um I am the I'm the office and I'm not I'm the shop I'm not I I I'm I'm the shop.* The lack of punctuation signals the fluidity of the speedy flow of language, without pause but with a change in intonation (*Ring ring*). With/in a generative reading it is as if the play is going too fast to seize, even momentarily; the play and the playing are elusive…

…which opens to closing this plateau. Play(ing) is elusive, but this is welcome in rhizo thinking: 'Movements, becoming, in other words, pure relations of speed and slowness, pure affects, are below and above the threshold of perception' (Deleuze & Guattari, 1987: 281). Flowing with Deleuze and Guattari, the plan(e) of games and their playing cannot be perceived at the same time as that which they compose or render…so, if play(ing) is intangible, indefinable, indescribable, this plateau can only emerge through a spandrel of adjoining relations of the multiplic-ity of texts, in a play(ing) of data, literature and the children's games and words, which opens to the *Matters of materiality* plateau further on…

Notes

1 School is compulsory for children from six years of age in Aotearoa New Zealand, although they may attend from age five; most children start school at five years of age.
2 This list is not exclusive. It is informed by personal communications (31 October 2012) with: Debi Futter-Puati, ex-Resource Teacher, Learning and Behaviour, who witnessed the demise of free play in new entrants classrooms in one particular area of Aotearoa New Zealand in the mid-1990s; June Anderson, primary teacher since the mid-1970s with extensive teaching experience in the early years of school; Jayne Ngariki, early childhood teacher, who has a knowledge of new entrant class programmes in her locality and remembers 'choosing time' in her early days at school; and Hamish Jones, parent of a five year old currently in a new entrants class.
3 This was a tacit, rhizo move in that I did it before this writing about doing it – the why and how came after the doing.
4 See Trueit's (2006) original text for her citations.
5 See http://en.wikipedia.org/wiki/Poiesis. For more on Poiesis, see Threadgold (1997).
6 Breaking with the academic formality of surnames seems appropriate in this destabilizing mo(ve)ment. With (un)certain familiarity, I continue.
7 This juxtaposed rhizo-poiesis was initially published in Sellers (2009a) (online at: http://ejournals.library.ualberta.ca/index.php/complicity/article/view/8819/7139).
8 See 'mythopoetic' in References.
9 See 'paedeia' in References.

Children playing
rhizo~methodology

Every voyage is intensive, and occurs in relation to thresholds of intensity between which it evolves or that it crosses.

(Deleuze & Guattari, 1987: 54)

nomadic flow

By rhizo~methodology, I mean working within the research as/with rhizome and following a nomadic flow. 'Rhizo' and 'methodology' in this plateau are joined with the tilde to foreground the workings of the co-implicated relations involved; elsewhere I use the term 'rhizomethodology' in respect of this as a research process. In flowing, nomads do not operate in fixed or closed space or follow specified routes, rather in rhizo ways they re-route pathways and narratives of the territory, a literal and figurative talking self into be(com)ing, (re)mapping the map as it is mapped. In this, doing and thinking become (un)doing and (re)thinking through a flow that is simultaneously energy, force and motion; this nomadic flow embodies becoming, heterogeneity, 'passage to the limit' and 'continuous variation' (Deleuze & Guattari, 1987: 363). Flow cannot be determined, only followed, or mapped thus working as nomad is about 'unhinging habitual and reactive thinking, regularity and normalized inscriptions… grow[ing] from the middle, the cracks, the voids, the hyphens, the slashes, and the outcrops…undoing…remapping a different space…a whole new virtual landscape featuring otherworldly affects, always marginal and transversal' (O'Riley, 2003: 29).

Working as nomad, working nomad or doing nomad opens (to) different ways of thinking, moving into spaces without boundaries to dream of other ways of be(com)ing and contemplate what it might mean to realize them. This goes outside a focus on what something might mean, for example, instead foregrounding questions like: How might meaning change? How have some meanings become normalized? How have others disappeared? (Richardson & St. Pierre, 2005: 969). Working nomadically is not about tracing straight paths in thinking, doing and be(com)ing, rather it is 'letting go of conventional wisdom and willful ignorance' (O'Riley, 2003: 21) and thinking outside over-coded (research) processes. The nomad works with de~territorialization (being without boundaries), destratification (being undefined and/or undefinable), and lines of flight (composed of unlimited directions in motion of both thought and thinking) in a trajectory that distributes people in open, indefinite space. In such spaces there are no points, paths, or land even. Rather, the nomad is always already in multidimensional, anti-genealogical, a-centred, non-hierarchical fluxive space with a network of interconnections processing from/through the middle, continually coming and going.

nomad~rhizome

Flowing nomadically with rhizome involves a complex interplay of following lines of flight and passaging through various territories, such as physical and imaginative space of the games children play and the relationships among players. Ceaselessly, more and more connections are generated through the rhizome, assembling as an a-centred milieu of perpetual and dynamic change without specific end or entry points, beginnings or endings. In this smooth space of nomad~rhizome, there are no points or positions, only lines, and working with these lines, as de~territorializing lines of flight, opens (to) possibilities for connecting what otherwise may be regarded as disparate thoughts, ideas and activity. In this way a network of interconnections forms – an amassing of middles amidst an array of multidirectional movement among open systems. Generating this nomad~rhizome assemblage, 'open and connectable in all of its dimensions' (Deleuze & Guattari, 1987: 12), disturbs the arborescently informed, linear, sequential progression of modernist thought and action that is always retraced through the same series of points of structuration and 'always comes back "to the same"' (p. 12).

Tracing (thinking) pathways arborescently, from trunk through branches and leaves, requires coming and going along the same tracks, with a fixed beginning (tips of roots or base of trunk) and ending (tips of leaves). While a tree trunk and branches may expand in length and girth, new pathways are formed only at the tips, and returning along pathways can only occur by re-tracing the route already travelled (Figure 7.1a).

In a burrow – a rhizome (Figure 7.1b) – there are infinite combinations of negotiable pathways through and back again; there is a multiplicity of entryways, which double as exits, with many pathways intersecting and ongoing possibilities for new pathways irrupting among and beyond those that already exist, de/re/territorializing liminal spaces between. (Re)turning to negotiate pathways as nomad~rhizome can happen in infinite ways.

mapping rhizo~methodology

Flowing as nomad~rhizome involves passaging towards never-ending peripheries and in this rhizo nomad flow, mapping rhizo~methodology becomes an activity of continual con/di/vergence of processing around and about, linking, interconnecting through thinking and doing the interminable *and...and...and...* Working to generate a rhizo mapping of the children at play (in the *Children performing curriculum complexly* plateau) it becomes apparent that, as well as rhizo~methodology

Figure 7.1a Arborescent tracing
(photograph by Warren
Sellers)

Figure 7.1b Burrow~rhizome
produced by crustaceans
in the Middle Jurassic
period (http//en.
wikipedia.org/wiki/File:
ThalassinoidesIsrael.JPG)

informing the data, the children show how rhizo~methodology works – they work it and make it work, merging rhizo and methodology into an inseparable multiplicity. There is a flow of rhizo~nomad, an assemblage of game~setting~players. Generating the data with the children, we flow freely through the setting, following lines of flight in a video-ed assemblage of their play(ing). Lines of flight appear within the strong girls game, made perceptible through a multiplicity of video camera operators – Chloe, Abi, Lisa, Libby, Lee, Eve and me. Although this ruptures the flow, new irruptions emerge, enriching the data as moments are captured through many eyes. In this, it becomes apparent that the children and I are no longer ourselves, and it is no longer important who I~we are or who is I~we (Deleuze & Guattari, 1987). In bringing Deleuzo-Guattarian imaginaries to the rhizoanalysis to foreground the children's representations of curricular performativity, I become aware of their tacitly playing out various imaginaries – rhizo mapping their nomadic flow, flowing as nomad, in rhizo ways negotiating smooth spaces. A de~territorializing mo(ve)ment then happens and their rhizo performativity both informs the methodology and illuminates the rhizo~methodology and rhizoanalysis at work. As the methodology informs the data generation, the data inform the rhizoanalysis; what the children are doing in the data shows the workings of the methodology in the rhizoanalysis. Flowing with their curricular performativity makes perceptible the embodiment of their thinking~playing. As in a Mobius strip (Figure 7.2), such de~territorializing mo(ve)ments are on the same

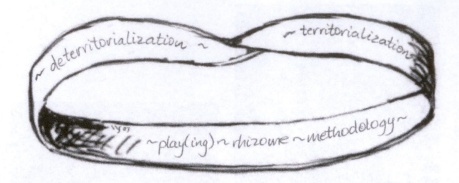

Figure 7.2 De~territorialization, always already at on(c)e on the same plane (drawing by Warren Sellers)

plane, continuously (e)merging; epistemology, ontology, performance, performativity emerge and merge in the play and play of rhizo~methodology.

rhizo~mapping the children's play(ing)[1]

Video snippets of the strong girls game, played out by Libby, Lee and Alice, are captured over two days as they negotiate smooth spaces of the game, their play(ing), their imaginations and the setting. Smooth spaces enable unstructured, non-striated opportunities for the children to work and play, uninterrupted and unhurried, flowing through space-times of setting and programme. Smooth spaces of the play(ing) of the game(s) are illuminated in the performativity of (e)merging storyline(s) – in contrast to a (pre)scribed scripted performance. The strong girls' intention of 'saving the world outside' is a de~territorializing mo(ve)ment as in the game of Go.

Deleuze and Guattari use the game of Go to explain smooth spaces of nomadic de~territorializing lines of flight in contrast to the occupation of the ordered, striated spaces of chess:

> in chess, it is a question of arranging a closed space for oneself, thus of going from one point to another, of occupying the maximum number of squares with the minimum number of pieces. In Go, it is a question of arraying oneself in a open space, of holding space, of maintaining the possibility of springing up at any point: the movement is not from one point to another, but becomes perpetual, without aim or destination, without departure or arrival. The 'smooth' space of Go, as against the 'striated' space of chess…The difference is that chess codes and decodes space, whereas Go proceeds altogether differently, territorializing or deterritorializing it…
>
> (Deleuze & Guattari, 1987: 353)

Rather than capturing the space and eliminating occupiers, as chess does, the Go player encircles the territory and both spaces merge; the outside space is territorialized from within, by territorializing a bordering space. All at once the space is de~territorialized by this sha(tte)ring of ownership of the territory, by renouncing oneself by going elsewhere to further territorialize adjacent territory. And so the flow continues, creating a 'milieu of exteriority' (Deleuze & Guattari, 1987: 353), avoiding battles, battle lines and battles over power; it is about mobility not occupation. As the strong girls negotiate the physical territory indoors and the playground outside and the imaginative territory of their game, they follow de~territorializing lines of flight conversationally and de~territorializing lines of flight within the storyline of their game. They explore folds and surfaces – physical and imaginative – upon which they happen, they slip and slide through discursively intra-active spaces of relations among themselves and the game. Similarly, other children and I flow with the video camera, recording the game and, later, I flow through the video-recorded snippets uncovering resonances between the children's play(ing) and rhizo~methodology.

the strong girls as nomad~rhizome

Flowing as nomad~rhizome through smooth spaces, Libby, Lee and Alice de~territorialize spaces of their game. There is 'a flow of children; a flow of walking with pauses, straggling and forward rushes...a collective assemblage... one inside the other...plugged into an immense outside that is a multiplicity' (Deleuze & Guattari, 1987: 23). Within this multiplicity, involving forty other children, several adults, the physical surroundings, artefacts and the uninterrupted space of the curricular programme of the setting, the children 'space themselves out and disperse...jostle together and coexist...begin to dance' (pp. 23–4) as the game continues to emerge. There is dynamic ebbing and flowing of ideas and energy, as the tracing of their pre-conceived game is continually plugged into the (e)merging strong girls map for saving the world outside, the strong girls game itself (e)merging from/with/in an earlier game of Mums and Dads.

> Libby, Lee and Alice invite Chloe to join their game.
> Libby: *Alice wants to be the little sister. Lee wants to be the big sister and I wanna be the Mum, and you wanna be the baby? 'Cos we're playing Mums and Dads.*
> Chloe listens but says nothing so they abandon that line of flight and follow another, running outside to play the game without her. They skip across the playground, making their way over and through various pieces of climbing equipment and into a large wooden cube.
> Libby: *Hey, this here is our place in here.*
> Lee, climbing into an adjoining cube: *No. No. I know...this could be the house and that could be our bedroom.*

Alice follows Lee and they climb through to join Libby, going with her line of flight in regard to which cube is to be their home. They sit on the ledges inside and discuss where to sleep and the kinds of snoring noises they can make.

They have started up the territory for the Mums and Dads game, but their attention moves to the world outside the game – the videocamera~me. They tell me about their characters and confirm amongst themselves that it is a Mums and Dads *people* game, not Mums and Dads butterflies.

While my presence may have interrupted the flow of their game, the rupture generates an opportunity to confirm the storyline and the characters they each play. Both interiority (inside elements of their game) and exteriority (the outside camera~me) ebb and flow in continual relations with the other. Another i(nter)ruption occurs as Lee reaches to brush some bark chips off Libby's tights; they discuss their clothing and their status in the world.

> Libby: *...hey it looks like looks like we're pretty girls.*
> Lee: *Yeah we're pretty...I'm the prettiest girl in the world.*

Lee's claim goes uncontested; as pretty girls they play together. The imaginary game is merging with actual artefacts and happenings, these merging with their imaginary world as their game emerges. Flowing as nomad~rhizome, they are negotiating their actual and imagined worlds all at once; actual and imagined operate on the same plane in this smooth space, continually (e)merging in different ways. Libby decides it is now morning as they wander around outside their home and inside their game. Suddenly, another de~territorializing line of flight starts up.

> Libby runs up to the others and proclaims: *We better be strong girls!*
> Lee says: *No!* Alice says nothing.
> Libby shouts: *We can be strong girls now...and...WE...CAN...DO...IT!* (punching her arms in the air)...*We have to have maps to see where to go.*
> Despite Lee's objection and Alice's silence, they follow Libby's line of flight and run inside to the drawing table to make maps.

Flowing as nomad~rhizome they have negotiated disparate spaces of ideas and activity – with the Mums and Dads game, its relation to butterflies, interacting with the videocamera~me, discussing their clothing and what matters in terms of being pretty, then segueing from Mums and Dads to strong girls. They continually de~territorialize actual and virtual spaces of their game.

mapping nomad~rhizome flow

These children's use of mapping similarly makes perceptible a tacit understanding of rhizome as they negotiate (e)merging space-times of their game. Always already they are moving through virtual~possible, actualizing~realizing (Deleuze, 1993) mapped spaces: through the map of the imaginary game; through deciding they need to create an actual map; through mapping the next part of their game; through collaborating around their drawn maps. They flow in rhizo ways through (a) Deleuzo-Guattarian milieu(s), negotiating virtual and possible spaces of the game and of the world outside. Mapping becomes a way of affirming the characters they each play and exploring their relationships with one another, of confirming the mo(ve)ments of the emerging storyline of their game, of working out which part of the playground they will flow into next, of exploring their understandings of the physical and social context(s) they are playing with/in and how this relates to the outside world.

> Libby leads the map making: *Now we can draw a map...OK! Now!*
> She draws a stick figure in the centre bottom of her page, and Lee replicates Libby's figure (Figure 7.3a & b). Alice watches but draws a more detailed figure that takes up most of her page, positioned as portrait whereas Libby and Lee's is landscape.

Although Lee objects occasionally to Libby's decision making, she flows with Libby, following Libby's lines of flight with few deviations. Alice quietly flows with the others, but more openly incorporates her preferences for her map, such as the orientation of her paper.

Libby draws a line, leading from her person, a line that wiggles and zigzags and loosely follows the edge of her page. As she draws, she explains: *You need to do [...] in here so we know where to go...we go through the prickly grass...by the tree* (Figure 7.4a). She joins another line to the first, indicating the prickly grass with zigzags along the top of her page and the tree by a thinner zigzag in the top right corner. The line then loops back onto the initial line around the page. Lee draws a line surrounding her person, a pathway with less detail and without explanation (Figure 7.4b).

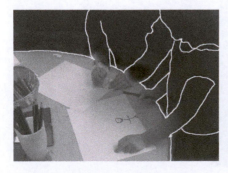

Figure 7.3a Libby leads the map making

Figure 7.3b Lee replicates Libby's figure

Figure 7.4a So we know where to go...   *Figure 7.4b Lee draws her pathway*

Alice continues with her own understanding of the interiority of the map. Her figure is large and her pathway pictured as a series of disjointed squiggles. She flows as nomad~rhizome within nomad~rhizome, following Libby's lead...*and*...following her own desire for the game...*and*...all three girls are embodied in processes of mapping their understandings of how the game should process (Figure 7.5).

We are now presented with three mappings of one game; three understandings of how they each envisage the game will proceed. Their maps indicate the pathway they intend to negotiate as strong girls. Libby talks about her pathway as she draws it, communicating her ideas for the game, ideas that unfold in the drawing. She creates a pathway with no beginning or ending, one that crosses over itself several times, suggesting they will process through a middle~milieu. Lee's is a simpler pathway and Alice's is different again. Alice's map is dominated by the figure,

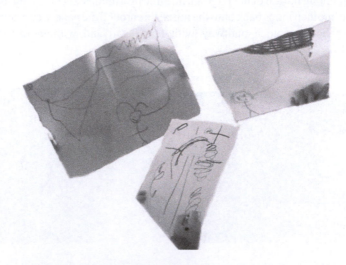

Figure 7.5 Three mappings of one game

surrounded by several unconnected wiggles – that her pathway is disjointed is of no concern to any of them.

Just as this game does not begin as being one about strong girls – the strong girl storyline starts up in the Mums and Dads game – there appears to be no explicitly planned endpoint either. What seems important are the various spaces through which they will flow – de~territorializing spaces, lines of flight to be followed. Then, another line of flight emerges. They move from the smooth space of their game to the striated space of literacy and numeracy and back again to the smooth game space.

> They each write their name on the back of their maps, then spend several minutes conversing about the similarities and differences in the spelling. They fold their maps and because of the different paper orientations, Libby and Lee make a lengthwise fold while Alice folds hers crosswise.
>
> Lee notices the difference and points this out: *She did a long one.*
>
> Libby responds: *That's OK. She's fine...C'mon, let's go...to save the world outside.*

In this mo(ve)ment, discursive understandings of curriculum, in conventional terms, are perceptible as they share their understandings about reading and writing. Blended into one is literacy, numeracy and social learning as they affirm one another's capabilities in forming various letters, affirm one another as people and acknowledge the different orientations of the paper folding. While they enjoy the interchange about their literacy and numeracy skills and knowledge, Libby is mindful of all three being included as successful performers of their curricular understandings and the rhizo performativity of their game. It is of no consequence that Alice's map looks different; it still works to constitute the play(ing) of the game and the players.

> Once outside Libby pauses, pointing to her map: *Start there and y' go all the way round...We need to go to the playground...it said playground* (Figure 7.6a & b).

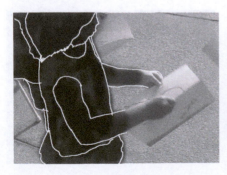

Figure 7.6a *Start there and go all the way round*   Figure 7.6b *We need to go to the play-ground*

They twist and weave through the playground, pausing to play on various pieces of equipment, to interact with other children and with the videocamera~me and seat themselves on a large log (Figure 7.7a & b).

Libby does the map-reading (Figure 7.8a): *Our map says to go to um to go to...*(her speech tails off; and later) *Treasure...the treasure is here...see the little x here* (and later still) *Hey...hey, wanna go to the pool? If you want to go to the pool, that's OK.*

They continue on their way, negotiating the outdoor equipment – over, under, through, across, balancing, jumping... (Figure 7.8b)

And so they continue mapping their play(ing), flowing through the milieu of their game, a flow of walking running skipping swinging jumping pausing rushing, singularly and severally an assemblage, with/in a multiplicity. They dance through their game, playing out their understandings of themselves as children with/in childhood(s) and/with/in a performativity of curricular experiences, flowing together as one – each a singularity; together as several (Figures 7.9a & b).

Figure 7.7a Weaving through the play-ground

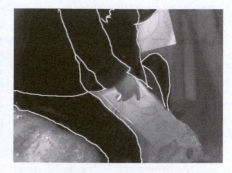

Figure 7.7b Seated on a log

Figure 7.8a Our map says to go...

Figure 7.8b Negotiating the outdoor equipment

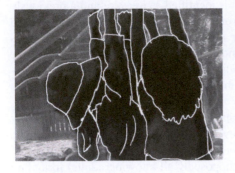

Figure 7.9a Swinging

Figure 7.9b Flowing together

Figure 7.9c Each a singularity, together
as several

children performing nomad~rhizome

The children perform as nomad~rhizome in their play(ing), uninterrupted and unhurried within a programme less formalized, one that does not dictate specific times and places for adult-identified teaching of imposed stuff to be learned. Both children and curriculum in this setting operate as nomad~rhizome, generative of enriched learning~living space-times. Not overwhelmed by adult conceptions of what's necessary to curriculum, Libby, Lee and Alice, typical of others in the kindergarten, flow through spaces of the setting, the programme, with/in relationships they encounter, through the territory of the physical environment and their un/conscious imaginary territories, following lines of flight conversationally with one another and lines of flight within their strong girl game, de~territorializing actual and imagined folds and surfaces (physical and imaginative) as happened upon, slipping in and out of discursive space-times. They play Mums and Dads, outside in the large boxes; they flow inside to the drawing table to make maps as their game segues into strong girls, then outside again to follow the pathways of their maps. They track through the outdoor equipment, pausing to hang from the bars, to re(read) their maps – an 'x' is identified as treasure and a previously unmarked swimming pool appears. Through their informal, improvised, enacted storying of games, they open out their imaginary worlds. As Mums and Dads they discuss their home, their clothing and their gendered understandings; and, the strong girls theme emerges with a mission to save the world outside. They generate productive learning spaces through making maps and then work with them to map their play.

When perceived as nomad~rhizome players, these children perform differently from the rational human beings that developmentalism dictates. In modernistic terms, Libby, Lee and Alice might be perceived as skimming the surface of 'real' learning, such as their unattended (by supposedly all-knowing adults) foray into literacy and numeracy learning. They might be perceived as sorting themselves into a social order that demands a certain kind of leadership, namely one person in charge all of the time. However, a generative rhizo reading illuminates them as differently sensible and sense-able, but not necessarily reasonable, as they un/consciously – tacitly and with conscious decision – seemingly randomly negotiate various curricular territories and/with/through (e)merging lines of flight. Throughout the rhizo performativity of their game, they de~territorialize smooth spaces of their singular and several desires to play the game, ameliorating any un/intentional individualized control. Despite Libby working to include all, there are moments when Lee might have walked away from the game, such as when her objection to the flow of the storyline was ignored by Libby. But, as well, Lee does not persist with objecting and Alice quietly plays out her resistance to totally conforming. Together they flow through the actual and imagined territories of their game, pausing, rushing, straggling, dispersing, jostling, co-existing, dancing...

There is nothing static or fixed about the children, the game, the geographical or discursive territories to be negotiated, the way they communicate (verbally through language and visually through their maps) and the space-time of the game. The game neither begins nor ends; it is always already continuing on from or opening to another. The strong girls game and the generative mapping emerges from within a middle~milieu~plateau of their play (Mums and Dads) and eventually merges with yet another plateau, as their play(ing) continues on past this data snippet. In the middle of the plateau, along the way, the game and the children follow other lines of flight. They decide that they need a map and in the process of drawing it, they intensify the map of the game. They follow lines of flight pictured on their drawn maps and move through middles of mappings not pictured. Through map-making, the children express their desires for playing the game and mark the territory to be negotiated. In drawing the continuously (e)merging maps, they follow and map lines of flight in their thinking, making personal connections with/in the territory they would negotiate and with one another's maps and ideas expressed through/with/in them. As they flow through their mapping, they pause literally (to rest on the log and to swing from the bars) and figuratively on plateaus to contemplate processes of, and the procession of their learning.

playing rhizo~methodology

Following St. Pierre (2001), I am 'not much interested in any search for origi-
nary and correct meanings' (p. 150) of their play(ing), but I am interested in the
multiplicity that their game both becomes and operates within, as in rhizo ways
I similarly negotiate territories of their games. This involves bringing together
seemingly disparate discourses – Deleuzo-Guattarian philosophy and children's
map making. It involves following lines of flight (theirs in playing; mine in
research methodology), as mapped on paper, imaginarily mapped and played out
similar to their maps but also differently through their ongoing imaginings processing through de-territorializing lines of flight. This is akin to my negotiating
a milieu constituted of and through my researching with Deleuzian philosophy,
putting rhizo~methodology to work and continuing the inquiry through writing
the rhizo~methodology and through a rhizoanalysis – in this, everything is always
already becoming-something different. Intra-activity among discursive systems
within texts and discourses themselves does not operate as traceable straight lines,
nor does it presume a simply striated text. Everything (e)merges (im)plausibly,
(im)perceptibly, connecting and crossing over. In this way Libby, Lee and Alice
illuminate generative spaces of rhizo~methodology through the play(ing) of their
game. As the storyline of the game is always already narrated and (e)merging,
so Deleuzo-Guattarian figurations inform the research. In narrating and project-
ing the storyline, the children are putting the tracing back on the map; tracings
of conventional theories of children, childhood and curricular performativity are
always already transposed on mappings of rhizo~methodology. Immersed in the
(e)merging complexity, through their map making and their enacted mapping, they
make perceptible pathways and spaces that are/will be negotiated in the course of
their game. Flowing with them in writing the methodology and in the rhizoanalysis I follow lines of flight, attentive to tacit understandings of becoming-something
different, opening (to) possibilities through juxtaposing text, images, transcripts
and commentaries, for example, within the rhizoanalysis throughout the various
plateaus. The children explicate characters in the unfolding of their games, inviting and inciting calling them(selves) into be(com)ing, announcing their strong girl
storyline to the outside and singularly and severally generating desiring-spaces
for the game. In a similar way, my becoming-researcher (e)merges through intra-
activity with outside (writers of) the literature and inside participant-children in
generating the data.

As I map a way through the snippet of data of children playing in rhizo ways
– playing out rhizome – the mapping illuminates moments of con/di/vergence,
with connections gesturing towards sense-able readings of contradictory and conflicting discourses. On the surface, the prospect of linking in any productive way
children's map(pings) or play(ing) with philosophical understandings of research
methodology may seem unlikely. However, what becomes apparent through a
rhizoanalysis of the texts of the data is that young children unaware of Deleuzian
figurations or rhizo methodologies enact complex understandings of these. The

intensity of this complexity is different from taken-for-granted versions of possible childhood understandings outlined in many curriculum texts. As Deleuze (1997) puts it: 'Children never stop talking about what they are doing or trying to do: exploring milieus by means of dynamic trajectories and drawing up maps of them' (p. 61). So, there is no need to be surprised about their tacit understandings of nomad~rhizome. To be surprised or amazed is to dismiss the sophistication of their knowledge, the complexity of their curricular understandings and their conceptions of living~learning. Throughout the rhizo methodology foregrounded here, possibilities are generated for processing in a similar way to the children's performativity...inquiring about the inquiry about inquiring about the inquiry and inquiring...on a de~territorializing epistemological~ontological plane...

Note

1   See also Honan and Sellers (2006) and Sellers and Honan (2007) for different rhizo-analyses of the children's curricular performativity within the data snippet used here.

Becoming-child(ren) becoming-power-full

Children's questions are poorly understood if they are not seen as question-machines.

(Deleuze & Guattari, 1987: 256)

opening to power-fullness

Using the notion of 'power-fullness' as a way of problematizing conventional notions of power, being powerful and empowerment (Sellers & Honan, 2007), in this plateau I foreground the power relations between Tim as child-research participant and me as adult-researcher in an attempt to flatten the modernist adult|child hierarchy and promote intra-active researcher~participant relations.[1] All too often young children's expressions of how they understand the workings of their worlds are either not understood or not listened to. Generating the data of the research project was a conjoint endeavour with the children and within this the children expressed their power-fullness in ways both perceptible and imperceptible to my adult~researcher situation. When my actions compromised their space-times, they communicated this by ignoring me or through a direct challenge. For example: When my questioning about their play no longer engaged their interest, Fleur, Lucy and Maria continued with what they were doing as if I were not there (see the *Play(ing)* plateau); and in the data of this plateau, Tim tires of being followed with the video camera and establishes a boundary that clearly I am not to cross. These children's forthrightness makes perceptible how, all-too-easily a (mis)placement of powerrelations can simultaneously compromise and enable their flows and expressions of power-fullness.

The idea of children becoming power-full draws on Deleuzian and Foucauldian notions of power – or power-fullness – as force and affect to which we all have access; it does not assume a top-down imposition. This opens (to) a critique of the notion of empowerment in *Te Whāriki* (Ministry of Education, 1996). In foregrounding Tim's expressions of power-fullness, common understandings of empowerment are disrupted. His challenging and presumably rhetorical question~statement directed at me on two different days – *You following me everywhere we go!* and *You're following us! Why are you following us?* – is arguably a directive to not follow him and his friends. Yet, it took two exchanges for me to comprehend this; I was locked in a power-relations space that may have compromised his power-fullness but at the same time it opened possibilities for it to flow. This is not to justify my imperceptibility but to illuminate this space-time as opening an expression of Tim's power-fullness. In the first situation, I am closed to the machinics of unequal power relations at play and thus to his expression of flows of power-fullness. Through the second interchange, I open to a power-full possibility as I come to actually understand Deleuze and Guattari's lucid statement, 'Children's questions are poorly understood if they are not seen as question-machines' (Deleuze & Guattari, 1987: 256). The moments here elucidate Tim's accusations/questions as desiring machines of his power-full flows.

Both Foucault and Deleuze work with the understanding that power is a force in perpetual motion that flows through social networks, an affect that is operational. So, Tim's and my relationship is (im)partial, just part of the network of power relations at play in the two data snippets used in this plateau. In these, my attention is with making perceptible how the connecting flows of becoming-power-full work in relation to one another. In expressions of power-fullness he disturbs pervasive discourses that position children as incapable, immature, weak and needy, this in turn disrupting the adult|child binary and any associated hierarchical privileging. He opens possibilities outside the potentially agentic child towards understanding always already becoming-child(ren). He works with power as relational and operational. His question-machine – *Why are you following me everywhere we go?* – opens to/through power-full expressions of curricular performativity.

disrupting empowerment

Empowerment is a modernist concept implying someone doing something for someone else in a hierarchical, top-down relationship; a dictionary definition states that empowerment is the 'action of empowering; the state of being empowered' (*Oxford English Dictionary*, Online).[2] In this, power is conceived as a form of hierarchical control, as pressure exerted from above so that those above oppress those below, enforcing submission; alternatively, a more powerful body may bestow power on a powerless body in a gesture of empowerment. That is, power and authority for a purpose or to a specific end is invested, imparted, authorized, licensed, permitted, enabled. This implies someone greater and stronger doing something for someone in a weaker position and communicates an authoritarian, deterministic notion of control even as one body claims authority to *free* another from a state of powerlessness. Within these terms of 'giving over' empowerment conceived as a process of liberating bodies from a position of powerlessness – bodies that are (supposedly) oppressed, repressed and disempowered – is commonly accepted. Empowerment is thus considered a desirable, liberatory force for individuals affecting control in/of their lives with power understood as a thing, as something some people have more of than others, as something a body grants or is granted. Thus regarded, empowerment is a state of being that young children *need* to be *endowed* with by the adult world.

To think about empowering children in relationships and learning sustains the adult|child binary, positioning adults over children. In conditions of empowerment adults presume power ideologically; children are assumed inferior, as needy beings, less fit than adults. In order to catch up and be admitted to a more advanced adult positioning requires that decisions are made for and on behalf of children about what they supposedly 'need' to know, how they 'need' to go about acquiring certain knowledge and skills, and how they 'need' to behave. In this regard, empowerment assumes in/competence to (not) know for themselves what is important for them to know or how to operate; as well as in/competence being a culturally bound, arborescent tracing, children are regarded as lacking in knowledge and skills, as being unknowing. At best, they are perceived as having *immature* understandings – having little, limited or no understanding of why certain knowledge and ways of operating are productive to relationships and learning of curricular performativity; and, they are perceived as incapable of articulating such knowledge and deploying such skills.

Within this structuralist view, children supposedly 'need' to have advocates to empower them, that is, well intentioned and undoubtedly caring adults to decide what they 'need' to know and to provide an environment conducive to behaving in 'appropriate' ways. Regardless of whether empowerment is granted to children in that they are presented with opportunities that *allow* or *enable* them to engage positively in power relations, empowerment remains a thing that adults provide for children to satisfy the needs legacy of developmental approaches to children and childhood. As Holt (2004) says, empowerment 'seems to be clearly located within modernist imperatives to emancipate' (p. 15). However, pretending to be fully conscious of all desires and motivations and the forces and constraints that operate on them is to deny the (im)partiality of the accounts and an understanding of subjectivity. Thus I admit to being unstable and dynamically changing in a power-fullness that is subjectively my own; also, while endeavouring not to impose this on others, to entirely avoid such mo(ve)ments is likely impossible.

whakamana

One of the four guiding principles of *Te Whāriki* is empowerment, which in this bicultural document parallels the Māori concept of whakamana. However, given that language works to express beliefs of any given culture and that language does not fully cross through differing cultural understandings, a traditional Māori understanding of whakamana can only be authentically represented in Te Reo Māori (the Māori language) and cannot be completely defined in English terms. Thus, an explanation in English albeit mediated by usage by Māori in English texts is always already (im)partial. However, it appears that a traditional Māori understanding of whakamana is subtly different from empowerment. In *The Reed Dictionary of Modern Māori* (Ryan, 1997) the prefix *whaka* is translated as 'cause to do, in the direction of, towards' and *mana* as 'integrity, charisma, prestige, formal, jurisdiction'. In these terms whakamana communicates a somewhat intangible movement towards respecting power-fullness. Royal Tangaere (1999) suggests it is not something to be imparted by a higher authority; rather it operates in a middle space of collaborative negotiations. He explains whakamana as: 'listening, guiding and supporting [that] does not model a bureaucratic system' (p. 8), more about leading than leadership. Durie (2006) talks of whakamana being the *capacity* to empower that bodies experience. It is a 'function that facilitates the entry of members of the whānau into the wider community, as individuals and as Māori' (p. 5), whānau or extended family being the threshold for fully participating in the Māori world and in wider society. These are operational concepts, conveying a sense of movement towards space-times of personal and communal power-fullness.

Within these operations there is a sense of reciprocity, an always already connected awareness by the individual *and* recognition from the world, so that the inside and outside are simultaneously working to create space-times in/through which the uniqueness of children – their gifts and traits – can (e)merge; whakamana thus problematizes a conventional understanding of empowerment as the flip side of relations of power, as something not necessarily imposed but at least enabled from the outside. However, while this outsider-activated conception of empowerment is central to *Te Whāriki*, the sense of reciprocity and capacity of insider operations conveyed by Royal Tangaere and Durie is evident: 'Children learn through *collaboration with* adults and peers, through *guided* participation' (Ministry of Education, 1996: 9, italics added). But, although the Māori concept of whakamana is part of the whāriki gifted by Te Kōhanga Reo to the early childhood curriculum, it is the English understanding of empowerment that commonly informs early childhood practice in Aotearoa New Zealand. This discourse of empowerment that works to constitute the minds and bodies of children is part of a network of westernized, modernist power relations that pervade various bodies, such as, early childhood education and curriculum.

Deleuzian and Foucauldian power relations

For Deleuze and Foucault, power is understood as a continuous force of relations, fluidly moving back and forth among people and institutions so that no singular person or institution holds or exerts power in a static and fixed way. Power in this sense is 'diffuse and unformed' (Deleuze, 1988: 73). It is not a thing with which some bodies are endowed; it is a force or affect that flows through relationships, affecting other related forces and affected by others. Foucault (1980) considers power as 'a *productive* network that runs through the whole social body, much more than a *negative* instance whose function is repression' (p. 120, italics added). Power is always already everywhere, extending boundlessly through social relations, a force that is never isolated. Thus, power is not positioned in either adult or child, for example, rather, it becomes perceptible in the social arrangements of adults and children that are commonly worked with. As a force it is accessible to child and adult, although most often, exacerbated by the prevailing modernist adult|child binary, forces of power are interpreted as negative affects for children to the extent that 'disruptive' or 'challenging' behaviour is mediated rather than welcomed as children's expressions of power-fullness.

Deleuze explains Foucault's conceptualization of power thus:

> An exercise of power shows up as an affect, since force defines itself by its very power to affect other forces (to which it is related) and to be affected by other forces. To incite, provoke and produce…constitute *active* affects, while to be incited or provoked, to be induced to produce, to have a 'useful' effect, constitute *reactive* affects. The latter are not simply the 'repercussion' or 'passive side' of the former but are rather 'the irreducible encounter' between the two, especially if we believe that the force affected has a certain capacity for resistance. At the same time…each force implies power relations: and every field of forces distributes forces according to these relations and their variations.
>
> (Deleuze, 1988: 71, italics added)

Deleuze and Guattari (1987) discuss power in terms of *pouvoir* and *puissance*. *Pouvoir* relates to the actual, *puissance* to the virtual. Their use of *pouvoir* is similar to Foucault's as 'an instituted and reproducible relation of force' (Massumi, 1987b: xvii), a realm of power and domination. Different, but nevertheless part of the Foucauldian network of power, *puissance* describes 'a *range* of *potential*…"a *capacity* for existence," "a *capacity* to affect or be affected"…a *scale* of *intensity*' (p. xvii, italics added). Powers of becoming, as in children's becoming-power-full, as illuminated by Tim in the data that follows in this plateau, addresses *puissance* as powers of intensity, constituting and constituted by affects and a capacity to affect and be affected. This becomes perceptible in Tim's expressions of power-fullness around his playmates and towards me as adult-researcher.

When power is perceived as complex and non-linear in ongoing operations of relations with/in a multiplicity of forces rather than a singular force acting on specific bodies, different possibilities for conceiving power-fullness emerge around/with/in/through encounters of relationships – in this I use 'power-fullness' to problematize modernist assumptions of power as a controlling, top-down effect, desired by all and possessed by few, the 'fullness' of the term signalling a condition of power common to all. Power-fullness responds to Deleuze's (1988) provocation to ask not what power is and where it comes from, but to ask, 'How is it practiced?' (p. 71). Power-fullness also destabilizes modernist notions of empowerment, the adult|child binary and developmental, behaviourist interpretations of children and their childhoods. Thinking of children as power-full alongside adults they engage with and the institutions they operate within, disentangles child and adult from a disabling modernist understanding of unequal power relationships, instead recognizing that any body is embodied in any other body's expressions of power-fullness – a manifestation of becoming-children becoming-adult. The now disrupted adult|child dualism marks both child and adult, (re)conceiving the relationship as a-hierarchical and problematizing the modernist view that children need advocates to empower them. Instead, children are (re)conceived in operations of always already becoming-power-full.

expressions and flows of becoming-power-full

For Deleuze and Guattari (1987) becoming is a dynamic movement of change, a continual flow through unique mo(ve)ment of constantly changing space-times. Nothing stands still in our thinking or be(com)ing; everything slip-slides. The present is only ever understood from within past experiences and in anticipation of particular futures; memories of the past change as our lived experiences in the present accumulate; the momentary present (e)merges as/with the future. Thus, as with children, power-fullness is always in process of becoming – becoming-children becoming-power-full. Within the data there is a multiplicity of becomings expressed in many ways. For example: becoming-Tim manifests as the becoming-child of singular children; children working severally with their subjectivities, together making maps and playing games manifest as becoming-children. These become perceptible as expressions of power-fullness of each child and as flows of power-fullness of their severalty – alone and together everyone is always already becoming-power-full, an entangling of power-fullness of children and adults. Becoming and power-fullness are inextricably entwined. To explain the becoming of children's power-fullness, I open (to) Tim's power-fullness as he problematizes power relations passing through him. This in turn problematizes common assumptions of empowerment explicit in *Te Whāriki* that arguably sustain inequitable power relations.

In the following data snippets, Tim performs power-fullness, affectively and to good effect, as he confronts the complex network of power relations of participant-child and adult-researcher. Through this relationship, Tim works his power-fullness. His activity of becoming-power-full and the condition of power-fullness his activity produces emerge from/with/in the following transcriptions, the first from the dinosaur spider hunt and the second from the bad guys hunt a few days later.

expressions of becoming-power-full ~ 'You're following us! Why are you following us?'

Zak is pulling a trolley, in which Tim is seated, holding their hobbyhorses. Going down a rise, the trolley travels too fast for Zak to control. Tim yells: *Stop! Stop! Stop!* The trolley crashes into the wooden edging of the adventure playground area (Figure 8.1a). Zak lifts his hobbyhorse out of the trolley. Tim sits for a moment then stands in the trolley, looks around the surrounding area and announces: *This is our parking spot!* (Figure 8.1b).

> Tim suddenly points at me (Figure 8.2a): *You're following us! Why are you following us?*
> Hands on his hips, he stares at me (Figure 8.2b).

Figure 8.1a The trolley has crashed to a halt   *Figure 8.1b* *This is our parking spot!*

Figure 8.2a *You're following us!*   *Figure 8.2b* *Why are you following us?*

MS: *Oh because I'm making a video of you. Is that OK?*
Zak (without hesitation): *Yeah, that'll be OK.*
MS: *I can show it to you later on the TV screen.*
Zak trots off astride his hobbyhorse: *I like watching TV.*
MS: *OK, when you've been on your dinosaur spider hunt.* Tim jumps off the
   trolley, sits for a moment on the end of it, and then follows Zak.
Zak pauses, looks back towards Tim, calling: *C'mon (...) it'll be all right.*
Tim's reply is inaudible as he picks up his hobbyhorse and follows.

Thinking back on my response to Tim, my concern at the time was with openly
answering his questions, to ensure the data generation process was transparent
and their participation voluntary. My pragmatic answer to: *Why are you following us?* focuses on 'why' and misses Tim's words as a request to leave them
alone. I respond with the obvious, which did not need stating: I am video-recording their game and, if they want they can watch it later. However, in this defining
mo(ve)ment of replying in terms of the research task and the possibility of later

viewing the video, I fail to (co)operate as adult-researcher in the 'border(less) work the children were engaged in'.[3] While not appreciating the significance of Tim's removal tactics as an expression of power-fullness I understand that my presence is unwelcome and stop video-recording their game. However, I miss the significance of the accusatory statement, *You're following us!*

In an expression of power-fullness, Tim signals I am not welcome in the territory while Zak expresses his power-fullness differently, perhaps as mediator working to continue the game and assure Tim that my presence is incidental. Zak also communicates an understanding that each expression of power-fullness matters and does not matter when he says, *Yeah, that'll be OK...C'mon...it'll be all right.* In commingling flows of expressions of power-fullness both communicate differently that I am to be ignored. Zak calmly walks off and Tim, initially confrontational, follows muttering inaudibly. In a severalty of power-fullness they close down the intra-activity by excluding me from the territory of the game. These de~territorializing mo(ve)ments of power-fullness – becoming-child(ren) becoming-power-full – disrupt the pervasive adult propensity to dominate. While the power relations are on the surface unequal, considering the expressions of power-fullness flowing through the intra-activity, it is perhaps less about specific moments of unequal power relations and more about dynamic mo(ve)ments inevitably (im)balanced. In varying flows, power-fullness irrupts and disrupts, opening opportunities for power-full expressions of others.

In (mis)interpreting *You're following us! Why are you following us?* I become aware of the confessional 'I' of a behaviourist that Jackson (2010) transgresses towards a generative 'becoming-I'. This 'plays with a limit that is never reached and forces the reader into new ways of seeing/hearing/listening/imagining' (p. 584). Following Jackson, the reading of the data and the reading here is thus provoked through questions like: Are readers caught in conventional, governing, controlling discourses of representation and do they want/need/desire to 'hear' the children? Might readers, as becoming-I, negotiate the text and not depend on the writer (me) to tell them what to think? How might readers experience becoming-I as they engage with the representation? Might Tim's becoming-power-full move readers towards rethinking their own power-fullness?

Tim's flow of becoming-power-full ~ 'You following me everywhere we go!'

Tim confronts me again a few days later and this time the flows of power-fullness operate differently. Tim is on a bad guys hunt with Piri, but their game is interrupted in the adventure playground by challenges from several children around the equipment they have gathered. Josh takes an innovative approach towards being included in the game.

Josh: *Oh yeah, and I'm the baddie and I stole your stuff.*
Tim resists: *I'm going to call the bad boss to take you away.*

Josh clarifies: *Oh, so you want to get me away.*

Others also want Tim and Piri's equipment. Aware that Josh has stolen Piri's stuff, Tim arranges his phone, camera, small wooden stop sign on the top of a large wooden reel. Rory then jumps him from above, glaring at him at close range while Lex, who has rushed in from another direction, grabs at the camera, saying: *Can I have that? I need it I need a camera.*

Tim clutches the camera tight against his body and they retreat.

Adam then arrives and debates ownership of the camera.

Adam: *You don't really need that.*

Tim: *Yes we do, we take pictures of us. We take pictures of each other.*

Adam: *OK just give me the camera.*

A complex array of becoming-children becoming-power-full becomes perceptible through de~territorializing flows of intra-activity. Piri's power-fullness manifests as he stands by and lets Josh steal his equipment, ensuring there is a bad guy to hunt. Tim claims his power-fullness as firstly he arranges his equipment – for all to see and maybe, in its visibility, for safekeeping – and then in asserting he will phone the bad boss. In another power-full move he does not respond to Josh who asks if he wants him to go away – Josh, in his power-fullness, seems to know there needs to be a bad guy if there is to be a bad guys hunt and has maybe noticed the discrepancy in how Tim is enacting the storyline at this moment. Maybe Tim notices as well or maybe in an expression of power-fullness he neither replies nor phones the bad boss. Rory, Lex and Adam are playing a game of their own and it seems from the power-full demands they make of Tim to hand over the camera that they are short of equipment. Tim in his power-fullness refuses to accede. Severally, these expressions of singular power-fullness are diffuse and unformed, producing a network of activity that passes through them all.

Then, Tim and Adam are embodied with/in a power-full play of wanting and not wanting the camera; their power-fullness slips and slides: Adam demands the camera and Tim refuses to hand it over; Tim offers it and Adam refuses to take it; Adam again demands it and Tim refuses him; Adam stalks off and Tim runs after him trying to give the camera to him; Adam turns and points his hand, as if a gun, at Tim. Tim seems confused as he wanders after Adam. Throughout the entangled relations of games and players, no one player or game has totalizing power over any other. In this seemingly closing mo(ve)ment Adam may be signalling that he thinks he has control of the progress of the commingling games as he stalks off, pointing his hand/'gun' at Tim, but Tim still has the camera and ensures the storyline of his game, as he understands it will continue. Differently, singularly and severally, through intra-active relations both are embodied in mutual conditions of power-fullness.

Shortly after, Tim is standing alone in the adventure playground, his back to the videocamera~me, staring in the direction that Adam, Lex and Rory disappeared. Tim is amidst an arrangement of reels, planks and boxes. The mapping (Map 8.1)

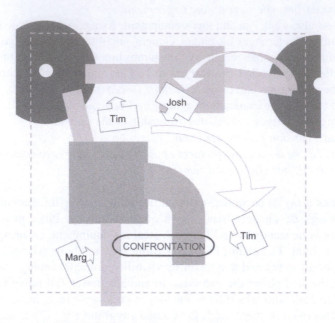

Map 8.1 The scene of the pending confrontational expressions of power-fullness

pictures the arrangement of children, adult and artefacts that constitute the scene of Tim's confrontational expression of power-fullness.

> Josh runs up a plank and jumps onto the cube beside Tim (Figure 8.3a). Tim remains motionless, staring into the distance. Josh, still intent on engaging with Tim says: *I need to show you something.*
> Tim looks up at Josh: *What?*
> Josh: *Shall we hide from the teachers?* (Figure 8.3b).

Figure 8.3a Josh jumps onto the cube beside Tim

Figure 8.3b Shall we hide from the teachers?

Tim says nothing, but walks past Josh, around the slide, then, feet astride, he turns to face the videocamera~me, nodding decisively in my direction. He is holding the phone by the aerial (Figure 8.4).

MS (wondering whether Josh's reappearance is hassling him): *Are you all right Tim?*

He points the phone at me and shouts: *You following me everywhere we go!*

As he speaks, he gestures with the phone, holding its aerial and swinging it wildly (Figure 8.5); at 'we' he looks in the direction of Josh, apparent now as friend not foe.

Figure 8.4 Tim turns to face the videocamera~me

Figure 8.5 Tim gestures with the phone

MS, referring to my video-recording him: *Is that annoying you?*
He emphatically nods his head twice (Figure 8.6).
MS: *OK, I'll stop.*

Tim, grinning, strides off, out of range of the videocamera~me (Figure 8.7).

Tim's flow of power-fullness in the bad guys hunt

When Tim unequivocally expresses his annoyance at my following him in the bad guys hunt, similar to his earlier expression of power-fullness, my perception in the moment is that he is frazzled by the series of challenges to his game and disputes over his equipment. In a misplaced behaviourist (mis)interpretation of confessional-I, I think that the challenges Tim encountered precipitate his challenging comment to me. But, as becoming-I thinking with Deleuze and Foucault about this confrontation, Tim's ongoing condition of power-fullness is clearly illuminated otherwise.

Figure 8.6 Tim emphatically nods twice

Figure 8.7 Tim strides off

Tim is decidedly unhappy about my video-ing his game, his exasperated tone and gesture make this clear and the presumption that Tim needed my protection marks the pervasiveness of conventional, governing, controlling discourses of power. However, Tim and Josh severally make perceptible their intact power-fullness, together working to slip away – Josh suggests hiding and Tim forthrightly problematizes my position by confronting me directly. Josh is now a different part of the game, my presence opening a possibility for him to make his way in on different terms. As comrades they dismiss my intervention, clearly asserting that I am invading the territory of his game – the playing and the playground. My presence is marked as hierarchical adult|child and researcher|participant relations, which all at once compromises and opens the children's power-fullness in terms of closing me down and in regard to following a new line of flight – the rhizome ruptures and erupts elsewhere – Josh becomes part of the game in a way that is now acceptable to Tim. Each works his power-fullness to constitute active and reactive affects.

flows of power-fullness in researching with children

While video-recording, I was aware of Tim's constant playing out of his power-fullness alongside other children's, however, it was not until writing my way through the rhizoanalysis that my part in Tim's becoming-children~becoming-power-full opened in my thinking. Despite attempting to flatten out the all-too-frequently unequally power-imbued researcher-participant relations, I had slipped into presuming power as the 'all-knowing researcher' and into the 'institutional ethics discourse' that relentlessly reduces children agentially in terms of knowing and knowledge.[4] In the first analysis of the ~~thesis~~, the confessional-I wrote of being surprised by Tim's confrontation, admitting I should not have been; the confessional-I was disturbed, as supposedly respectful researcher about disregarding invasive practices. However, questions open about slip-sliding relations of videocamera~me invading their territory as 30 minutes later Tim purposefully dances in front of the camera.

> MS: *Hello, Tim. I thought you were tired of me following you with the camera.*
> Tim: *We're, we're not any more.*

So it seems that in asserting his desires in/for his space-time Tim displaces any supposedly misplaced confessional-I thoughts of the pervasive all-knowing researcher and reductive institutional ethics discourse. While these exist Tim power-fully negotiates a way through. The confrontation becomes a productive moment of Tim's power-fullness, disrupting the reproduction of unequal power relations.

Somewhat (im)perceptibly, expressions of power-fullness flow in rhizo ways through the intra-activity of several children, the playing of the game, the playground, the videocamera~me. As rhizome, Tim, Josh and I negotiate lines of flight of intra-activity, as singularly and several. In the mapping (Map 8.2), Tim's

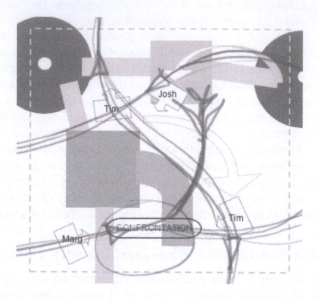

Map 8.2 Rhizo flows of power-fullness

attention is with something or someone in the distance. Josh, slip-sliding through the centre and periphery of the game, has followed Tim and is now suggesting they hide. I am trying to keep a respectful distance as I video the activity. Then, as our lines of flight intersect, flows of powerfull-ness around/through/with/in Tim, Josh and me are entangled with (e)merging expressions of rhizo flows of power-fullness displacing any possible determinist analysis of a confrontational clash.

Tim and Josh flow as rhizome through the(ir) game(s) and the intra-active spaces in-between. Both are protagonist in their own games and antagonist in that of the other, as Tim hunts bad guys and Josh is a baddie. The game(s) they are embodied with/in commingle when Josh suggests they hide and Tim nods in agreement. Tim moves around past Josh, I come into view and Tim confronts me. The entanglement continues as I am drawn in as antagonist in their games and with them as protagonists – participant~researchers – in data generation processes. The assumption of confessional-I, that I subverted Tim's flows of power-fullness, is imbued with behaviourist expectations of working to dispel his anger and frustration in my concern to respond to the 'why' of his statement – *You're following us! Why are you following us?* This response marks the pervasiveness of the adult|child binary, that is, assumed adult control over children's emotions and imposition of adult rules for the setting. This is not to deny that adult concerns for peaceable environments do not matter, it is to open (to) possibilities for respectfully negotiating children's emotions and power-fullness with an understanding that peace-able arrangements are not always peace-full, as in the arrangement precipitated by Tim shouting at me.

Becoming-I transgresses confessional-I through understandings that Tim's power-fullness is in no way compromised as he segues through space-times where my following him does and does not matter and as he morphs through mo(ve)ments of saying nothing about my following him and yelling at me not to. This is an irreducible encounter of relations of power-fullness as both Tim and I incite, provoke and produce both active affects and useful effects of power-fullness distributed through our singular and several selves. 'Power' flowing back and forth through intra-active conditions and expressions of 'full-ness' renders 'empowerment' per se redundant. In expressions of power-fullness – becoming Tim becoming-power-full – Tim is not a needy child. He does not need empowering through operations of a modernist world-view, in which adults assume the right and obligation to provide for supposedly needy children. As becoming-adults living~learning with becoming-children we flow through/with/in planes of conditions and expressions of power-fullness, with adults neither more nor less than young children.

re(con)ceiving becoming-child(ren) becoming-power-full in curriculum

Generating a multiplicity of becoming-power-full disrupts the pervasiveness of modernist discourses of power. In a rhizo way power as affect is embodied in relations of becomings: 'a constellation of affects, an intensive map, is a becoming' (Deleuze, 1997: 64). Affective happenings or becomings of affect are forces entangled in all forms of social production, in dynamic mo(ve)ments of change, the continual flow through unique space-times of a constantly changing present. So, Tim's expressions of becoming-power-full can only be conceived as a constantly changing assemblage of forces, always already in flux, as a flow of expressions de~territorializing intra-active relations. So, how does it work? How might children in conditions and flows of becoming-power-full participate in the work of re(con)ceiving children in early childhood curriculum, where curriculum is understood as the human~material activity (see the *Materiality matters* plateau) involving every person, situation, event and artefact commingling and co-implicated with/in conditions and capacities of/for learning?

Philosophically, it is relatively easy to map relations of intra-activity involved in becoming-power-full flows. But, living the experiences of always already becoming, such as becoming-power-full, amidst dichotomous tracings of modernist power relations is challenging. It is not easy to (re)move dominating developmental perspectives within our thinking; it is not easy to see things in the middle; and, we must always plug the tracing back into the map. Even talking about becoming-power-full is unwieldy, yet if we want to change the way we think, to learn to think differently, learning to use words differently matters, and when words no longer work to use images to think with/through. Warren Sellers (2008) presents picturing as a rhizo-imaginary for thinking differently; for him using pictures to think about wor(l)ds generates a turn in/of thought. Periodically, I turn to picturing my thoughts with lines, although these are generally marked with words. Working with such picturing~thoughts (Maps 8.1 and 8.2) around Tim displaying his power-fullness as participant~researcher makes perceptible that words of the transcription and writing alone fall short. Confrontation as a rhizo flow of power-fullness erupts from within the picture (Map 8.2). This picturing along with the imagery of Tim in the video opens (to) possibilities for thinking differently; it opens (to) possibilities for force-full expressions, which recursively intensify mo(ve)ments of possibilities. As he problematizes the power relations at play and disrupts the notion of empowerment, the becoming child of becoming-Tim becomes perceptible in rhizo flows becoming-power-full.

Deleuze (1988) explains the complexity at play here: 'Power has no essence; it is simply operational. It is not an attribute but a relation: the power-relation is the set of possible relations between forces which pass through the dominated forces no less than the dominating' (p. 27). Within power as affect, Tim is neither disadvantaged nor needy as he works to express this condition. From within this space-time of entangled lines of flight amidst the intra-active relations of children and adult, flows of becoming-power-full (e)merge. A multidimensional multiplicity of power-fullness becomes perceptible as flows, flowing through/with/in/among the flowing of the game(s), the flowing lines of flight, the flowing of the video recording and flowing relationships among one another. Tim's expressions of power-fullness force-fully emerge, perturbing developmentally positioned behaviourist cause and effect-type discourses of power and empowerment.

Notes

1   Intra-active relations go beyond interactive relationships among humans; intra-activity involves the forces and affects of relations among human and nonhuman (organic and material) worlds (see Lenz Taguchi, 2010).
2   See 'empowerment' in References.
3   Bronwyn Davies, thesis assessor, alerted me to this. This thought-wave continues to diffract throughout the following conversation of this plateau.
4   Bronwyn Davies, thesis assessor, comment.

Matters of materiality ~ materiality matters

opening the plateau...

My wondering as I wander through my thinking intensifies, continually shattering with/in expressions of (e)merging becoming-researcher~writer~thinker that are entangled with conditions of becoming-research~writing~thinking. In an incipiently different diffractive way I (re)turn to the Deleuzian questions: How do things work? What new thoughts become possible to think? (Massumi, 1992). Travelling while seated alongside St. Pierre (2004), as nomad I (re)consider in an intra-active way questions posed in the opening plateau (*Preceding echoes~foreshadowing*): What else might there be *with/in* the space of the playing and *with/in* play-space? What else might there be *with/in* these spaces? What spaces might there be other than the physical surroundings and the enacted play? What might be happening *with/in those other intra-active spaces*? What opens is a milieu of affective relations generated in-between as the force of things materializes through the energy of humans and the energy of matter diffracts through human forces... *and...* embodied in the milieu is a relational materiality of intra-active human~nonhuman encounters of thinking~reading~writing as thoughts emerge and words materialize on both computer screen and paper.

In thinking~writing about materiality matters I ponder how to work the ideas into the text in this newly (e)merging plateau about human/material relations and how to format the writing of the plateau. I want ideas from the literature and data to emerge from and merge with the materiality of the text, not for the data to be an add-on as that returns to the linear. A colleague says, 'Just write it and work out the formatting later.' But, in this mo(ve)ment of relational matters, I realize that the materiality of the writing process is as important as what I want to say. In the same way that I cannot write about rhizome without becoming rhizome and doing rhizome, neither can I write about relations with matter without engaging with the materiality of the wording of my ideas. Another colleague suggests a page that unfolds, 'Like an envelope,' she says, without knowing about my working with an enfolded-ness of ideas. In a creative eruption of possibilities, I suggest a palimpsest of data on semi-transparent paper; then, alternate pages of theory and data to disrupt the linearity. 'But that might be confusing for readers,' I think aloud...

simultaneously she adds, 'Isn't that how rhizome works?' So, without intending to incite confusion, rather, to open the rhizome and invite diffractive possibilities, I set up a doubled page, enabling a slip-sliding reading of the theoretical exploration and the exploration of data. In this way neither engaging with the literature nor making a rhizome with the data leads or takes precedence; the tracing is on the map, one becoming the other. This eases my flow of thinking~writing~reading, but will it work for the reading~thinking? At least, the material agency of formatted page becomes perceptible...*and*...I realize that in putting rhizome to work, materiality is always already illuminated throughout the plateaus...*and*...it is impossible to keep theory and data apart...*and*...where to place this plateau...I want to make a rhizome...risk failure, fail...failures are always already faltering, ebbing and flowing de~territorializing lines of flight of the plan(e)...

Matters of materiality ~ engaging literature

'Thing-power' perhaps has the rhetorical advantage of calling to mind a childhood sense of the world as filled with all sorts of animate beings, some not, some human, some not, some organic, some not. It draws attention to an efficacy of objects in excess of the human meanings, designs, or purposes they express or serve.

(Bennett, 2010: 20)

Rhizo thinking is a never-ending (ad)venture; it is always already open to putting things together differently in ongoing commingling processes, not to fill any 'gaps' but to engage with different sites of emergence. (Re)thinking data in this plateau using ideas of materiality is an attempt to flatten out remnants of the pervasiveness of arborescent analysis, to plug more of the tracing into the map. Although I have worked to map ideas that decentre psychological and developmentally causal approaches throughout the plateaus, I am now in a thinking space-time that alerts me to the anthropocentric, sociocentric and logocentric tracings that (un)thinkingly I adopted. 'Un-thinkingly' signals that it was not until writing this plateau that this particular space-time of thought opened.

Through a body of work about various material, posthumanist turns (Alaimo & Heckman, 2008), I become interested to understand the material constitution of social relations

Materiality matters…making rhizome…

The Deleuzian question is: How does it work? Understanding that materiality matters and that matters of materiality, an assemblage of thing-power, are always already at play with/in young children's play(ing) of games, I (re)turn to (re)generate the rhizoanalysis, turning things inside out to consider engagements with matter, having worked with matters of engagement in other plateaus.

Following Karin Hultman and Hillevi Lenz Taguchi's (2010) relational materialist turn, I consider becoming-children as emerging in a '*relational field,* where *non*-human forces are equally at play' (p. 525, original italics). Without intending to privilege either the material or the social, the nonhuman or the human, I (re)turn to the data to disrupt anthro-, socio- and logocentric readings and to illuminate power-full affects of material, nonhuman forces enfolded in the social interactions of the play(ing).

Throughout the data generation the children become more familiar with the videocamera and I work to ensure my visibility without imposing myself on their play spaces, but in illuminating the intra-activity with materiality, different things are discernible. Even when operating (im)passively in the periphery of their play-spaces, it is impossible to be there without the materiality of my body being an imposition in the and the social constitution of materiality (Orlikowski, 2006). Included is Hillevi Lenz Taguchi's (2009) relational materialist approach that decentralizes anthropocentrism and logocentrism in favour of an interdependent co-existence; also Karen Barad's (2007) entangled intra-activity of relations with material worlds; and, Jane Bennett's (2010) ecology of matter that foregrounds materialistic agency. As I engage with this work I realize that while I work towards decentralizing adult understandings of curriculum and bringing young children's into play throughout the other plateaus, I perpetuate other hierarchies by valorizing human social relationships in ways that dismiss relational aspects of materiality. As for Hultman and Taguchi (2010), my 'perceptual style and...habits of seeing' (p. 525, original italics) remained inscribed by humanist notions that my poststructuralist thinking sought to escape; despite my attempt to disrupt the adult|child binary in the other plateaus, a human|nonhuman[1] binary flourishes.

In becoming attentive to matters of materiality, I come to understand that the power to affect and be affected involves all bodies, material as well as human. Deleuze (1992) says: 'all power bears with it a corresponding and inseparable capacity to be affected...that of acting, and that of suffering action' (p. 93). Thus, in different ways in every mo(ve)ment everyone and everything affects and is affected by everyone and everything.

physical space...and...the camera also de-territorializes the space, materializing as both virtual and actual. As periphery and centre of the games are fluid, when the children involve me in their conversation I am drawn into the centre, the camera being a part of me. At times they glance up without interrupting the flow of the conversation or activity of their game and without interacting directly with either camera or me. Foregrounding material relations, this transgresses a simple expression of familiarity with technology; it is a discernible moment of their perception of material relations. In such mo(ve)ments the children and camera~me operate as one; nonhuman~human boundaries blur.

These slip-sliding human~nonhuman relations are perceptible through the slippage of people through butterflies in a data snippet from the *Children performing curriculum complexly* plateau:

Libby, Lee and Alice are in the adventure playground negotiating the storyline of their game.
Libby: *...and we're playing Mums and Dads*
Lee: *And not Mums and Dads butterflies, eh? Mums and Dads people.*

Although Lee clarifies that as players in the game they are people, not butterflies, the intra-active space of playing the game in terms of being Mums and Dads emerges as the

Acknowledging Bennett's (2010) warning that 'thing-power' is liable to 'overstate the thinginess or fixed stability of materiality' (p. 20), my intention is to explore what matter *does* rather than what its essence is; to foreground *force* (rather than entity), *energy* (rather the stuff). I also deploy *event* as an energy producing movement and *affect* as an intensity of encounters generated in-between. The Deleuzo-Guattarian sensibilities – force, event and affect – work all-at-once with energy of matter through productive encounters that open ongoing possibilities for becoming-something different. As with Deleuzo-Guattarian imaginaries, none comes before any other, each is enfolded in the others, merging with and emerging from.

Force is explicated by Stagoll as:

any capacity to produce a change or "becoming"...All of reality is an expression and consequence of interactions between forces...colliding in some particular and unpredictable way...Every force exerts itself upon others. No force can exist apart from its inter-relationships with other forces and, since such associations of struggle are always temporary, forces are always in the process of becoming different or passing out of existence, so that no particular force can be repeated.

(Stagoll, 2005: 107, original italics)

energy of the event. In this in-between space the imagined game materializes. Apparent also is an affective happening of human~material relations and how every body – human and nonhuman – enfolds and is enfolded in every other body. No force is separable or replicable; the milieu is always already contingent and complex. Continuing with their conversation, the emerging game and the materiality of the playground force-fully affect an event of the becoming-strong girls through movements of energy:

Libby: *Hey we better be strong girls...we can be strong girls now* (raising her arms in air). *We can be strong girls* (bringing hands to chest) *and...we...can...do...it!* (pumping her arms in the air with each word). Libby runs off and Lee and Alice follow, jumping up onto and then over the corner of some wooden decking, then circling back over a swing bridge constructed only of ropes – a carefully negotiated de~territorializing flow.

Attending to the human~nonhuman relational intra-activity, within which both human and material worlds become intelligible to the other in movements of becoming-with the other, it is hard to overlook the link between Libby's strong girls proclamation and accompanying gestures and activity of her leading the others in demonstrating their physical strength – running, jumping and negotiating the swing bridge. The forces and energy of her choice of movement is expressed through

Forces are always already in process of becoming different; there are thus no fixed 'things-in- themselves'. Rather, what we consider to be the stuff of matter is perceptible only in the constantly changing relations with other bodies, human and material. In this sense, things do not have an 'independent existence or essence', rather, through ongoing mo(ve)ments of energy, that is, lines of flight or flows of de~territorialization, the human~materiality entanglement is constantly changing; the milieu we~they operate in is 'contingent and infinitely complex' (Stagoll, 2005: 106–8). Events as energy producing mo(ve)ments within this milieu, are also characterized as change – 'an event is not a particular state or happening in itself, but something made actual in the State or happening' (p. 87). It is a milieu of becoming in which the happening itself is the thing; there are no specific outcomes, only mo(ve)ments of openings to possibilities for forces and energy to be generated anew – becoming-child, happening-thing.

(E)merging from/with/in understandings of force and event is affect, similarly experienced as flows among bodies. Colman (2005b) says that affect is the change or variation that happens with/in encounters between bodies, through processes, forces, powers and expressions – 'affective happenings [are] occasions where things and bodies are altered' (p. 12). Affects are the activity of encounters, happenings of the in-between of and...and...and... in this mo(ve)ment a ceaseless intra-activity of forces always already dynamic and fluxive. Alluding to

the agency of the decking and bridge and in relation to what the materials require of her physical prowess – in this event the decking and bridge as phenomena 'produce effects and alter situations' (Bennett, 2004: 355). The children's collective performativity as a severalty of becoming-strong girls is all-at-once affected by, and is an affect of the decking and the bridge – children and materiality intelligibly respond and are responsive to the other. Decking and bridge, along with the game itself, becomes a site of emergence of the becoming-strong girls' performativity of power-fullness and strength. This redistribution of agential forces materializes not as a body of discrete subjects and objects but as a proliferation of 'movement and rest, speed and slowness between unformed elements' (Deleuze & Guattari, 1987: 266). With/in the intra-activity of encounters of affective spaces in-between, human and material agency slip-slides and congeals through power-fully different expressions of indiscrete bodies.

Back to the data, Libby and Lee both demonstrate an understanding of experiential forces among human~nonhuman bodies:

Lee: ...and we can need maps.
Libby: ooh yeah we have to make maps to be strong girls.

In proclaiming that they need maps to be strong girls, they indicate that only through the affective force or agency of the maps can they become strong girls – entangled performativity the a-subjectivity of affect as being without form or structure, Deleuze and Guattari (1987) explain affects as becomings. Affective happenings thus circulate as events, energy mo(ve)ments and forces in which human~material bodies collide and are altered; force and affect are (im)perceptible expressions of events, constituted of movement or speed. Always already in motion, force, energy, event and affect are singularly and severally elusive, operating in a milieu of slip-sliding, rhizo-relational intra-activity and opening possibilities anew for a-humanist[2] readings of matters of materiality in a redistribution of embodied human~material agency.

Possibilities open, transgressing logocentric manifestations of culture and matter – culture can no longer be exclusively figured as discourse, language or ideology, for example, nor matter equated only with lived experience. Disrupting the life|matter binary, in turn dominated hierarchically by the *adult* human world, also disrupts subject|object, in which people trump things; also disrupted is the discursive|material that promotes words of minds over the materiality of matter. The stuff of things now emerges from the shadows, as hierarchical relationships are cast aside and incipiently different relations open in rhizo unruliness of matter and humanity. Human and nonhuman commingle, inseparable within this flattened responsiveness to matter and a renewed sensitivity opens to an assemblage of forever growing relations.

of becoming-children (e)merging with/through the materiality of mapping. While the mapping of the game in their imagination (the virtual) and on paper (the actual) is a way of negotiating the game-plan and the plane of playing the game, it is the agency of the maps that actualizes the game – an affective assemblage redistributing children, game, maps and the artefacts they depict.

In another mo(ve)ment of redistributed agency that de~ territorializes (supposedly inert) material and (lively) human relations, the life|matter and discursive|material binaries are flattened. Within the Goldilocks game, Libby, discussing the significance of the bowl of sand as Goldilocks' porridge, places it on the sandpit edging beside Kane, an entangled Willy Wonka~monster~bear. Turning agency in on itself in an a-humanist reading, the relations among the players of the intertwined games cannot happen without material forces being considered active agents. Affective forces of materiality become perceptible through the placement of the *bowl* on the *sandpit edging* and the ensuing seemingly chaotic flight through the *sandpit*. There is a materialization of intra-active forces as Libby, Lee and Alice enact their embodied victim~strong girls power-fullness. Also, what presents as chaos in the constantly changing direction and the yelling – including Kane's – of their flight, is a lively materialization of the agential force and affect of the entangled chocolate factory~monster~Goldilocks games. Human and material in enfolded matters of vibrancy of stuff and

Matters of materiality and the materiality of matter involves re-thinking the object, (re)turning to *it*, turning *it* around multidimensionally in a hybrid reconstitution of nonhuman worlds that we de-territorialize. It involves casting aside matter as inert and considering the stuff of *it* as 'vibrant' (Bennett, 2010), alongside a living and 'lively humanity' (Anderson & Tolia-Kelly, 2004: 669). Discussing the vibrancy and vitality of matter, Jane Bennett (2010) considers thing-power as 'the curious ability of inanimate things to animate, to act, to produce effects dramatic and subtle' (p. 6). Also, in moving towards 'ecological sensibility', which works with a shared, vital materiality of persons and things, 'human power is itself a kind of thing-power' (p. 10). But Bennett asks: Is this claiming more than it is possible to know? Questioning the possibility of making too much of materiality becomes redundant when open to a diffractive encounter. Barad (2007) explains diffraction as a wave rushing towards the shore being disrupted by a rock. The water parts around the rock only to come together again, producing a different kind of wave that still (re)produces the activity of the pre-rock encounter. Considering diffraction, in terms of object~people relations, involves an ongoing, entangled activity of co-existence, embodiment and mutual interdependence: 'What is manifest arrives through humans but not entirely because of them' (Bennett, 2010: 17). For example, the force of things materializes through the energy of people and is perceived as affective encounters of intensities generated in-between... *and*...the energy of matter diffracts through human forces,

vitality of humanity.

But, like Jane Bennett, I ask: Am I at risk of making too much out of this (re)reading of children's relations with materiality in the playing of their games? This is not a *reflective* question that considers more of the same through a move that bends back on itself. Rather, it is *diffractive*. In a shattering and scattering move, things/ideas are interrupted and (re)distributed differently; on this differential plane shadows of the tracing are always already on the map.

Flying over Victoria, from Melbourne to Adelaide, I look down on country marked by winding contours of ancient creek beds long since dried up and absorbed into pastoral land, the pasture marked as paddocks by a grid of fences. I see a smooth map of old rivers embodied in the tracing of striated paddocks. It is not that either map or tracing reflects the other; each is (in) the other. Diffraction.

There are moments in the children's play when diffractive mo(ve)ments of intra-active becomings – of children and matter – is perceptible. Kane is attempting to organize five children into a different chocolate factory game (in the *Rhizo-mapping* plateau). He is talking the game into being – in itself a relational materialist move, also diffractive – as they all draw maps:

manifesting as affective relations in an assemblage of relational materialism. This relational ontology is an always already changing assemblage of intra-activity of people~thing-power, an overlapping of human being and thing-ness slip-sliding, colliding, eliding.

Barad (2008) also presents matter as an active agent – '*matter is substance in its intra-active becoming – not a thing, but a doing, a congealing of agency*' (p. 139, original italics, underline added). Thus, agentic capacity becomes differentially distributed throughout the activity of human and material relations. Neither is privileged over the other, rather, agency is constituted through an intra-activity of bodies and forces in processes of interconnecting and interfering one with others. Within human~materiality relations, people and things are enfolded as performative agents, as interdependent bodies always affecting and being affected. As Latour (1996) says, people and things 'exchange properties and replace one another' (p. 61), this displacing the thing-ness of subject and object with activity of events. The subject|object binary dissolves and what becomes important are the relations in-between. Similarly, the material|discursive binary fades within an ongoing, mutually constitutive engagement of mind and matter. Matter and meaning are entangled in an assemblage of agentic forces of *things human* and *things material*, generating a human~ materiality milieu of performativity perceptible only as flows through/with/in intra-activity with others and characterized

Kane: *So we have to go past the chocolate waterfall, back past me, and then we go up the river, and then we go... 'Scuse me, watch what the map's gonna tell you. You go past the chocolate waterfall. Hey everybody look at the map!*

Although Kane may be announcing his desire for leadership through talking about his mapping ideas, he makes perceptible the agency of the materials at hand and, at least momentarily, disrupts the life|matter binary as he passes his (desired) authority to the map. For him, the map has a life of its own; it is a heterogeneous body; it talks, so watch it to see what it says! Simultaneously, Nadia dismantles the discursive|material hierarchy in presenting the agency of her map; she has made it and now illuminates the authority it has become. In few words she promotes materiality of matter (the agency of her map) over words of minds (Kane's *talk* about his intentions):

Nadia rolls up her map: *This is the map where we get lost, OK?*
Kane, rolling his map: *Well this is the map.*
Nadia, adding more to her map: *Yeah, but this is the map where we get lost.*
Kane: *Mmmmm and this is the map where we know where to go.*
Nadia hands her map to Kane and, signalling the maps are made, she leads the way outside.

The notion that she may be conceding authority to Kane does not fit with the assertive becoming-Nadia at work. A relational only by ongoing shifts and de~territorialization of relational movement.

What is different here to how we generally think about our interactions with the material world, and particularly children's interactions with artefacts and materials of their play(ing), is the idea that both human and material worlds are agentic – things are not a priori constructs, rather they are 'agentially enacted' (Barad, 2007: 150). As with discursive practices, matter is understood in 'dynamic and productive terms – in terms of intra-activity' (p. 150). Matter is not perceived as an array of particular things and fixed substances; it is understood as the relations of one thing among many others. In movements with/ in moments – mo(ve)ments – matter is perceptible in recursive relations among bodies in intra-active processes of ongoing materialization. Matter becomes substance only in its intra-active becoming.

Lenz Taguchi aptly summarizes Barad's contention that materials of material worlds are performative agents: 'Everything is taking part in a dynamic process of intra-activity and materialisation as an ongoing flow of agency, through which a part of the world makes itself intelligible to another part of the world' (Lenz Taguchi, 2010: 29). Organisms and matter of both human and nonhuman worlds are inextricably intertwined in matter(s) and wor(l)ds of materiality. Barad (2007) says, '*the material and the discursive are mutually*

materialist reading suggests she is making her map agentic alongside Kane's, that she understands that she is always already embodied in heterogeneous relations with materiality. Human~material bodies exchanging properties and becoming the other are differentially, diffractively distributed, always already an assemblage.

The proliferation of ebbs and flows of speed and movement, in dynamic flows of de~territorialization of human and material worlds at times is overwhelming – in this thinking~writing, human~material, virtual~actual (ad)venture. Also for Tim enmeshed in the actual human~material experience of his bad guys hunt game with Piri (in the *Becoming-child(ren) becoming-power-full* plateau). Tim and Piri have each collected more stuff than they can comfortably carry – camera, phone, map and small wooden traffic sign. This stuff opens an intra-active space of encounters amidst a complex of human, material and discursive forces when their game is challenged by Josh, Rory, Lex and Adam who are vying for Tim's camera, which they want for their game:

Having taken Piri's stuff from him, Josh tries to join the game: *Oh yeah, and I'm the baddie and I stole your stuff.*
Tim resists: *I'm going to call the bad boss to take you away.*
Josh: *Oh, so you want to get me away.*
Josh has admitted the theft and Tim now openly arranges his equipment on the top of a reel. Rory jumps on the reel from

implicated in the dynamics of intra-activity' (p. 152, original italics). Lenz Taguchi (2010) explains it thus: 'The material affects our discursive understandings just as much as our discursive understandings affect the material reality around us' (p. 30). In other words, organisms and matter come together as an assemblage of relations in intra-active spaces of mutual agency, so that children's games, their maps, camera and other play materials have a relational affect, not only because of the children's interactions with them and their choice of engaging with them but also because of their materiality. The materials themselves may seem inert, but what happens within the in-between spaces of encounters is a mutual embodiment.

Transgressing pervasive binarial discourses opens (to) possibilities for considering relational non–human forces as a plane of redistribution of agency among social relations and materiality. In this horizontal move, a plane of proliferation amasses, constituted through 'relations of movement and rest, slowness and speed between unformed elements' (Deleuze & Guattari, 1987: 266); the plane is a-centred, a-hierarchical, always already in flux, generating assemblages through arrangements of speed within a multiplicity of space-times. This is a plane of immanence, in which subjects (e.g. children, adults) and objects (e.g. nonhuman materials) are not perceived as structured forms, rather they are embodied subjects–objects made perceptible through movements with others. It is a milieu of affects, of embodied relations, whereby the material world

above, glaring at Tim at close range while Lex, who has rushed in from another direction, grabs at the camera, saying: *Can I have that? I need it, I need a camera.* Tim clutches the camera close to his body and Josh, Rory and Lex retreat.
Adam arrives and eyes the camera: *You don't really need that.*
Tim: *Yes we do, we take pictures of us. We take pictures of each other.*

Adam: *OK just give me the camera.*

As Law (2003) says, 'the social is nothing other than patterned networks of heterogeneous materials... the stuff of the social isn't simply human' (p. 2); it involves materiality as well. In a chaotic assemblage of speed and movement, of human and nonhuman dynamically changing subject–object relations a messy rhizo sensibility is all there seems to be as desired ownership of the camera then oscillates: Adam demands the camera and Tim refuses to hand it over; Tim offers it and Adam refuses to take it; Adam again demands it and Tim refuses him; Adam stalks off and Tim runs after him trying to give the camera to him; Adam turns and points his hand, like a gun, at Tim. Tim seems confused as he wanders after Adam... (im)perceptibly confusing materiality matters of human relations...

In this slip-sliding writing alongside, words about playing and the play(ing) with/in words becomes a way of expressing materiality matters and matters of materiality. Flowing with becomes agentic...*and*...the intra-activity among human and material worlds (e)merges through the performativity of human beings...*and*...non/human forces becoming intelligible, each to the other. Enfolded non/human forces in the data include: the games children imagine and play out; artefacts relating to those games, such as, maps, the playground space and the resources available; materials used for generating maps; materials used for playing their games and engaging with their maps; maps as tools for engaging with the playground; the video camera... *and*...the materiality of the data merges with the discursive the theorizing...

Harker (2005), opening to affective time-spaces of material relations is a gesture towards a more nuanced approach to play(ing) and becomes another way of avoiding inhabiting the notion of play and of reducing children's playing to things fixed, definable and identifiable even. With/in children's curricular performativity and this performativity of (my) adult curricular understandings everything is always already elusively flowing and changing...becoming-child(ren) becoming-something different becoming-embodied-I...curriculum as (a) milieu(s) of becoming in matters of engagement and engagement with matter...

leaving the plateau...

Through this juxtaposition of an engagement with matter that moves outside the more common focus of matters of engagement an incipiently different assemblage (e)merges – a plane of immanence proliferates in which 'form is constantly being dissolved' (Deleuze & Guattari, 1987: 267). Thing-ness is made (im)perceptible, as elusive, dynamic and changing as human subjectivity. Events are not *things* that happen, they are *happenings* of speed, rest, flow and movement; similarly embodied in mo(ve)ments of becoming, humans are perceptible as becoming-children~becoming-adult. In becoming intelligible each to the other, human and material worlds are always already an intra-activity of encounters among becoming-something different and matters of materiality – a becoming-thingness – all operating as commingling happenings of energy forces (im)perceptible only as affect. Bringing some of the data alongside the literature involves furthering a material~discursive engagement with the literature. In these slip-sliding rhizo mo(ve)ments the form the data characterizes within the right-hand column is dissolved; and the form of juxtaposing literature with data dissolves as two stories both same and different alongside one another, in similarly different ways tell the same story, diffractively, of human~material relations. Boundaries and categories are no longer, all becoming in conditions of becoming-thingness~becoming-children~becoming-adult. That developmental psychology, for example, tries to think about children only as a human entity and that conventional approaches to curriculum attempt to operate primarily on a material plane becomes (im)perceptibly impossible. The *Te Whāriki* description of curriculum opens (to) incipiently different possibilities involving mean materiality matters (the potentiality for these italicized)...

> the sum total of the *experiences*, *activities*, and *events*, whether direct or indirect, which occur within an *environment* designed to foster children's learning and development...curriculum is provided by the people, *places*, and *things* in the child's environment; the adults, the other children, the *physical environment*, and the *resources*.
>
> (Ministry of Education, 1996: 10–11, italics added)

...*and*...what is perceptible is that the affective encounters in-between of non/human worlds materialize in other space-times, such as with/in the thinking~writing relations circulating through my (our) thoughts and thinking, the writing of my (our) thoughts and thinking, the written word, the keyboard and computer screen, the emerging book~assemblage amassing through plateaus that are always already constantly changing, singularly and severally, all (a) milieu(s) of becoming...*and*...in approaching the end of this plateau, it becomes apparent that I must (re)turn to the other plateaus to re-site the concept of interactivity and reflection and recite a discourse of intra-activity and diffraction, which may be confusing as I may then be using it before explaining it. Rhizome at work; the rhizome intensifies, defying linearity, as what comes after affects, is affected by and is an affect of what comes before...*and*...I (re)turn, yet again, to the notion that becoming is beyond before...*and*...in the same mo(ve)ment an *Aftrwrding* unfolds...

Notes

1   Any use of 'nonhuman' here refers to material worlds.
2   Thinking 'a-humanist' displaces the humanist primacy that arguably lingers in a 'posthumanist' approach.

Aftrwrdng

What matters with putting rhizo research, rhizomethodology and rhizoanalysis to work is what (e)merges from/with/in the middle of (the) rhizome – the illuminations that diffract through what is happening in the shadows like momentary glimpses of dappled pools of light shifting with the sun, light fading in and out, coming and going through windblown shadows, clouds (e)merging and dissolving, everything de~materializing, de~territorializing. Thoughts, ideas, thinking that cannot be captured or seized; all are elusive, only momentarily (im)perceptible because everything is always already becoming-something different. The notion of 'seizing' characterizes what this assemblage of plateaus is not: to seize is to take *hold* of an *object firmly*, to take *advantage* of something, to take *official possession* of something, to take somebody into *custody*, to become *jammed* as a *result* of *pressure*, to become painfully *stiff* or *immobile*, to come to a sudden and *permanent halt*, to endow with *ownership*, to *tie* or *secure* (*Encarta World English Dictionary*, 1999).[1] But, there is no fixed structure or definitive ownership marked in this book~assemblage; in its a-centredness the expectation is that every reading will open differing curricular understandings, for every reader with every reading. However, seize also means to understand an idea or concept especially quickly and this notion of speed, of momentarily grasping or glimpsing, is embodied in the text throughout, at times overwhelmingly so in the writing. Every part and process of the thinking~writing resists being pinned or tied down, hence, my proffering the notion of curriculum as (a) milieu(s) of becoming, in which 'becoming is beyond before'.[2]

Re(con)ceiving children in curriculum is a poststructuralist, transgressive project, negotiating a multidimensional multiplicity of thought~thinking towards un/en/folding what is (im)perceptibly elusive. In early childhood curriculum, developmental psychology informed perspectives of children and childhood have dominated the past century. Although *Te Whāriki* sought to break from these in the mid-1990s, the sociocultural ideals it aspires to continue the co-constructivist yet structuralist endeavour of *scaffolding* children into rationalized, mature adulthood and the *what* and *how* of curriculum pervades. Curriculum as a learning~living (ad)venture is promoted in *Te Whāriki* workings of a strengths-based approach incorporating flowing with children's interests, but thirty years on from the emergence of the reconceptualist conversation a modernist perspective, accompanied by the adult|child binary, is sustained. So, my question is: What of *receiving* children in curriculum?

Receiving children in curriculum involves different ways of (re)thinking understandings of children – what children's understandings are and how we think about children, their understandings and their childhood(s). It involves thinking of children living~working~learning *with* adults – an embodied severalty of children and adults – some merely younger or older than others. Disadvantaging children on the grounds of their younger age begs questions around the less stratified concept of adulthood. Young adults and the elderly may be regarded separately in certain circumstances, but discernible degrees in the 50 years or so of the dominating middle mass of adulthood are less marked by an ageist agenda. Thus, bringing children (with young adults and elderly people) and their understandings into this unmarked middle is a viable proposition. If there are no explicit boundaries in the middle mass of adulthood, why have limits at either end? Young children continually display their capacity in regard to their understanding of learning~living. For example, Marcy's 'disruptive behaviour' (in *Preceding echoes*) provides a glimpse into what she understood she needed of curriculum – in her desired curricular performativity Marcy has the right to express these as 'needs'. Even in developmental terms, supporting her desire to do a puzzle is arguably more significant for her in that moment than sitting at a table listening to a story while waiting for morning tea to be served; and, in sociocultural terms, the ideals of agentic subjectivity uphold her right to be in charge of her own learning and to set her own curricular agenda. Tim (in *Becoming-children becoming-power-full*) is another power-full example of children expressing understandings of what matters for (his) learning~living. He clearly communicates his desires for his curriculum performativity.

But, as the middling of this text unfolds, Tim and Marcy's activity of singularly becoming-child and severally becoming-children is perceptible – they knew *what* they needed to do, *how* to go about it, that is, what capacities to deploy and *why* it mattered to their learning~living. In various mo(ve)ments Tim and Marcy and every child in the data snippets here work continually with singular and several desires for their living~learning as becoming-child(ren) – Marcy's attempt to finish her puzzling was as much a condition of power-fullness as Tim's explicitly confronting me was an expression of his. Through conditions and expressions of subjectivity they endeavour to become something different in a de~territorializing line of flight of the multidimensional becoming-one of singularity and becoming-one of several. Considering children as responsible and response-able thinkers~learners with sophisticated understandings about learning~living opens possibilities for them and their desires, and for respect and dignity as young human beings within (a) milieu(s) of curricular performativity.

What is curriculum then for becoming-child(ren)? Curriculum as (a) milieu(s) of becoming generates space-times for becoming-child(ren) to negotiate their becomings, in flows of becoming-power-full becoming-intense becoming-imperceptible

– response-ably made perceptible by the severalty of children in the intersecting games in the *Children performing curriculum complexly* plateau, for example. Curriculum as (a) milieu(s) of becoming also becomes a space-time where(by) the adult|child binary is dissolved into commingling child~adult expressions of curricular performativity in doing~learning~living. Also disrupted in milieu(s) of becoming, are the life|matter and discursive|material binaries through entangled intra-activity of becoming-child(ren)~becoming-adult~becoming-materiality (in *Materiality matters*). All are enmeshed in the *Te Whāriki* definition of curriculum and, in regard to curricular performativity, perceptible through the entangled living~life experience that children bring to early childhood settings and the possibilities that open for becoming-children to further work their experience in those settings. Young children becoming curriculum becomes discernible.

Te Whāriki presents early childhood curriculum as opening opportunities for 'new learning' and 'alternative ways of doing things', 'making connections across time and place' and 'establishing different kinds of relationships' (Ministry of Education, 1996: 9). In promoting children as life-long learners – becoming-child(ren)~becoming adult(s) – it is stated that 'children need both the confidence to develop and capacity to continue acquiring new knowledge and skills' (p. 18). This constitutes a multidimensional picture of what early childhood education might be for young children working with different ways of doing learning that connect in various relations of different space-times. But, to analyse these and evaluate what they mean for young children and their learning runs counter to keeping the whāriki open and connectable in all its becomings. What matters is to make more of the matting through commingling matters of curricular performativity of both children and adults – adults and children operating diffractively in their situated contexts, working through areas of connectivity of an array of human~material~discursive relations of the becoming-milieu of curriculum, always already becoming-something different. This may sound overwhelming but it happens.

Recently in an Aotearoa New Zealand kindergarten I was some of a milieu of vibrant human, more than human, material relations involving the kindergarten children, siblings passing through, teachers, parents, grandparents, caregivers, rabbit, birds, gardens, autumn leaves, sand, mud, puddles, grass, trees, hillside, pathways (and more) and a multitude of readily accessible materials and resources, inside and out, momentarily affecting and being affected by others in-between – a milieu of complexly intra-active relations of curricular performativity. In the programme and physical surroundings of such early childhood settings there is much open space – unhurried and uninterrupted space-times of uncluttered play spaces, with intentional plans and spontaneous planes open to surprise, unrestricted inside~outside flow and accessibility to materials and relationships. In de~territorializing lines of flight of these space-times children negotiate social, natural and material worlds in intra-active, commingling relations of the in-between. Relations (e)merge as assemblages of children, various adults, particular animals in the setting, materials (paint, dress-ups, books and many kinds of tools, such as brushes, hammers, iPads, cameras to name a few) and the natural world

(sand, water, grass, hillside, trees, puddles, wind, sun). In human~material relational areas of connectivity, who or what instigates which mo(ve)ment is inde-
terminable and is unnecessary to decide – a priori agency dissolves within the
flattened binary. It may look like chaos as children flow through space-times of the
setting, pausing to attire themselves in dress-ups, flowing into art spaces, making
artworks before moving on, some spilling into the block corner, others pausing to
play with ephemeral materials to create temporary works of stones, glass baubles,
feathers, leaves, sticks, shells, (re)grouping in a flow outside, reading books and
conversing with a teacher along the way, racing into the adventure playground,
slip-sliding virtually through an imaginary game related to their chosen dress-ups
and slip-sliding in the muddy ground outside. Inviting spaces of materiality set
up by the teachers are enriched by parents, other adults and younger siblings and
time takes on different meanings – what is measurable as a tracing of about thirty
minutes in the chaotic flow described here, also becomes a complex mapping of
play(ing), a performative space-time continually de~territorializing, perceptively
productive to non/human learning~living of/by the becoming-child(ren).

So much is happening
in this mixed milieu of desiring-
machines
that it becomes hard to see force and
affect of intra-activity…
so I (re)turn to a poeitic juxtaposition to negotiate a way through,
towards making perceptible what
matters…in mo(ve)ments of this
space-time…

It seems that what matters is
trying to understand re(con)ceiving
children in curriculum, not from
a top-down, adult(erated) exterior
perspective but from interior
areas of connectivity whereby
young children in their becomings
are situated with/in their curricular
performativity.
No longer either|or, now
and…and…and…
The child|adult binary disrupted.

All of us, becoming-
children~becoming adult, opening (to)

De~territorializing non/human and
material worlds
children, adult researcher, plateaus,
texts and space-times in-between
attempting to unfold a lucid conversation towards generating possibilities
for thinking differently
in the virtual worlds of the texts of this
book~assemblage
in the actual worlds of becoming-
children learning~living in early childhood settings.

I feel like the fictitious young Aborigi-
nal Australian, supposedly inarticulate
in (post)colonial terms, described by
author Alex Miller:

'Shelving the information by whatever
means he possessed for cataloguing
such things, niched among the
galleries and tenements of his thought,
arranged in an order scarcely to be
imagined, *either of an infinite sim-
plicity or complex beyond systems of
ordering and structure. A mystical*

opportunities for learning a/new, doing things differently, always already connecting in space-times that transgress conventional understandings of time and place, immersed, entangled in a multiplicity of a-centred, a-hierarchical relations among people, animals and things in non/human~material worlds.

Children operating in rhizo becomings, constantly becoming-something different, in oscillating mo(ve)ments of confidence and timidity make perceptible their flowing capacity of desire in their understandings, enhancing their always already erudite knowledge and skills; adults in these becomings open (to) possibilities for re(con)ceiving children and curricular performativity and intensifying in rhizo ways the power-fullness of the living~learning of becoming-child(ren).

landscape of dreams and visions, fluid and irreducible, repeated upon itself infinitely, the problem of storage and retrieval overcome.' (Miller, 2002: 184, italics added)

But is this arguably complicit, simplicity~complexity a default mechanism of my struggle to 'seize' ideas from/with/in this site of emergence? Or is it a machinic assemblage of desirable thoughts and thinking, unavoidably elusive, constantly in motion, moving multidirectionally, never-endingly multidimensional, always already becoming-intensities of liminality? In trying (not) to seize the machinics of the (im)possible, am I generating a mechanical seizure of thoughts in my attempt to hold fast to certain ideas? Put the tracing back on the map say Deleuze and Guattari. Assemble a multiplicity of texts on the same plan(e) in conditions and expressions of ongoing performativity...

Put rhizome to work. Turn the woven mat inside out, into rhizo-matting, mapping a play(ing) of rhizomethodology, rhizomapping, becomings-, curricular performativity to negotiate the milieu of principles, strands, goals, programmes, philosophies and differing early childhood settings envisaged within the curricular possibilities that *Te Whāriki* opens. The intention of the curriculum developers, Margaret Carr and Helen May with lead Māori writers Tamati and Tilly Reedy to present curriculum as a dictionary of possibilities, not a book of recipes, continues with/in the plateaus of this book~assemblage. De~territorialize the plan(e) – the plan of the tracing and the plane of the map. If there is an obsession, it is with the question, 'How does it work?' How does curriculum work in the contextually appropriate plan(e)s with/in which all early childhood educationists work? How do becoming-children operate in these plan(e)s? How might these plan(e)s be never-ending sites of emergence, continually opening (to) possibilities, generating intensities of becoming-child(ren)~becoming-adult(s) in matters of non/human~material relations? If there are any answers, they are yours to un/en/fold as you along with other readers negotiate the thought~thinking of these plateaus. In matters of materiality, the plateaus speak for themselves, each (re)telling a story of re(con)ceiving becoming-child(ren) in mo(ve)ments of curricular performativity.

At the ~~beginning~~, I wrote a *Letter to Marcy*, noting that the book~assemblage gathered together here is but a postscript to the complex storying of her puzzling mo(ve)ment. Pausing within the milieu of plateaus assembled here, I contemplate the ~~end~~ of this *Aftrwrdng* as merely momentarily leaving the space-times of an infinity of commingling doing~living~learning of rhizome. Writing an *Aftrwrdng* free of constraints of linearly informed decisions or conclusions is challenging, hence the poietic juxtaposition deployed here. It is more than difficult to 'describe' some 'thing' that 'makes sense' while saying something different in regard to curricular ideas; it is (im)perceptibly (im)possible. However, I persist, not with making sense but with thinking differently. At the ~~end~~ of the *Children perform-ing curriculum complexly* plateau I present some supposedly simple ideas made perceptible with/in the children's curricular performativity of the games they are playing. I write that children thrive within the complexity of their spontaneous play(ing) and that linear processes are not necessary to the productive play(ing) of generative learning~living experiences; that children are adept at responding to possibilities that open through flowing with notions of *and... and... and...* I allege that linear processes obstruct and are destructive to generativity. I rehearse a rhi-zoanalysis of gendered performativity of the embodied victim~strong girls and suggest that their expressions of power-fullness opened (to) a generative line of flight, which de~territorializes the game, their subjectivities and adult understand-ings of (non-)gendered activity. I work with the notion that the children's leader-ship subject positionings are similarly fluid.

Yet some may say that modernist thought arguably oozes from the cracks albeit in offerings of different 'interpretations' of 'behaviour', now 'classified' in rhizo ways, for example. However, in the plan(e)s of thinking here my intentions are not about interpreting or assigning specific meanings but with attending to con-nectivity and how things work. With/in this, children's behaviour is perceived as expressions of desire and power-fullness, all attempting to avoid modernist cod-ing, adult(erated) positionings and concretizing but inevitably slip-sliding through these. Thinking differently outside modernist – behaviourist, structuralist, positiv-ist – analyses, involves putting the tracing back on the map, not replacing the trac-ing with a map. Disrupting the binary with *and... and... and...* rather than reversing its either|or-ness to create another binary. Other generative space-time possibilities of becoming now open – space-times of becoming-child(ren)... *and...* space-times of becoming-adult(s), in conditions here of becoming-researcher~becoming-reader~writer~thinker. It is (less) about arriving at (new) thoughts... *and...* (more) about learning to process thought and thinking in other ways otherwise through/ towards thinking differently. As we continue to ask 'How does it work?' thoughts outside currently structuralist repertoires may then emerge from the shadows through thinking (with)... *and... and... and...*

From/with/in the shadows of intra-active, in-between space-times, some different ideas for re(con)ceiving children in curriculum have become perceptible, in rhizo

ways of thinking differently rather than in producing different thoughts with/in the
commingling plateaus of young children becoming curriculum. In ideas plan(e)s
of de~territorializing curricular performativity through negotiating rhizo ways of
thinking~writing~doing I have worked to foreground the idea that there is always
already more happening with/in the shadows. For example, ideas perceptible as
engendering becoming-child(ren)... *and*...their childhood(s*)...and*...their curriculum performativity...*and*...adult perceptions of these...*and*...the incompleteness
of the txt-ese of this *Aftrwrdng* itself signalling incompleteness. There is always
already more happening, more to be happened upon. In leaving the space-times
of this shadowy thinking, I (re)turn to write again to Marcy in this now flattened
plane of becoming-child(ren)~becoming-adult(s). As with the opening letter, the
language is mine towards young children becoming curriculum, resonating with
re(con)ceiving children in curriculum through their curricular performativity.

Dear Marcy,

I write to you as all becoming-child(ren) in all space-times of Aotearoa New Zealand
early childhood educational settings and beyond. There have been (im)perceptibly
difficult mo(ve)ments to negotiate in producing this book~assemblage, it being a
mere postscript to my initial letter to you; not least, difficulties of modernist thoughts
pervading my supposedly poststructuralist ways of operating. In the commingling
doing~learning towards un/en/folding the question 'How does it work?' some of
these seepages I noticed and either wrote out or wrote into explications of rhizo
ways of thinking. But there are likely other seepages that I have not (yet) noticed,
their (im)perceptibility be(com)ing an ongoing challenge to generating ways for
thinking differently. However, while learning to think differently embodies virtual
thoughts about children, childhood(s) and curricular performativity, the actual
wor(l)ds that constitute the space-times of your learning~living are still fraught with
difficulties.

   Curricular performativity or doing~learning for you is similarly challenged from/
with/in limited and limiting modernist discourses extensively coded by classifica-
tions and categories, sequential ordering of developmental skills and standardized
ways of achieving these. This is demanding and tiring, sapping energy of children and
adults as conformity necessarily and adversely impacts productive learning~living
in such striated spaces. Flattening the adult|child, material|discursive binarial walls
of this modernist prison of thought, concerned with control and confinement of
curriculum, children and childhood(s), opens (to) possibilities for spaces of co-
existence in/through/which becoming-child(ren)~becoming-adult commingle, freely
mobile, singularly and severally. In such de~territorializing space-times children's
expressions of dissatisfaction about adult imposed expectations for curricular
performativity (e)merge differently. For you, Marcy, your actions of communicating
that your sitting at a table to listen to a story as neither a desire nor a priority for you
in that moment, means that neither you nor your behaviour is labelled disruptive,
rather that you have a responsible and response-able agenda to be respected.

There is no attempt to interrupt this, knowing that when you are hungry you will eat; knowing also that if sitting at a table is a skill necessary to school classroom learning – still three years away for you – you will learn to do that there. Early years are for your early childhood education; school readiness is about school being ready for you. Other binaries (e)merge from/with/in these closing words as hierarchical worlds of compulsory and formal learning of schools are made perceptible as attempting authority over non-compulsory, informal learning of early childhood settings – but another space-time awaits for flattening that one...

Doing away with hierarchical positioning, adults have no reason to interpret actions such as yours as being against them, their ideals and their aspirations for you. Rather, in these de~territorializing space-times your activity flows as expressions of *your* becoming-child(ren), expressions of *your* desires for ongoing becomings of *your* singular and several subjectivity. For educationists – practitioners, researchers, scholars – space-times are opening to practices and practising for thinking differently, through/with/in possibilities outside conventional discourses. In early childhood education, possibilities are with (simply) flowing with, or following de~territorializing flows of children in the complexity of their play(ing), so that children are no longer dependent on adults for curriculum provision and (supposedly) for their learning. In this, children are understood as learners ~researchers~curricularists embodied in recursive, responsible and productive teaching~learning relationships, always already becoming-child(ren) in relations with becoming-adults, with non/human~material worlds around about and with curricular wor(l)ds.

Historically, Marcy, Aotearoa New Zealand early childhood education has progressed through adult-centred teaching, child-centred learning into current trends of co-constructed child-adult shared learning experiences. The aspirations of co-construction reflect reciprocity but the inherent pedagogy separates children's and adult worlds. In a similar ways, formalized early childhood settings operating as striated sites of consumption, remediation and preparation for school distance the open, smooth spaces of less formalized settings where early childhood education is valued as significant matters of early learning~living years; also distanced is informal family/whānau/community learning. However, generating ways for thinking differently here, albeit inevitably an affect of my westernized subjectivity opens (to) possibilities for transgressing boundaries and for being situated alongside various eastern philosophies and Indigenous cultures, for example. Such possibilities (re)cites~sites curriculum as curriculum-ing, as embodied learning~teaching relations (re)turning to Deleuzo-Guattarian becoming, in which there is a commingling of becoming-child(ren) with/in dynamically changing processual negotiations that intensify expressions of monad~nomad singularity ~subjectivity. From/with/in my singular understandings, this way of re(con)ceiving children and their childhood(s) resonates with the curricular performativity of your doing~learning~living, Marcy, and with that of the children's play(ing) throughout the data of the research used here.

In an inside~outside mo(ve)ment of eversion, theorizing the pedagogy of play becomes a serious endeavour that benefits from a play-full approach (as in the *Play(ing)* plateau). Play is seriously children's doing~learning~living and in a play-full way it is elusive and definable only in terms of its complexity. As I flow with various children's play(ing) in processes of video-ing, transcribing the data and then engaging with a rhizoanalysis of the play(ing) of the data, everything becomes perceptible as inextricably entwined. Yet, in persisting with *not* trying to untangle what play is, instead operating through its de~territorializing flows, play's complexity is illuminated in a becoming of (im)perceptibility. Thus, in a similar way I avoid a factual analysis here of how practitioners can engage with this way of working to understand children, their childhood(s) and curriculum through their play(ing). Instead I suggest that it is in processual intra-active relations with children and their curricular performativity that ideas are illuminated; in mo(ve)ments of curricular performativity, in doing~learning with children we come to understand how things might work differently and how we might be(come) differently with children.

Through his play(ing) Tim foregrounds what matters for his power-full expressions of desire for his becoming-child(ren) and to his doing~learning~living; also what matters for (my) adult (mis)interpretations of what matters for him, other children nearby and adults in the setting operating in teaching~researching worlds. Learning to think as/of children embodied in conditions of power-fullness in respect of their desires for their power-fullness transgresses adult|child and material|discursive binaries and the authoritarian positioning that this high ground has unfairly afforded adults through many era. It also transgresses developmental/behaviourist analyses. Letting go of the familiar may be challenging, as what we are stepping into may not always be clearly definable as the same. Yet is stepping into a stream of flowing water ever the same? Rocks, sand, water and flow are always already becoming-something different; banks are undermined and the flow speeds through the middle. Stepping into space-times of becoming-something different opens (ourselves) (to) differing possibilities for reconceiving children and childhood(s) and for receiving children's curricular understandings towards generating incipiently different ways of theorizing curricular performativity. Diffractive possibilities open as waves emerge form and merge with preceding waves, waves that emerged before.

As for the rhizo of the inquiry, rhizomethodology and rhizoanalysis of research, *Rhizo-mapping* and *Children playing rhizo~methodology* are some of my workings of these. In operations of 'How does it work?' there is a multiplicity of multidimensional space-times of research~writing~thinking always already unfolding.

Marcy, it is time to leave this space-time of rhizo thought and thinking. It's not that the curricular conversation is over – it is never-ending. I think perhaps I will be forever in conversation with you as I continue working to receive young children in curriculum through reconceiving curricular performativity in (a) milieu(s) of becoming. So, this is but an ebb in the flow of the intermezzo…with/in in-between liminal spaces of interstiality, de~territorializing lines of flight, e/ir/dis/inter/ruptions of rhizomethodology…*and*…young children becoming curriculum…*and*…

Me he manu motu i te mahanga

As the bird escapes the snare, for you Marcy, I joy-fully escape the limitations of authoritarian modernist, linear, arborescent thought to fly freely with you and intensify the rhizome of/through this play-full becoming-thinking around re(con)ceiving children and curriculum differently.

Yours respect-fully, in power-full flows of play(ing) with/in our singular and several curricular performativity of becoming-child/ren~becoming-adult/researcher~becoming-curriculum.

Marg

P.S. The next moment is (y)ours[3]…for thinking differently…

Notes

1 See Soukhanov (1999).
2 Warren Sellers is the author of this phrase (personal conversation, 23 December 2011).
3 Making more of Daignault (1992, cited in Pinar *et al.*, 1995: 847).

References

Ailwood, J. (2003) Governing early childhood education through play. *Contemporary Issues in Early Childhood*, 4, 286–99.

Alaimo, S. & Hekman, S. (2008) *Material Feminisms*. Bloomington & Indianapolis: Indiana University Press.

Anderson, B. & Tolia-Kelly, D. (2004) Matter(s) in social and cultural geography. *Geoforum*, 35, 699–74.

Apple, M. (1979) *Ideology and Curriculum*. London: Routledge & Kegan Paul.

Ayers, W. (1992) The shifting ground of curriculum thought and everyday practice. *Theory Into Practice*, 31, 259.

Barad, K. (2007) *Meeting the Universe Halfway: Quantum Physics and the Entanglement of Matter and Meaning*. Durham, NC: Duke University Press.

Barad, K. (2008) Posthumanist performativity: toward an understanding of how matter comes to matter. *In* S. Alaimo & S. Hekman (eds) *Material Feminisms*. Bloomington: Indiana University Press, 120–54.

Bennett, J. (2004) The force of things: steps toward an ecology of matter. *Political Theory*, 32, 347–72.

Bennett, J. (2010) *Vibrant Matter: A Political Ecology of Things*. Durham & London: Duke University Press.

Biesta, G.J.J. & Osberg, D. (2007) Beyond re/presentation: a case for updating the epistemology of schooling. *Interchange*, 38, 15–29.

Bird, L. (2003) Seen and heard? Moving beyond discourses about children's needs and rights in educational policies. *New Zealand Journal of Educational Studies*, 38, 37–48.

Bishop, R. (2008) Freeing ourselves from neocolonial domination in research: a Kaupapa Māori approach to creating knowledge. *In* N.K. Denzin & Y.S. Lincoln (eds) *The Landscape of Qualitative Research*. 3rd edn. Los Angeles: Sage Publications, 145–84.

Bloch, M.N. (1992) Critical perspectives on the historical relationship between child development and early childhood education research. *In* S.A. Kessler & B.B. Swadener (eds) *Reconceptualizing the Early Childhood Curriculum: Beginning the Dialogue*. New York & London: Teachers College Press, 3–20.

Bloch, M.N. (2007) Reconceptualizing early childhood education and childhood studies: new theoretical frameworks and implications for early childhood research. Rethinking Early Childhood Education Conference, National Chengchi University, Taiwan.

Borgnon, L. (2007) Conceptions of the self in early childhood: territorializing identities. *Educational Philosophy and Theory*, 39, 264–74.

Boundas, C.V. (2005) Intensity. *In* A. Parr (ed.) *The Deleuze Dictionary*. Edinburgh: Edinburgh University Press, 131–2.

Braidotti, R. (1994a) *Nomadic Subjects: Embodiment and Difference in Contemporary Feminist Theory*. New York: Columbia University Press.

Braidotti, R. (1994b) Toward a new nomadism: feminist Deleuzian tracks; or, metaphysics and metabolism. *In* C.V. Boundas & D. Olkowski (eds) *Gilles Deleuze and the Theater of Philosophy*. New York & London: Routledge, 159–86.

Braidotti, R. (1994c) Sexual difference as a nomadic political project. *Nomadic Subjects: Embodiment and Difference in Contemporary Feminist Theory*. New York: Columbia University Press, 147–72.

Braidotti, R. (1996) Nomadism with a difference: Deleuze's legacy in a feminist perspective. *Man and World*, 29, 305–14.

Braidotti, R. (2000) Teratologies. *In* I. Buchanan & C. Colebrook (eds) *Deleuze and Feminist Theory*. Edinburgh: Edinburgh University Press, 156–72.

Braidotti, R. (2001) Becoming-woman: rethinking the positivity of difference. *In* E. Bronfen & M. Kavka (eds) *Feminist Consequences: Theory for the New Century*. New York: Columbia University Press, 381–413.

Braidotti, R. (2003) Becoming-woman: or sexual difference revisited. *Theory, Culture and Society*, 20, 43–64.

Bredekamp, S. (ed.) (1987) *Developmentally Appropriate Practice in Early Childhood Programs Serving Children From Birth Through Age 8*. Washington, DC: National Association for the Education of Young Children.

Bredekamp, S. & Copple, C. (eds) (1997) *Developmentally Appropriate Practice in Early Childhood Programs*. Washington, DC: National Association for the Education of Young Children.

Bruner, J.S. (1986) *Actual Minds, Possible Worlds*. Cambridge, MA: Harvard University Press.

Bruner, J.S. (1996) *The Culture of Education*. Cambridge, MA: Harvard University Press.

Bruns, A. (2007) Produsage: towards a broader framework for user-led content creation. *Creativity and Cognition 6*. Washington, DC.

Butler, J. (1990) *Gender Trouble: Feminism and the Subversion of Identity*. New York: Routledge.

Cannella, G.S. (ed.) (1997) *Deconstructing Early Childhood Education: Social Justice and Revolution*. New York: Peter Lang Publishing.

Cannella, G.S. (1998) Early childhood education: a call for the construction of revolutionary images. *In* W.F. Pinar (ed.) *Curriculum: Toward New Identities*. New York: Garland Publishing, Inc., 157–84.

Cannella, G.S. (2005) Reconceptualizing the field (of early care and education); if 'western' child development is a problem, then what do we do? *In* N. Yelland (ed.) *Critical Issues in Early Childhood Education*. Maidenhead, Berkshire: Open University Press, 17–39.

Cannella, G.S. & Kincheloe, J.L. (eds) (2002) *Kidworld: Childhood Studies, Global Perspectives, and Education*, New York: Peter Lang.

Cannella, G.S. & Viruru, R. (2004) *Childhood and Postcolonization: Power, Education, and Contemporary Practice*. New York: RoutledgeFalmer.

Carr, M. & May, H. (1993) Choosing a model. Reflecting on the development process of *Te Whāriki*: national early childhood curriculum guidelines in New Zealand. *International Journal of Early Years Education*, 1, 7–21.

Charlie and the Chocolate Factory (2005) Feature film. Directed by Burton, T. USA: Warner Brothers.

Clark, R. (2004) The imaginary. *The Literary Encyclopedia* [online].

'cobweb, n.' OED Online. June 2012. Oxford University Press. Online at: http://www.oed.com/view/Entry/35246?redirectedFrom=cobweb (accessed 15 August 2012).

Coetzee, J.M. (2007) *Diary of a Bad Year*. London: Harvill Secker.

Cole, M. & Wertsch, J.V. (1996) Beyond the individual-social antimony in discussions of Piaget and Vygotsky. *Human Development*, 39, 250–6.

Colebrook, C. (2002) *Understanding Deleuze*. Crows Nest, NSW: Allen & Unwin.

Colebrook, C. (2005) Introduction. *In* A. Parr (ed.) *The Deleuze Dictionary*. Edinburgh: Edinburgh University Press, 1–6.

Colman, F.J. (2005a) Rhizome. *In* A. Parr (ed.) *The Deleuze Dictionary*. Edinburgh: Edinburgh University Press, 231–3.

Colman, F.J. (2005b) Affect. *In* A. Parr (ed.) *The Deleuze Dictionary*. Edinburgh: Edinburgh University Press, 11–13.

Concise Oxford Dictionary (1999) 10th edn. Oxford: Oxford University Press.

Conley, T. (2005) Singularity. *In* A. Parr (ed.) *The Deleuze Dictionary*. Edinburgh: Edinburgh University Press, 251–3.

Corsaro, W. (1997) *The Sociology of Childhood*. USA: Pine Forge Press.

Cullen, J. (2003) The challenge of *Te Whāriki:* catalyst for change? *In* J.G. Nuttall (ed.) *Weaving Te Whāriki: Aotearoa New Zealand's Early Childhood Curriculum Document in Theory and Practice*. Wellington, NZ: New Zealand Council for Educational Research, 269–96.

Dahlberg, G. & Moss, P. (2005) *Ethics and Politics in Early Childhood Education*. London & New York: RoutledgeFalmer.

Dahlberg, G., Moss, P. & Pence, A.R. (1999) *Beyond Quality in Early Childhood Education and Care: Postmodern Perspectives*. London: Falmer.

Dalli, C. (1999) Starting childcare before three: narratives of experience from a tri-partite focus. Unpublished PhD thesis, Victoria University of Wellington.

Damon, W. (ed.) (1998) *Handbook of Child Psychology*. New York: John Wiley.

David, M.E. (1980) *The State, the Family and Education*. London: Boston: Routledge & Kegan Paul.

Davies, B. (1989) *Frogs and Snails and Feminist Tales: Preschool Children and Gender*. Sydney: Allen & Unwin.

Davies, B. (1990) Agency as a form of discursive practice. A classroom scene observed. *British Journal of Sociology of Education*, 11, 341–61.

Davies, B. (1994) *Poststructuralist Theory and Classroom Practice*. Geelong: Deakin University.

Davies, B. (2003) *Frogs and Snails and Feminist Tales: Preschool Children and Gender*. Revised edn. Cresskill, NJ: Hampton Press, Inc.

Davies, B., Browne, J., Gannon, S., Honan, E., Laws, C., Mueller-Rockstroh, B. & Petersen, E.B. (2004) The ambivalent practices of reflexivity. *Qualitative Inquiry*, 10, 360–89.

Davis, B. (1996) *Teaching Mathematics: Toward a Sound Alternative*. New York: Garland Publishing Ltd.

De Castell, S. & Jenson, J. (2003) Serious play: curriculum for a post-talk era. *Journal of the Canadian Association for Curriculum Studies*, 1, 47–52.

Deleuze, G. (1988) *Foucault*. London: Athlone.

Deleuze, G. (1992) *Expressionism in Philosophy: Spinoza*. New York: Zone Books.

Deleuze, G. (1993) *The Fold: Leibniz and the Baroque* Minneapolis: University of Minnesota Press.

Deleuze, G. (1994) *Difference and Repetition*. London: Athlone Press.

Deleuze, G. (1995) *Negotiations: 1972–1990*. New York: Columbia University Press.

Deleuze, G. (1997) What children say. *Essays Critical and Clinical*. Minneapolis, MN: University of Minnesota Press, 61–7.

Deleuze, G. (2004) *Difference and Repetition*. London: Continuum.

Deleuze, G. & Guattari, F. (1976) *Rhizome*. Paris: Minuit.

Deleuze, G. & Guattari, F. (1987) *A Thousand Plateaus: Capitalism and Schizophrenia*. Minneapolis: University of Minnesota Press.

Deleuze, G. & Guattari, F. (1994) *What is Philosophy?* London & New York: Verso.

Deleuze, G. & Parnet, C. (1987) *Dialogues*. London: Athlone Press.

Dept of Education Employment and Workplace Relations & Council of Australian Governments (2009) *Belonging, Being & Becoming: The Early Years Learning Framework for Australia* [online]. Dept of Education, Employment and Workplace Relations for the Council of Australian Governments. Online at: http://www.deewr.gov.au/Earlychildhood/Policy_Agenda/Quality/Documents/Final EYLF Framework Report-WEB.pdf (accessed August 2012).

Dewey, J. (1943) *The Child and the Curriculum, and, the School and Society*. Chicago: University of Chicago Press.

Doll, W.E., Jr (2006) Method and its culture: an historical approach. *Complicity: An International Journal of Complexity and Education*, 3, 85–9.

Dosse, F. (2010) *Gilles Deleuze & Félix Guattari: Intersecting Lives*. New York: Columbia University Press.

Due, R. (2007) *Deleuze*. Cambridge, UK: Polity Press.

Duhn, I. (2006) The making of global citizens: traces of cosmopolitanism in the New Zealand early childhood curriculum, *Te Whāriki. Contemporary Issues in Early Childhood*, 7, 191–202.

Durie, M. (1998) *Te Mana, Te Kāwanatanga: The Politics of Māori Self-Determination*. Auckland: Oxford University Press.

Durie, M. (2006) Measuring Māori wellbeing. New Zealand Treasury Guest Lecture Series. Wellington.

Edwards, S. & Nuttall, J. (2005) Getting beyond the 'what' and the 'how': problematising pedagogy in early childhood education. *Early Childhood Folio*, 9, 34–8.

Egan, K. (1978) What is curriculum? *Curriculum Inquiry*, 8, 65–72.

Egan, K. (2003) Retrospective on 'What is curriculum?' *Journal of the Canadian Association for Curriculum Studies*, 1, 17–24.

'empowerment, n.' OED Online. June 2012. Oxford University Press. Online at: http://www.oed.com/view/Entry/61400?redirectedFrom=empowerment (accessed 15 August 2012).

Fleer, M. (ed.) (1995) *DAP Centrism: Challenging Developmentally Appropriate Practice*. Watson, ACT: Australian Early Childhood Association.

Foucault, M. (1980) *Power/Knowledge: Selected Interviews and Other Writings 1972–1977*. London: Harvester Wheatsheaf.

Foucault, M. (1990) *The History of Sexuality Volume II: The Use of Pleasure*. New York: Vintage Books.

Foucault, M. & Deleuze, G. (1980) Intellectuals and power: a conversation between Michel Foucault and Gilles Deleuze. *In* D.F. Bouchard (ed.) *Language, Counter-Memory,*

Practice: Selected Essays and Interviews by Michel Foucault. Ithaca, NY: Cornell University Press, 205–17.

Gadamer, H.-G. (1982) *Truth and Method*. New York: Crossroad.

Gadamer, H.-G. (1998) *Truth and Method*. 2nd revised edn. New York: Continuum.

Gibbons, A. (2007) Philosophers as children: Playing with style in the philosophy of education. *Educational Philosophy and Theory*, 39, 506–18.

Gough, N. (2006a) Foreword [sous rature]. *In* I. Semetsky (ed.) *Deleuze, Education and Becoming*. Rotterdam: Sense Publishers, ix–xv.

Gough, N. (2006b) Rhizosemiotic play and the generativity of fiction. *Complicity: An International Journal of Complexity and Education*, 3, 119–24.

Grieshaber, S. & Cannella, G.S. (eds) (2001) *Embracing Identities in Early Childhood Education: Diversity and Possibilities*. New York & London: Teachers College Press.

Grosz, E. (1994a) A thousand tiny sexes: feminisms and rhizomatics. *In* C.V. Boundas & D. Olkowski (eds) *Gilles Deleuze and the Theatre of Philosophy*. New York: Routledge, 187–210.

Grosz, E. (1994b) *Volatile Bodies: Toward a Corporeal Feminism*. St Leonards, NSW: Allen & Unwin.

Grumet, M. (1976a) Existential and phenomenological foundations. *In* W.F. Pinar & M. Grumet (eds) *Toward a Poor Curriculum*. Dubuque, IA: Kendall/Hunt, 31–50.

Grumet, M. (1976b) Toward a poor curriculum. *In* W.F. Pinar & M. Grumet (eds) *Toward a Poor Curriculum*. Dubuque, IA: Kendall/Hunt, 67–88.

Grumet, M.R. (1988) *Bitter Milk: Women and Teaching*. Amherst: University of Massachusetts Press.

Grumet, M.R. (1999) Autobiography and reconceptualization. *In* W.F. Pinar (ed.) *Contemporary Curriculum Discourses: Twenty Years of JCT*. New York: Peter Lang, 24–9.

Grumet, M. & Stone, L. (2000) Feminism and curriculum: getting our act together. *Journal of Curriculum Studies*, 32, 183–97.

Guss, F. (2005) Reconceptualizing play: aesthetic self-definitions. *Contemporary Issues in Early Childhood*, 6, 233–43.

Hand, S. (1988) Translating theory, or the difference between Deleuze and Foucault [translator's introduction]. *In* G. Deleuze (ed.) *Foucault*. Minneapolis, MN: University of Minnesota Press, xli–xliv.

Harker, C. (2005) Playing and affective time-spaces. *Children's Geographies*, 3, 47–62.

Hatch, J.A., Bowman, B., Jor'dan, J.R., Morgan, C.L., Hart, C., Soto, L.D., Lubeck, S. & Hyson, M. (2002) Developmentally appropriate practice: continuing the dialogue. *Contemporary Issues in Early Childhood*, 3, 439–57.

Henriques, J., Hollway, W., Urwin, C., Venn, C. & Walkerdine, V. (eds) (1998/1984) *Changing the Subject: Psychology, Social Regulation, and Subjectivity*. London & New York: Routledge.

Hill, E. (2006) Guest editorial: play as a response to life. *The First Years Nga Tau Tuatahi New Zealand Journal of Infant Toddler Education*, 8, 3–4.

Hodgkin, R.A. (1985) *Playing and Exploring*. London & New York: Methuen.

Holt, L. (2004) The 'voices' of children: de-centring empowering research relations. *Children's Geographies*, 2, 13–27.

Honan, E. & Sellers, M. (2006) So how does it work? – rhizomatic methodologiesed. Engaging pedagogies: Australian Association for Research in Education International Conference, Adelaide, SA: AARE.

Honan, E. & Sellers, M. (2008) (E)merging methodologies: putting rhizomes to work. *In* I. Semetsky (ed.) *Nomadic Education: Variations on a Theme by Deleuze and Guattari.* Rottterdam: Sense Publishers, 111–28.

Hultman, K. & Lenz Taguchi, H. (2010) Challenging anthropocentric analysis of visual data: a relational materialist methodological approach to educational research. *International Journal of Qualitative Studies in Education*, 23, 525–42.

Hyun, E. (1998) *Making Sense of Developmentally and Culturally Appropriate Practice (DCAP) in Early Childhood Education.* New York: Peter Lang.

Irigaray, L. (1985) *This Sex Which Is Not One.* Ithaca, NY: Cornell University Press.

Jackson, A.Y. (2003) Rhizovocality. *Qualitative Studies in Education*, 16, 693–710.

Jackson, A.Y. (2010) Deleuze and the girl. *International Journal of Qualitative Studies in Education*, 23, 579–87.

Jipson, J. (1992) The emergent curriculum: contextualizing a feminist perspective. *In* S.A. Kessler & B.B. Swadener (eds) *Reconceptualizing the Early Childhood Curriculum: Beginning the Dialogue.* New York & London: Teachers College Press, 149–64.

Jipson, J. & Johnson, R.T. (eds) (2001) *Resistance and Representation: Rethinking Childhood Education.* New York: Peter Lang.

Jordan, B. (2003) Professional development making a difference for children: co-constructing understanding in early childhood centres. Unpublished PhD thesis, Massey University.

Kennedy, D. (2002) The child and post modern subjectivity. *Educational Theory*, 52, 155–67.

Kessler, S.A. (1991) Alternative perspectives on early childhood education. *Early Childhood Research Quarterly*, 6, 183–97.

Kessler, S.A. & Swadener, B.B. (eds) (1992) *Reconceptualizing the Early Childhood Curriculum: Beginning the Dialogue.* New York: Teachers College, Columbia University.

Kincheloe, J.L. (1997) Introduction. *In* G.S. Cannella (ed.) *Deconstructing Early Childhood Education: Social Justice and Revolution.* New York: Peter Lang Publishing, vii–viii.

Kincheloe, J.L., Slattery, P. & Steinberg, S.R. (2000) *Contextualising Teaching.* New York: Longman.

King, N.R. (1992) The impact of context on the play of young children. *In* S.A. Kessler & B.B. Swadener (eds) *Reconceptualizing the Early Childhood Curriculum: Beginning the Dialogue.* New York: Teachers College, Columbia University, 43–61.

Kitchin, R. & Dodge, M. (2007) Rethinking maps. *Progress in Human Geography*, 31, 331–44.

Kitchin, R., Perkins, C. & Dodge, M. (2009) Thinking about maps. *In* M. Dodge, R. Kitchin & C. Perkins (eds) *Rethinking Maps: New Frontiers in Cartographic Theory.* Abingdon: Routledge, 1–25.

Lather, P. (1992) Critical frames in educational research: feminist and poststructural perspectives. *Theory into Practice*, 31, 87–99.

Latour, B. (1996) *Aramis, or, The Love of Technology.* Cambridge, MA: Harvard University Press.

Law, J. (2003) *Making a Mess with Method* [online]. Centre for Science Studies, Lancaster University. Online at: http://www.lancs.ac.uk/fass/sociology/papers/law-making-a-mess-with-method.pdf (accessed February 2009).

Lee, N. (1998) Towards an immature sociology. *Sociological Review*, 46, 458–82.

Lenz Taguchi, H. (2009) Writing practices in Swedish teacher education and the inclusion/exclusion of subjectivities. *Critical Studies in Education*, 50, 145–58.

Lenz Taguchi, H. (2010) *Going Beyond the Theory/Practice Divide in Early Childhood Education: Introducing an Intra-active Pedagogy*. London & New York: Routledge.

Lero, D.S. (2000) Early childhood education: an empowering force for the twenty-first century? *In* J. Hayden (ed.) *Landscapes in Early Childhood Education: Cross-National Perspectives on Empowerment – a Guide for the New Millenium*. New York: Peter Lang, 445–57.

Liebschner, J. (1992) *A Child's Work: Freedom and Play in Froebel's Educational Theory and Practice*. Cambridge: Lutterworth Press.

Lorraine, T. (2005a) Plateau. *In* A. Parr (ed.) *The Deleuze Dictionary*. Edinburgh: Edinburgh University Press, 206–7.

Lorraine, T. (2005b) Lines of flight. *In* A. Parr (ed.) *The Deleuze Dictionary*. Edinburgh: Edinburgh University Press, 144–6.

Lubeck, S. (1991) Reconceptualizing early childhood education: a response. *Early Education & Development*, 2, 168–74.

MacNaughton, G. (2000) *Rethinking Gender in Early Childhood Education*. St Leonards, NSW: Allen & Unwin.

Mara, D. (1998) *Implementation of Te Whāriki in Pacific Islands Early Childhood Centres. Final Report to the Ministry of Education*. Wellington.

Marshall, J.D., Sears, J.T. & Schubert, W.H. (2000) *Turning Points in Curriculum: A Contemporary American Memoir*. Upper Saddle River, NJ: Prentice-Hall.

Massumi, B. (1987a) Translator's foreword: pleasures of philosophy. *In* G. Deleuze & F. Guattari (eds) *A Thousand Plateaus: Capitalism and Schizophrenia*. Minneapolis & London: University of Minnesota Press, ix–xv.

Massumi, B. (1987b) Notes on the translation and acknowledgments. *In* G. Deleuze & F. Guattari (eds) *A Thousand Plateaus: Capitalism and Schizophrenia*. Minneapolis & London: University of Minnesota Press, xvi–xix.

Massumi, B. (1992) *A User's Guide to Capitalism and Schizophrenia: Deviations from Deleuze and Guattari*. Cambridge, MA: MIT Press.

Massumi, B. (2002) *Parables for the Virtual: Movement, Affect, Sensation*. Durham, NC: Duke University Press.

May, H. (2002) Aotearoa-New Zealand: an overview of history, policy and curriculum. *McGill Journal of Education*, 37, 19–36.

May, H. & Carr, M. (2000) Empowering children to learn and grow – *Te Whāriki*: the New Zealand early childhood national curriculum. *In* J. Hayden (ed.) *Landscapes in Early Childhood Education: Cross-national Perspectives on Empowerment – a Guide for the New Millennium*. New York: Peter Lang, 153–69.

Mayall, B. (2002) *Towards a Sociology for Childhood: Thinking from Children's Lives*. Buckingham/Philadelphia: Open University Press.

Mayhew, K.C. & Edwards, A.C. (1966/1936) *The Dewey School: The Laboratory School of the University of Chicago, 1896–1903*. New York: Atherton Press.

McLeod, L.S. (2002) Leadership and management in early childhood centres: a qualitative case study. Unpublished PhD thesis, Massey University.

Miller, A. (2002) *Journey to the Stone Country*. Great Britain: Hodder & Stoughton.

Miller, J.L. (1982) The sound of silence breaking: feminist pedagogy and curriculum theory. *Journal of Curriculum Theorizing*, 4, 5–11.

Miller, J.L. (1992) Teachers, autobiography, and curriculum: critical and feminist perspectives. *In* S.A. Kessler & B.B. Swadener (eds) *Reconceptualizing the Early Childhood Curriculum: Beginning the Dialogue*. New York & London: Teachers College Press, 103–22.

Miller, J.L. (1999) Curriculum reconceptualized: a personal and partial history. *In* W.F. Pinar (ed.) *Contemporary Curriculum Discourses: Twenty Years of JCT*. New York: Peter Lang, 498–508.

Ministry of Education (1996) *Te Whāriki: He Whāriki Mātauranga mō ngā Mokopuna o Aotearoa: Early Childhood Curriculum*. Wellington: Learning Media.

Moss, P. (2002) Time to say farewell to 'early childhood'? *Contemporary Issues in Early Childhood*, 3, 435–48.

Moss, P. & Penn, H. (1996) *Transforming Nursery Education*. London: Paul Chapman Publishing.

Moss, P. & Petrie, P. (2002) *From Children's Services to Children's Spaces: Public Policy, Children and Childhood*. London: RoutledgeFalmer.

'mythopoetic, adj.' OED Online. June 2012. Oxford University Press. Online at: http://www.oed.com/view/Entry/235090?redirectedFrom=mythopoetic (accessed 15 August 2012).

Nuttall, J.G. (2004) Why don't you ask someone who cares? Teacher identity, intersubjectivity, and curriculum negotiation in a New Zealand childcare centre. Unpublished PhD thesis, Victoria University of Wellington.

Olsson, L.M. (2009) *Movement and Experimentation in Young Children's Learning: Deleuze and Guattari in Early Childhood Education*. London & New York: Routledge.

O'Riley, P.A. (2003) *Technology, Culture, and Socioeconomics: A Rhizoanalysis of Educational Discourses*. New York: Peter Lang.

Orlikowski, W.J. (2006) Material knowing: the scaffolding of human knowledge ability. *European Journal of Information Systems*, 15, 460–6.

Osberg, D., Biesta, G.J.J. & Cilliers, P. (2008) From representation to emergence: complexity's challenge to the epistemology of schooling. *Educational Philosophy and Theory*, 40, 213–27.

'paideia, n.' OED Online. June 2012. Oxford University Press. Online at: http://www.oed.com.ezproxy.lib.rmit.edu.au/view/Entry/135951?redirectedFrom=paedeia (accessed 15 August 2012).

Parr, A. (2005) Deterritorialisation/reterritorialisation. *In* A. Parr (ed.) *The Deleuze Dictionary*. Edinburgh: Edinburgh University Press, 66–9.

Pearsall, J. (1999) *The Concise Oxford dictionary*. 10th edn. Oxford: Oxford University Press.

Perkins, C. (2009) Playing with maps. *In* M. Dodge, R. Kitchin & C. Perkins (eds) *Rethinking Maps: New Frontiers in Cartographic Theory*. Abingdon: Routledge, 167–88.

Pinar, W.F. (1974) *Currere*: toward reconceptualization. *In* J.J. Jelinek (ed.) *Basic Problems in Modern Education; the Second Yearbook of the Arizona Association for Supervision and Curriculum Development*. Tempe, AZ: Arizona Association for Supervision and Curriculum Development, 147–71.

Pinar, W.F. (1975a) *Currere*: toward reconceptualization. *In* W.F. Pinar (ed.) *Curriculum Theorizing: The Reconceptualists*. Berkeley, CA: McCutchan Publishing Corporation, 396–414.

Pinar, W.F. (1975b) The method of 'currere'. Annual Meeting of the American Educational Research Association, Washington, DC.

Pinar, W.F. & Grumet, M. (1976) *Toward a Poor Curriculum*. Dubuque: Kendall/Hunt.

Pinar, W.F., Reynolds, W.M., Slattery, P. & Taubman, P.M. (1995) *Understanding Curriculum: An Introduction to the Study of Historical and Contemporary Curriculum Discourses*. New York: Peter Lang.

Podmore, V.A. & May, H. (2003) 'The child questions': narrative explorations of infants' experiences of Te Whāriki. *Australian Research in Early Childhood Education*, 10, 69–80.

Postman, N. (1994) *The Disappearance of Childhood.* New York: Vintage Books.

Prout, A. (2005) *The Future of Childhood.* London; New York: RoutledgeFalmer.

Quintero, E.P. (2007) Critical pedagogy and qualitative inquiry: lessons from working with refugee families. *In* J.A. Hatch (ed.) *Early Childhood Qualitative Research.* New York & London: Routledge, 109–28.

Ranz-Smith, D.J. (2007) Teacher perception of play: in leaving no child behind are teachers leaving childhood behind? *Early Education & Development*, 18, 271–303.

Readings, B. (1996) *The University in Ruins.* Cambridge, MA: Harvard University Press.

Reedy, T. (2003) Toku rangatiratanga na te mana-mātauranga 'knowledge and power set me free...'. *In* J. Nuttall (ed.) *Weaving Te Whāriki: Aotearoa New Zealand's Early Childhood Curriculum Document in Theory and Practice.* Wellington: NZCER, 51–77.

Rhedding-Jones, J. (2003) Questioning play and work, early childhood and pedagogy. *In* D.E. Lytle (ed.) *Play and Educational Theory and Practice.* Westport, CT: Praeger, 243–54.

Rhedding-Jones, J. (2007) Who chooses what research methodology? *In* J.A. Hatch (ed.) *Early Childhood Qualitative Research.* New York & London: Routledge, 207–22.

Richardson, L. (1992) The consequences of poetic representation: writing the other, rewriting the self. *In* C. Ellis & M. Flaherty (eds) *Investigating Subjectivity: Research on Lived Experience.* Thousand Oaks, CA: Sage, 125–37.

Richardson, L. (2000a) Writing: a method of inquiry. *In* N.K. Denzin & Y.S. Lincoln (eds) *Handbook of Qualitative Research.* 2nd edn. Thousand Oaks, CA: Sage Publications, 923–48.

Richardson, L. (2000b) Skirting a pleated text: de-disciplining an academic life. *In* E.A. St. Pierre & W.S. Pillow (eds) *Working the Ruins: Feminist Poststructural Theory and Methods in Education.* New York: Routledge, 153–63.

Richardson, L. (2001) Getting personal: writing-stories. *International Journal of Qualitative Studies in Education*, 14, 33–8.

Richardson, L. & St. Pierre, E.A. (2005) Writing: a method of inquiry. *In* N.K. Denzin & Y.S. Lincoln (eds) *The Sage Handbook of Qualitative Research.* 3rd edn. Thousand Oaks, CA: Sage Publications, 959–78.

Rinaldi, C. (2006) *In Dialogue with Reggio Emilia: Listening, Researching and Learning.* London/New York: Routledge.

Ritchie, J. (2001) Reflections on collectivism in early childhood care and education in Aotearoa/New Zealand. *In* S. Grieshaber & G.S. Cannella (eds) *Embracing Identities in Early Childhood Education: Diversity and Possibilities.* New York & London: Teachers College Press, 133–47.

Roffe, J. (2005) Multiplicity. *In* A. Parr (ed.) *The Deleuze Dictionary.* Edinburgh: Edinburgh Univerity Press, 176–7.

Rogoff, B. (1998) Cognition as a collaborative process. *In* D. Kuhn & R.S. Siegler (eds) *Handbook of Child Psychology.* 5th edn. New York: John Wiley, 679–744.

Rogoff, B. (2003) *The Cultural Nature of Human Development.* Oxford: Oxford University Press.

Royal Tangaere, A. (1999) He tāonga, te mokopunaed. First Transitions Seminar, Children's Issues Centre, Dunedin.

Ryan, P.M. (1997) *The Reed Dictionary of Modern Māori*. 2nd edn. Auckland, NZ: Reed.

Schubert, W.H. (1986) *Curriculum: Perspective, Paradigm, and Possibility*. New York & London: Macmillan Pub. Co./Collier Macmillan Publishers.

Sellers, M. (2005) Growing a rhizome: embodying early experiences in learning. *New Zealand Research in Early Childhood Education*, 8, 29–42.

Sellers, M. (2009a) A rhizo-poiesis: children's play(ing) of games. *Complicity: An International Journal of Complexity and Education*, 6(2), 91–103.

Sellers, M. (2009b) Re(con)ceiving children in curriculum: mapping (a) milieu(s) of becoming. Unpublished PhD thesis, University of Queensland.

Sellers, M. (2010) Re(con)ceiving young children's curricular performativity. *International Journal of Qualitative Studies in Education*, 23(5), 557–78. Online at: http://ejournals. library.ualberta.ca/index.php/complicity/article/view/8819/7139; http://www.tandfonline.com.

Sellers, M. & Honan, E. (2007) Putting rhizomes to work: (e)merging methodologies. *NZ Research in Early Childhood Education*, 10, 145–54.

Sellers, W. (2008) Picturing *currere* towards *c u r a*: rhizo-imaginary for curriculum. Unpublished PhD thesis, Deakin University.

Semetsky, I. (2006) *Deleuze, Education and Becoming*. Rotterdam: Sense Publishers.

Silin, J.G. (1987) The early childhood educator's knowledge base: a reconsideration. *In* L.G. Katz (ed.) *Current Topics in Early Childhood Education*. Norwood, NJ: Ablex, 16–31.

Silin, J.G. (1995) Developmentalism and the aims of education. *In* J.G. Silin (ed.) *Sex, Death, and the Education of Children: Our Passion for Ignorance in the Age of AIDS*. New York & London: Teachers College Press, 81–110.

Silin, J.G. (2003) The future in question. *Journal of Curriculum Theorizing*, 19, 9–24.

Smith, A.B. (2003) Te Whāriki: diversity or standardisation? Innovative aspects of the New Zealand early childhood curriculum. Education in the Early Years: International Developments and Implications for Germany Conference, Munich.

Smith, L.T. (1999) *Decolonizing Methodologies: Research and Indigenous Peoples*. London/Dunedin, NZ: Zed Books/University of Otago Press.

Smitherman Pratt, S. (2006) Playing with our understandings. *Complicity: An International Journal of Complexity and Education*, 3, 91–5.

Sorin, R. (2003) Research with young children: a rich glimpse into the world of childhood. *Australian Journal of Early Childhood*, 28, 31–5.

Soukhanov, A.H. (1999) *Encarta World English Dictionary*. London & New York: Bloomsbury & St Martin's Press.

St. Pierre, E.A. (1997) Guest editorial: an introduction to figurations – a poststructural practice of inquiry. *Qualitative Studies in Education*, 10, 279–84.

St. Pierre, E.A. (2000) Nomadic inquiry in smooth spaces. *In* E.A. St. Pierre & W.S. Pillow (eds) *Working The Ruins: Feminist Poststructural Theory and Methods in Education*. New York and London: Routledge, 258–83.

St. Pierre, E.A. (2001) Coming to theory: finding Foucault and Deleuze. *In* K. Weiler (ed.) *Feminist Engagements: Reading, Resisiting and Revisioning Male Theorists in Education and Cultural Studies*. New York & London: Routledge, 141–63.

St. Pierre, E.A. (2004) Deleuzian concepts for education: the subject undone. *Educational Philosophy and Theory*, 36, 283–96.

St. Pierre, E.A. & Pillow, W.S. (eds) (2000) *Working the Ruins: Feminist Poststructural Theory and Methods in Education*. New York: Routledge.

Stagoll, C. (2005) Becoming. *In* A. Parr (ed.) *The Deleuze Dictionary*. Edinburgh: Edinburgh University Press, 21–2.

Suransky, V. (1982) *The Erosion of Childhood*. Chicago: University of Chicago Press.

Surtees, N. (2003) Unravelling the woven mat: queering Te Whāriki. *Waikato Journal of Education*, 9, 143–53.

Sutton-Smith, B. (1995) Conclusion: the persuasive rhetorics of play. *In* A.D. Pellegrini (ed.) *The Future of Play Theory: A Multidisciplinary Inquiry into the Contributions of Brian Sutton-Smith*. Albany, NY: State University of New York Press, 275–96.

Sutton-Smith, B. (1997) *The Ambiguity of Play*. Cambridge, MA: Harvard University Press.

Sutton-Smith, B. & Magee, M.A. (1989) Reversible childhood. *Play and Culture*, 2, 52–63.

Swadener, B.B. & Mutua, K. (2007) Decolonizing research in cross-cultural contexts. *In* J.A. Hatch (ed.) *Early Childhood Qualitative Research*. New York & London: Routledge, 185–206.

Te One, S. (2003) The context for *Te Whāriki:* contemporary issues of influence. *In* J.G. Nuttall (ed.) *Weaving Te Whāriki : Aotearoa New Zealand's Early Childhood Curriculum Document in Theory and Practice*. Wellington, NZ: New Zealand Council for Educational Research, 17–49.

Threadgold, T. (1997) *Feminist Poetics: Poiesis, Performance, Histories*. London & New York: Routledge.

Toscano, A. (2005) Chaos. *In* A. Parr (ed.) *The Deleuze Dictionary*. Edinburgh: Edinburgh University Press, 43–4.

Trueit, D. (2002) Speaking of ghosts... *In* W.E. Doll Jr & N. Gough (eds) *Curriculum Visions*. New York: Peter Lang.

Trueit, D. (2005) Complexifying the poetic: toward a *poiesis* of curriculum. Doctoral dissertation, Louisiana State University. Online at: http://gateway.proquest.com/openurl%3 furl_ver=Z39.88–2004%26res_dat=xri:pqdiss%26rft_val_fmt=info:ofi/fmt:kev:mtx: dissertation%26rft_dat=xri:pqdiss:3199765 (accessed November 2012).

Trueit, D. (2006) Play which is more than play. *Complicity: An International Journal of Complexity and Education*, 3, 97–104.

University of Chicago Laboratory Schools (2012) *Educational Program: Curriculum*. Online at: http://www.ucls.uchicago.edu/about-lab/welcome/curriculum/index.aspx (accessed February 2012).

Varela, F. (1987) Laying down a path in walking. *In* W.I. Thompson (ed.) *Gaia a Way of Knowing: Political Implications of the New Biology*. Great Barrington, MA: Lindisfarne Press, 48–64.

Varela, F.J., Thompson, E. & Rosch, E. (1993) *Embodied Mind: Cognitive Science and Human Experience*. Cambridge, MA: MIT Press.

Viruru, R. & Cannella, G.S. (2001) Postcolonial ethnography. *In* S. Grieshaber & G.S. Cannella (eds) *Embracing Identities in Early Childhood Education: Diversity and Possibilities*. New York & London: Teachers College Press, 158–72.

Vygotsky, L.S. (1978) *Mind in Society: The Development of Higher Psychological Processes*. Cambridge: Harvard University Press.

Walkerdine, V. (1992) Progressive pedagogy and political struggle. *In* C. Luke & J. Gore (eds) *Feminisms and Critical Pedagogy*. New York: Routledge, 15–24.

Walkerdine, V. (1998/1984) Developmental psychology and the child-centred pedagogy: the insertion of Piaget into early education. *In* J. Henriques, W. Hollway, C. Urwin, C.

Venn & V. Walkerdine (eds) *Changing the Subject: Psychology, Social Regulation and Subjectivity*. London & New York: Routledge, 153–202.

Walsh, D.J. (1991) Extending the discourse on developmental appropriateness: a developmental perspective. *Early Education & Development*, 2, 109–19.

Walsh, D.J. (2005) Developmental theory and early childhood education: necessary but not sufficient. *In* N. Yelland (ed.) *Critical Issues in Early Childhood Education*. Maidenhead: Open University Press, 40–8.

Wood, E. (2004) Developing a pedagogy of play. *In* A. Anning, J. Cullen & M. Fleer (eds) *Early Childhood Education: Society and Culture*. London: Sage Publications, 19–30.

Woodrow, C. (1999) Revisiting images of the child in early childhood education: reflections and considerations. *Australian Journal of Early Childhood*, 24, 7–12.

Woodrow, C. & Brennan, M. (2001) Interrupting dominant images: critical and ethical issues. *In* J. Jipson & R.T. Johnson (eds) *Resistance and Representation: Rethinking Childhood Education*. New York: Peter Lang, 23–43.

Wright, S. (2007) Graphic-narrative play: young children's authoring through drawing and telling. *International Journal of Education and the Arts*, 8(8), 1–28.

Yelland, N. (ed.) (2005) *Critical Issues in Early Childhood Education*. Maidenhead: Open University Press.

Index